More Hudson Valley UFOs

Including western Connecticut, northern New Jersey, and beyond...

Written by

Linda Zimmermann

Eagle Press

To contact the author, email: lindazim@optonline.net

Or write to:

Linda Zimmermann
P.O. Box 192
Blooming Grove, NY 10914

Website: www.gotozim.com

Facebook: Linda Zimmermann author page
            Hudson Valley UFOs

Other UFO books by Linda Zimmermann:

In the Night Sky
Hudson Valley UFOs

Go to Amazon.com to see the author's complete list of books on a wide variety of topics in both print and e-book formats.

Eagle Press, New York
ISBN: 978-1-937174-30-9

CONTENTS

Acknowledgements

Many thanks to John Schuessler for taking the time and effort to send me copies of the *SBI Report*.

Thanks also to Mike Panicello, MUFON Connecticut State Director, for speaking at the Danbury UFO Conference, and for directing me to some excellent cases.

And C. Burns worked tirelessly all day taking witness statements at the Danbury UFO Conference, not even stopping for lunch. Now, that's dedication!

Mark Packo was kind enough to send me his comprehensive report on his field investigations of the 1980s.

Special thanks to Michael Schratt for his amazing illustrations.

Thanks also to Aurelio Muraca of the Danbury Library for organizing the conference—hopefully the first of many.

And as always, my deepest gratitude to all of the witnesses who had the courage to share their stories, because without you, none of this would have been possible.

Introduction

It seems like only yesterday that I was deciding to take up the challenge of researching and writing about UFOs, and now here I am with my third book on the subject. But that's what the field of ufology can do to you—it draws you in and takes you ever deeper into a bizarre world that can sometimes be frightening, mystifying, exhilarating, or frustrating, but always fascinating and enthralling.

While I naturally chose to concentrate my field of study on the Hudson Valley where I have always lived, it has become increasingly clear that western Connecticut has experienced the same activity over the decades—often the same craft on the same night. (Aliens Without Borders, I like to call it!)

This prompted me to initiate the Danbury UFO Conference held in October 2016 at the Danbury, CT Library. In addition to spreading the word about Hudson Valley UFOs, my hope was that it would draw at least a few local witnesses to share their stories. In reality, there was a line at the door before the conference even started!

So, as we need to expand our minds to the concept of UFOs, I have had to expand the geography of the Hudson Valley phenomena to include western Connecticut. And I also took the liberty to include a few older cases from nowhere near the Hudson Valley, just because they were too good to resist, and illustrated the fact that these craft have been with us a long time.

I hope you enjoy *More Hudson Valley UFOs*, as in addition to the many eyewitness accounts from people I have personally interviewed, I have combed through newspaper archives and UFO databases looking for "all things Hudson Valley and Connecticut." I have also included a personal account which I still find extremely unsettling. Finally, there just may be a case of anti-gravity, or would that be too good to be true?

As always, you the reader, have the ultimate power to decide where the truth resides.

Linda Zimmermann
April 2017

Glossary

APRO: Aerial Phenomena Research Organization was started in January 1952 by Jim and Coral Lorenzen. Inactive.

MUFON: The Mutual UFO Network, currently active.

NICAP: The National Investigations Committee on Aerial Phenomena was active from the 1950s to the 1980s.

NUFORC: The National UFO Reporting Center began in 1974 and is still active.

Project Blue Book: This U.S. Air Force program to study UFO reports began in 1952 and ended in January 1970.

SBI: The Scientific Bureau of Investigation counted many law enforcement officers among its members. Active in the 1970s and 80s, its director and publication editor was Peter Mazzola.

1
1908-1910: The Mysterious Airships

I began the *Hudson Valley UFOs* book with a chapter on the "mysterious airship" sightings throughout the area in 1909. Many sightings occurred in the heart of the Hudson Valley in places such as Middletown, Goshen, Beacon, and Poughkeepsie, NY.

I have continued my research into this wave of sightings, and have found that it actually began a year earlier in Bristol, Connecticut, in July of 1908, and the range of these mysterious airships spread out from New England and the Hudson Valley to Canada and the Midwest. It is worth exploring these reports to fully understand the extent of this wave of sightings, and appreciate that modern UFO phenomena is not really that modern after all.

First, here are some facts to consider about the state of aviation in 1908. Please keep these numbers in mind as you read the following accounts and compare what was being reported with the extremely limited capabilities of human aviation at the time. And also be aware that *no known pilot had yet flown at night.*

The Wright Brothers state-of-the-art airplane in 1908 is being tested at Fort Myers in Virginia. On September 17, the plane crash landed, injuring Orville Wright and killing Lieutenant Thomas Selfridge—making him the first powered-airplane fatality. Aviation was dangerous business in broad daylight, let alone flying blindly in the darkness as these mysterious airships did with regularity.

- The record for the fastest speed in the world was set by Henry Farman in his Voisin Biplane on October 30, 1908, in France. And what was this record-breaking speed? A measly 40.26 miles per hour!
- The record for the farthest distance went to our own Wilbur Wright in the United States. On the last day of 1908, he managed to go 77.48 miles.
- One aspect of early flight that people often overlook when considering whether or not a mysterious airship could have been manmade is altitude. Today, we take it for granted when our flight attendants begin the beverage service at 35,000 feet, but when aviation was in its infancy, altitude was something to be envied. Remember this number then: On December 18, 1908, Wilbur Wright set the year's altitude record with just 361 feet!

Is It A Mysterious Airship?
The Sun, New York
November 1, 1908

A Bright Light, Traveling at Rapid Rate
Seen Passing Over New England

Boston, Oct. 31—Aeronauts are wondering if a mysterious airship, capable of navigating the skies no matter what the conditions are, is in existence and making the nightly trips over New England. Early this morning, two Bridgewater men, Phillip Prophett and John Flynn, undertakers of that town, while driving from West Bridgewater shortly before 4 o'clock, noticed a bright light in the sky above them. The light was not like that of a lantern, according to their reports, but resembled a searchlight. This light was traveling at a rapid rate, when suddenly it neared the earth.

The light was then played upon the earth beneath, as though operated by someone wishing to learn where he was. Then the light ascended, Prophett and Flynn say, until it reached a high elevation, when it disappeared in the direction of Plymouth. All of the balloons in which ascensions are made in this State were accounted for today, and a search through southeastern Massachusetts failed to reveal any further traces of the supposed airship.

Stories of a mysterious bright light, believed by those who have seen it to come from a balloon, have been heard all over New England. Last summer, several such reports came from the vicinity of Bristol, Ct., and later the same phenomenon was observed near Pittsfield, Ma.

Persons at White River Junction, Vt., have also told of seeing a similar light, and last week persons at Ware, Ma. reported that an illuminated balloon had passed over the town during the early hours of morning. In all these cases, however, no balloon could be found, all the known airships being accounted for at the time.

This article is a treasure trove of valuable information. To begin with, the newspaper rules out the possibility that these mysterious airships were balloons, because all balloons and airships had been "accounted for at the time." As airplanes were still quite primitive, were not yet flying at night, and carried no lights, they could also be eliminated from contention as the source of these numerous airship sightings.

So, what did that leave? What could these two undertakers have possibly seen on that early morning of October 31, 1908, that was capable of carrying a bright searchlight, move at "a rapid rate," and reach "a high elevation?" What type of manmade aircraft was possibly "capable of navigating the skies no matter what the conditions are," at that very early stage of aviation? Quite simply, there weren't any such manmade aircraft.

Another excellent example of the remarkable speed and maneuverability of these mysterious airships comes from the following article from 1909:

Saw A Mysterious Airship
Abilene Weekly Reflector, Abilene, Kansas
August 19, 1909

A Train Crew Reports a Race of 12
Miles With One Near Peoria, Illinois

Peoria, Ill., Aug. 12—Conductor Watkins in charge of a work train on the Rock Island railroad and members of his crew report an exciting race with a mysterious airship from Chillicothe, Ill., to the city limits of Peoria, a distance of 12 miles. The ship appeared to be almost 200 feet up in the air, bore lights on the front and rear end, and for several miles gave the train a lively race. Near Peoria, the ship took flight westward and disappeared over the bluffs. No one could be discerned on the craft, it being too dark, but the huge black body of the ship, which was described as cigar shape, was plainly visible. It was apparently under perfect control.

A ship with a "huge black body" that was "cigar shape" was able to race a train along the winding tracks for twelve miles, in the dark!? There was simply no aircraft in existence at that time that could have accomplished such a feat.

As I previously covered in *Hudson Valley UFOs*, the mysterious airship wave swept through the Hudson Valley during the summer of 1909, and then spread to Massachusetts in December. Thousands of people "thronged the streets" at night to watch the dark ship with its bright lights, and it is important to note that no one thought they were invaders from Mars or Venus, and no one was suffering from hysterical delusions. They just thought that some clever inventor had created a marvelous new aircraft that would revolutionize

The winding path of the train tracks from Chillicothe to Peoria which was easily navigated at high speed by a mysterious airship at night in 1909.

aviation, and they patiently awaited the announcement of this incredible new invention. And they waited. And waited.

No one ever came forward with this new aircraft, because it simply didn't exist as a human invention. Even a century later, no blueprints, prototypes, or evidence has ever been found to establish the mysterious airships as any work of man.

4

AIRSHIP OVER MONTCLAIR.

Residents There Puzzled by a Mysterious Machine in Flight.

Special to The New York Times.

MONTCLAIR, N. J., Aug. 23.—Residents of the north end of this town last evening again saw a mysterious aeroplane passing over that section of Montclair. The machine was seen before several days ago. The aeroplane flew high, and as it passed over Upper Montclair it emitted a great puff of smoke that observers thought indicated an explosion. The flying machine, however, was not halted in its course, though it came closer to the earth.

A number of people thought the aeroplane was that constructed by Alfred P. Morgan and Harold H. Dodd, young men of this town. They denied, however, that they have been making secret flights. Their airship, which they have at 15 Appleton Place, is not quite ready to fly. The motor arrived only to-day, and until this has been thoroughly tested no flights will be attempted.

The mysterious airship which was seen passing over the town last evening disappeared to the northward, and is believed to have come down in some isolated section of the country where some inventor has his headquarters.

The following clip from January 12, 1910 edition of *The Malone Farmer*, from Malone, NY, pokes fun at all of these airship witnesses, insinuating that they were all drunk.

It may be merely a coincidence that right after a lot of New England towns went "wet" the news of the mysterious airship, visible only at night, began to come.

AIRSHIP PASSES OVER CITY OF NORWICH (CT)
Willimantic Chronicle
Tuesday, 28 Dec 1909

Many People Saw it but They Were Unable to Tell
How Many Persons Were in it

That the "airship" that many Willimantic people saw or thought they saw last Thursday night may have been an airship after all, and that the stories sent out by local newspapermen were not such complete "fakes" as some persons would have the public believe, is indicated by the following account of an airship printed in the *Norwich Bulletin* this morning in its Norwich news:

"Between 7:30 and 8 o'clock Monday evening there were many in the central part of the city who were watching an airship as it passed over the city, going in a southerly direction. There was no noise to be heard and no particular demonstration with the searchlight, but the fact that the lights were moving attracted attention, and it was watched until it disappeared. It was not very high, but it was impossible to tell how many were in it. That it was not a star is the positive statement of those who saw it.

"It was not a steady level flight like that of a bird, but there was occasionally a dip to the airship and as it went along a second light now and then bobbed into view. It was a fine, clear bright night for a flight, but the operator must have been clothed like Perry on his Arctic trip, to defy the cold of the night."

The *New Haven Palladium* says: it was on the Christmas day just passed, that New Haveners witnessed for the first time in their home city an exhibition of the aeroplane, the invention of which was the real conquest of the air. A mysterious heavier-than-air machine circled the city during Christmas day, and at such a height that its real form, its pilot and its mechanics were not discernible, but it was properly enough within our vision to leave no doubt as to what the stranger was, it circled the air in a manner that is impossible for the balloon or the dirigible, and it was too large for any of the now known feathered inhabitants of the globe. Many of us have seen the aeroplane on exhibition in trial flights at low altitudes, but those who saw the mysterious stranger of Christmas were treated to the real thing in air conquests. It was a great spectacle in the skies. The aeroplane was generally believed to be the one which has been flying for many months past in New England, traveling incognito, as it were, for the stranger, while owned in Worchester, comes to earth and leaves it in parts unknown to the public. The owner claims that it is the greatest of all heavier-than-air contrivances, and after what we saw the other day we agree with him, if the Christmas day visitor was really Mr. Tillinghast in his greatest of airships. It was a stirring sight and encouraged our thoughts to the great achievements of mankind. In all of the seriousness of the incident there was also the humorous side to it, and no better shown perhaps than in the statement of the little newsboy who exclaimed, "That is nothing, only Santa Claus going home after a hard night's work."

Note: Wallace Tillinghast was a Massachusetts businessman who claimed he had built the mysterious airship. Amongst his outrageous assertions was that during a night journey from New York to Boston, he was actually able to crawl out of the cockpit and repair the engine in mid-flight. He never produced any airship or any proof to the public, and is now recognized as one of this country's greatest hoaxers.

Mysterious Airship at Essex
The Bennington Evening Banner, Bennington, VT
December 29, 1909

People Turn Out to See Brilliant
Lights in Western Sky

Essex Junction, Dec. 28—The populace was out in full force last night to view what was thought to be a mysterious airship. It was seen in the western sky where a brilliant light rose and fell and finally went out.

Light in the Skies
Daily Register, Sandusky, Ohio
July 23, 1909

Attracts Attention of Night Owls
Many Looked for Airship to Alight

A light believed by many to have been attached to an airship, attracted a great deal of attention in the northeastern skies about 11 o'clock Thursday night. One minute it would be large and brilliant and the next small and dim. It would remain apparently stationary for a while and then speed along in an easterly direction at a rapid rate.

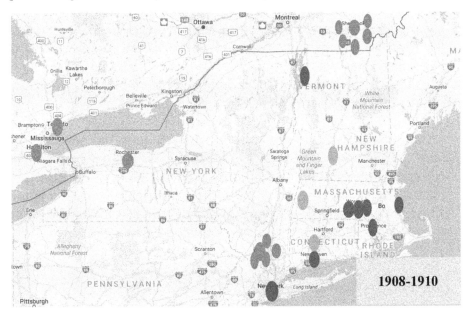

Locations of mass sightings of the mysterious airships from 1908-1910.

In 1909 and 1910, there were numerous reports of mysterious airships across Canada, most noticeably during the summer of 1909, just north of the New York and Vermont borders in Ontario. A summary of these events illustrates the range of reporting, from seriously dealing with the facts, to joking that the airships were nothing more than grasshoppers with lanterns.

August 12, 1909, *Sherbrooke Daily Record*
- "The lights appeared to be attached to something that was in motion, and going rapidly."
- "The airship was also seen in Coaticook…Observed three strange lights in the air…They were at an altitude of about 1,500 feet…appearing like a head light and a side and tail light. The object to which the lights were attached could not be seen, but it was traveling at a rapid rate in an easterly direction."
- Coaticook: "The chief topic of conversation here is about the airship." Six men "saw a cigar shaped airship sailing in a northerly direction two weeks ago last Tuesday."
- Waterville: "While Mr. and Mrs. Cardwell were walking out last Monday evening about nine o'clock, they saw an airship sailing along in a southerly direction, prettily lit up."

August 16
- "More Flying Machine News…it carried two lights…they were traveling about 10 or 12 miles an hour."
- "Thinks it was a Vermont Grasshopper: …it was two lights going fast through the air…from Holland, Vt. to Coaticook…Now I see two answers to this problem. One is that some kind-hearted American (who happened to have a flying machine) took a trip across to see if we were properly feeding the grasshoppers who emigrated from their country. Another is that it was a Holland, Vt. grasshopper…with lanterns attached so that they can work at night."

August 17
- "More News of Airship: A Waterville correspondent writes: "It was not a shooting star, neither a Vermont grasshopper, but a

genuine airship, loaded with U.S. undesirables who were bound to emigrate to Canada and took that method of travel to dodge Chief Davidson. A real Yankee trick."

August 23

- "Still Seeing Wonderful Airship--Residents of Cookshire Had a Good View of Flying Mystery--Green and Red Lights Could Be Seen Distinctly: for an hour and a half was the center of attention...seen travelling at an awful speed towards the East. These lights remained at the same distance apart and appeared to be fixed to some firm object...At times it would suddenly start downward, and then start up again...The entire population turned out." Some claimed that they viewed the dark, oblong craft through a telescope, and they were able to see a flagpole and flag at one end!
- "Was Also Seen at Beebe: he saw two lights quite plainly about ten o'clock...a number of others watched the strange lights in the heavens."

August 24

- "Probably an Advertising Scheme--Mysterious Lights in Sky seen By Sherbrookers: For hours the bright light hung high in the sky to the southeast. It was practically stationary all the evening, except at times it would disappear and a minute later come out as bright as ever...Is it that it is an advertising scheme on the part of some enterprising manufacturer, probably of tobacco, and that the 'comet' or 'airship' cigar or cigarette will appear on earth about exhibition week?"

August 31

- "Hamilton (Ontario) Sees the E.T. Airship--Mystified by Bright Light in Southeastern Sky--Planet Mars, Say Astronomers-- Yankee Airship is Another View: Those who have watched the strange light...say that the planet Mars was never known to manoeuvre around the skies like this mysterious red lamp, dipping down towards earth, suddenly ascending, and then drifting north and south towards the mountain and lake...All efforts so far to discover from whence this strange light comes from or where it goes have failed."

A year later, more red and green lights were seen across the length of Canada.

An Aerial Flying Dutchman
Niagara Falls (NY) Gazette
October 27, 1910

Toronto, Ont., Oct. 27 -- An aerial Flying Dutchman is making across Canada. That explains some of the reports that confused those who were searching for the missing balloon America, and raises the question whether some inventor of extraordinary genius isn't trying a secret trial trip before he startles the world with the story of his accomplishments.

The mysterious airship, carrying red and green lights, passed over Fort William and was seen by two train crews on trains some distance apart. It was still going westward.

Early this morning the airship was seen going over Saskatchewan from east to west, and it again carried red and green lights.

To cap the climax, Mrs. Grenfall, wife of the noted deep-sea missionary, writes that an airship was seen over St. Anthony's in far northern Labrador, a week ago.

The reports are confirmed from other places and appear absolutely reliable.

For centuries, apothecaries hung glass vessels in their windows containing brightly colored red and green liquids, often lit with lanterns, to indicate to illiterate people that this was where they could obtain medicine. Hence, the facetious title to this next mysterious airship article.

Drug Store Afloat in the Skies
Daily Capital Journal, Salem, Oregon
November 2, 1910

Mysterious airship, showing red and green lights,
seen at many points in British Columbia recently

Victoria, B.C., Nov, 2—British Columbia, as well as London, Berlin or Paris, has its bona fide airship mystery, and as yet no one has come forward to give a clue by which the mystery may be solved. Better still, the mystery appears to be drifting rapidly toward Victoria and the coast country generally, showing red and green lights, from which it may be inferred that a drug store has got afloat in the ether.

Since the ship passed over Calgary, reports from Swift Current, Medicine Hat and other cities have been received, all telling of the red and green lights.

So it is now clear that this mysterious airship wave expanded across most of North America—beginning in Connecticut in 1908, spreading across the Hudson Valley in summer of 1909 and New England and the Atlantic Coast later that year, and finally stretching to the Pacific Coast of Canada at the end of 1910.

Throughout the years of these sightings, reports remained consistent. Once we remove the wild claims and ridiculous excuses, the general picture emerges of a large, dark, oblong or cigar-shaped craft, with one to three bright white lights (sometimes red and green), usually producing no discernable sound, being capable of both hovering motionless and traveling "at a rapid rate" at elevations of at least 1,500 feet, witnessed by large populations of cities and towns across two countries.

If all this isn't convincing evidence that the UFO age did not begin in 1947 with Kenneth Arnold and Roswell, then consider the following from the airship wave of 1897, a full fifty years earlier:

Chicago Tribune, Bloomington, Illinois, April 11—An object believed to be the mysterious airship which has been sailing over Illinois was seen at noon today floating over Bloomington. It was going in a northeasterly direction at a great altitude. It was yellow in color and seemed to be rectangular in form.

A yellow, rectangular craft seen at a "great altitude" in broad daylight in 1897! Now *that* is a mysterious airship.

2
Discs

West Frankfort, Illinois
March/April 1927

From the APRO files, came this fascinating report of an interview conducted on December 26, 1969, of a grammar school principal who wished to remain anonymous, and who had been five years old at the time of his 1927 sighting. Even though this is not a Hudson Valley area case, I had to include it, as it is a very early saucer sighting—and I was so amused by the ending. Fear of ridicule is not the only reason why some people don't talk about their sightings!

Weather: Bright and sunny
Time: About 9:00 A.M, because the sun was at the observer's back in the East.

The observer reports that he was on his way to the store one block from his home. He happened to look to the west, and a bright, shiny disc flashed in the sky and he stood there and watched it as it approached in his direction. It finally came to a suspended, hovering stop over the house across the street from him, about 100 feet away. It was a big, round sphere almost as big as the house it was over. Estimated to be about 40 feet in diameter, made of a perfectly smooth, shiny material that reminded him of stainless steel. No seams or rivets were visible. The "gondola" underneath was attached. It appeared connected directly; no visible partition. As it approached, the whole sphere was revolving from right to left. At the time it came to a stop over the house, it also stopped revolving. Then four or five portholes around the gondola section all opened up at the same time. The inside of the gondola section appeared to be illuminated. The color of the light was blue white like a modern day arc light. There was no sound heard during the whole sighting. After hovering over the house for some time, the object drifted about 100 feet to the right and stopped. At this point the observer saw a thin line of something that reflected light, drop straight down from the bottom of the object. Terms like "glass rod" and "pencil-thin" pipe or wire were used. The next day when the area was looked at, it appeared to be as if a few gallons of oil had been poured on the ground and soaked it. After that, the object's portholes closed and it began to rotate again and departed in the same direction it came. The opening and closing of the portholes was an action like the iris shutter of a modern day camera. The whole sighting took about 30 minutes.

After 42 years the person reporting this incident remembers it vividly because his mother gave him a spanking for being gone so long and making up such big tales.

This might be the first case where a UFO witness received a spanking for telling his story! Unfortunately, however, this case does illustrate the sad fact that so many witnesses of all ages are afraid to tell their stories for fear of ridicule—or worse.

Richard Sweed
Norwalk, CT, 1950s and
Bakersfield, CA, 1927

The APRO files contained a newspaper article from *The Norwalk Hour*, from July 20, 1959, entitled *Space Flight Linked With Flying Saucers in Teacher's Letter* which begins with:

"There are frequent reports in the news about unidentified flying objects. A Norwalk man has written *The Norwalk Hour* expounding on the use of electro-magnetic power for use in manned and controlled space ships. Furthermore, the man relates how he saw a flying saucer take off in Arizona in 1927." [Note: This is incorrect. The sighting occurred in California, not Arizona.]

"Richard Sweed, a schoolteacher of the Carlton Court Apartments, South Norwalk, tells in his letter of his theories on the innovations pending in the field of flight."

Sweed's letter discusses the limitations of "chemical fueled rockets" and he believes that electro-magnetic power is the future of space flight, even though his friends said he was "insane" for having such theories of advanced forms of propulsion. If they thought his ideas were insane, they really must have loved what sparked Sweed's theories.

"The idea of electro-magnetic power came to me from an experience I had some 32 years ago.

"Why no reports of this experience? Well, what happened to reports given by commercial air line pilots? Also air force pilots and the numerous reports turned in by private citizenry?

"On October 18, 1927, on the way to Yuma, Arizona, on the outskirts of Bakersfield, California, I was fortunate to witness one of the Unidentified Flying Objects (flying saucers) on the take-off, although little was known or heard about them then. This was a space ship, not a rocket, propelled by some mysterious form or type of power. Why? Because it did not fume, flame or leave a gas or vapor trail on acceleration, such as combustion engines and rockets do.

"Construction of ship was round—60 ft. in diameter (more or less)—port holes (or round windows) with protruding metallic or ceramic objects resembling telescopic lenses. Color bluish gray, resembling metal heated and allowed to cool. Whining, humming, wheezing, swooshing sound on application of power thrust. Smooth, steady and terrific acceleration, rising at a 45 degree angle, and not straight up. Existence of some sort of magnetic pulling or attracting power. On reaching area of take-off, sand was fused like glass crystals.

"Now after relating to you my experiences, you can see why all these years I have believed in electric-magnetic power for manned and controlled space craft for solar system and lunar research."

This is a remarkable and very early sighting by this Connecticut schoolteacher of a "classic" flying saucer—round, about 60 feet in diameter, round windows, and no obvious signs of propulsion. Also, the fact that Sweed observed that the "sand was fused like glass crystals" is astonishing, as sand needs about 3,000 degrees Fahrenheit to melt into glass—certainly nothing that any aircraft in 1927 was capable of doing!

Sweed then goes on to speculate that perhaps there is an "Unknown Planet" that is obscured by the Moon which may be a source for these UFOs. This theory came about as the result of his many years of "telescopic observations." Sweed explains that "For the past 20 years of studying the moon" he has seen "illuminated objects leaving its area."

While we only have this newspaper article on which to base any conclusions as to the validity of these sightings, we can at least say that Richard Sweed had some credentials, being a teacher who stated that his life's work was "astronomy, cosmology, space medicine, space travel, solar and lunar research." His description of the flying saucer in California in 1927 is detailed, and his numerous observations made in Connecticut of "illuminated objects leaving" the area around the Moon in the 1950s is also well worth noting.

Dr. William Walton
Oak Park, Illinois
September 1929

At one of the UFO conferences in 2016, someone was telling me about his sighting, which involved a strong downward pressure bearing down on him from a craft in the sky above. He asked if I knew of any other cases of people feeling this type of pressure, and I couldn't think of any offhand at that moment. Coincidentally, however, a few weeks later when I was going through some APRO files, I did come upon such a case—and to my great surprise, it was from 1929! While this is obviously not a Hudson Valley case, its unique nature is well worth mentioning, and I hope others in the NY-NJ-CT area who may have experienced something similar will come forward and share their experiences.

It was a beautiful, moonless, star-filled, September evening in Oak Park, Illinois, at 10:30pm, when medical student William Walton was walking north on Euclid Avenue. Suddenly, he saw a "very bright yellowish-white diffused light; elliptically shaped like two saucers face to face." Walton's report states that the craft was "40' x 2'," and by that I assume he meant it was 40 feet in diameter and about 2 feet thick. It was moving "north to south at high speed; then veering to the southwest." The length of his sighting was about 30 seconds.

As remarkable as these facts are for a 1929 sighting, the full story of Walton's experience, recorded years later when he was a physician and surgeon is even more incredible:

Dr. Walton –then a young medical student—was walking home, going north on Euclid Street. As he diagonally crossed the street from the east to the west side, the light approached him – spreading itself across the width of the street and beyond. As it grew near, he heard a distinct humming, "like turbines" and felt both heat and pressure from above. The object passed directly over him at an estimated height of 100 feet. As it did, the pressure force knocked him to his knees. After it had passed, the

16

odor of sulfur was strong. Dr. Walton, although amazed and shaken, was not injured, and did not report the incident for fear of ridicule.

This case stands out for a variety of reasons. First, the incident appears to have been experienced by an educated, reputable individual, involving a very early and close saucer sighting. Then there is the fact of this intense pressure, which actually knocked the man down to his knees! The strong smell of sulfur, while unusual, has been reported over the years in a number of cases. Add to all of this the heat and turbine-like humming noise, and this becomes a very special case that was seen, smelled, and felt.

Frank Van Keuren
Beach Haven, NJ
Summer, 1933

Again, this is beyond the Hudson Valley area of northern New Jersey, but I can't resist these early cases!

In 1967, Frank Van Keuren of Denver, Colorado wrote a letter to NICAP about a sighting he had back in 1933, in Beach Haven, NJ. This is yet another example that there was substantial activity prior to World War II, especially regarding saucer-shaped craft.

(I have corrected some typos and added punctuation to make it more readable. And I particularly like to whom he addresses the letter.)

Dear Mr. Investigator:

We were fishing one night in the summer of 1933. The time was very late at night. We were in the inland waterways west of Beach Haven, N.J. It was a very clear dark night with the stars out, but no moon. All of a sudden, we were illuminated by a very brilliant floodlight from an object which couldn't have been more than 1,000 feet away in the air. This thing in the air, as I remember, didn't make any sound at all, and was traveling along like a slow plane. The best shape you could call it was like a disk. You couldn't tell anything else about it because it was too dark out. It played that floodlight on us for several minutes, and then proceeded to travel on toward some shortwave radio towers which were maybe 8 to 10 miles away. This thing played a group of floodlights all at once in that area and seemed to be circling there. We watched it for a while and probably lost interest.

I asked my dad what it was and he said it must be some kind of a plane used by the Coast Guard.

The unusual thing about it was it didn't have any running lights or make any sound.

Them days we didn't know what a flying saucer or UFO was. And I guess we still don't.

Mr. Van Keuren was certainly correct. In "them days" we didn't know what a UFO was, and 84 years later, we are still in the same situation.

***

It would have been nice if the reporter of this article had used a little more journalistic technique and acquired more facts of the sighting, rather than make light of the whole thing, but at least we have an account of multiple disks.

Mount Kisco, NY
New Castle Tribune
July 14, 1950

Rainy Weather, War Clouds, Flying Saucers, What's Next?

The $64 question in the mind of one Harriman Knolls dweller since Sunday night is "have the flying saucers at last visited Mount Kisco?"

The lady, who prefers to remain nameless, had spent a lazy Sunday evening, reading the newspapers. War clouds, murders, auto accidents, and hi-jinks of Mr. and Mrs. Moneybags, the stock market fluctuations, etc. The news surely was not conducive to a good night's sleep.

However, at about 11pm, she put out the cat, wound the clock and journeyed upstairs to court the elusive Morpheus. It was a hot night so the gal decided that the shades rolled to the top of both windows would help the cross ventilation.

As she relaxed in bed, mentally planning the next week's work and play, something very much like lightning lit up the eastern sky. Being extremely allergic to the stuff, milady decided to down the shades and in a hurry. Leaping from her bed, she was about to pull down the shade on the last window, when she noticed something which surely wasn't lightning. Five luminous disks, about twice the size of a one-pound coffee tin, sailed serenely and noiselessly, slightly above the house tops of the sleeping Harriman Knollers, from the direction of the Cook estate on Sarles Street on the south, losing themselves to her view over the Henry Mannix estate.

By this time, our gal was literally frozen to the spot and speech, which to that day had never failed her, was not to be invoked. Being a femme who imbibes nothing more devastating than aqua pura, or possibly a cup of tea, she knows it was not anything resembling the "pink elephant" parade so often experienced by the frivolous weekender.

So as we said, the $64 question is: "Did the lady see a flying saucer formation, or didn't she?"

"Want to try for the $64, General Omar Bradley?"

Mrs. William Airey
Albany, NY
October 1956, 7:15-7:25pm

While I was happy to find this 1956 Albany report in the APRO files, which promised a "diagram of sighting" on the back of the page, I was disappointed to find that the back of the page had not been copied and was not included in the online archive. Still, it is a good report, and I can just imagine the record-breaking run to the house!

While sitting on a hill overlooking several rows of houses, my friend and I observed three bright lights –the size and brightness of Venus at its brightest –maneuvering in the sky (it was dark out and other stars were clearly visible). We pointed out the "flying saucers" to each other and decided to watch them. A few minutes later we looked out over the horizon and observed a dark circular object over the houses. It moved in toward us slowly. It was completely circular, black, with what seemed to be small pits in the surface. When it was about 50' from us and parallel to us it seemed to be about 15' to 20' in diameter. At this range we were rather frightened and took off for home. Upon arriving there (having broken all our previous running records), we observed that the three lights were still maneuvering. We attempted to call our local observatory for the next two hours without getting through. There was nothing in the papers the next day about anyone else making a sighting. As we were both teenagers, we didn't think our report would account for much, so we never reported it.

Diagram of sighting on back.

3 in Katonah See Flying Saucer Tuesday Evening
Patent Trader, August 13, 1959

Katonah—Three persons in Katonah saw a flying saucer Tuesday night. The clearly observed object was visible for from one to two minutes and was then seemingly "swallowed up into the sky."

Mr. and Mrs. Irwin Stuart Block and Mrs. Block's sister, Dr. Lillian Wysocki, a medical doctor from Chicago, were sitting on the terrace of their home on Hook Road when the object appeared out of the eastern sky about 8pm, well before dark.

"It seemed like a round, elongated object with a flame glowing inside it," Mrs. Block said. "We followed its movement for a minute or two," she continued. "It seemed to be coming directly toward us when it suddenly made a right angle turn and disappeared, as though it was swallowed up into the sky."

Mrs. Block said the object had no wings and was completely noiseless. It traveled, she said, faster than a regular aircraft, but not as fast as a jet. In size it seemed to be somewhat smaller than the sun.

Tuesday night marked the beginning of the three-day annual Perseid meteor shower, a period when meteors are frequently seen during the hours of darkness. But the Blocks insisted that the object they saw could not have been a meteor.

"Meteors are not that large," Mrs. Block said, "and they travel much faster. Besides, it was still broad daylight." Nor, she said, could it have been a searchlight or a light reflection.

The Blocks called the radio station in Mount Kisco, and the occurrence was first reported Wednesday morning.

20

Mr. Block is a banker.

At 9:45pm the same night, two 14-year-old girls, Gloria Czepelka to Iris Koslozsky, saw an unidentified flying object cross over Czepelka's home on route 116, Somers. They described it as a great white light and observed it halfway across the sky; it dimmed out and "turned into" five little red circles of lights. In the rear there was a sixth light.

The girls were positive the object was not a meteorite. Its course, they said, was from north to south west.

***

The Wanaque Reservoir in New Jersey was a hotspot for sightings, particularly during the wave of 1966, which I wrote about in *In the Night Sky*.

Ringwood, NJ
July 1, 1965

NUFORC Report
Daylight sighting of silent hovering disc over Wanaque Reservoir

I was about 6 or so years old. Several of my brothers and sisters were with me when my mother brought us food shopping. She had been driving one of those old station wagons that had the back seat facing out the back window.

It was summertime, I remember because the back window was wide open. We were on our way home and I don't remember which of us were sitting back there but as Mom made a right turn we were facing the Wanaque reservoir.

All of a sudden, as Mom made that turn, we were staring straight at a silver disc hovering not more than 30 feet above the water, only about 50 feet away from us. I remember all of the kids screaming at Mom to stop the car. I just remember all of us screaming, but it wasn't really fear. More excitement, I believe.

Well, Mom had to drive up the road a short ways so that she could turn the car around, but by the time we got back there, it was gone. Mom did see it in the rearview mirror when she heard all the commotion we were making. The disc was about 50 feet long, shining silver and silent as it hovered. I, nor any of my family, reported it. I'm really not sure why.

For some strange reason, maybe because we were all so young (I'm second youngest of six) none of us discussed the sighting for years. I've talked to a couple of my siblings about it when we got older. We all remember it the same way.

I went to the Ringwood library to see if they had any information or old news clippings about that event. As it turns out, many people saw the same thing. UFOs seemed to make an appearance for that entire weekend. People from all over would park their cars around the reservoir day and night and many reported night sightings.

My mother, who has since passed, remembered men in dark suits, but she wasn't sure what they were doing there or how they knew what was going on that weekend. She was never approached by these men.

A few years ago, I read a book-*Above Top Secret*-by Mr. Good and sure enough, he had reports in his book about the Wanaque reservoir sightings. Since then, I have spoken to a few "old" Ringwoodites about whether they had ever had sightings, and to my surprise, many had. But none had seen a daylight sighting. Only the night sightings.

Barbara
West Point Military Academy
Summer c.1966

Barbara's father, a captain and doctor in the Army, was stationed at West Point in the mid-1960s. She and her mother were walking across a cobblestone courtyard in front of a four story, L-shaped, brick building one clear, summer's day, when suddenly "men in uniforms" came streaming out of the building, and nearby buildings, filling the courtyard.

I heard them shouting things such as, "I've heard of these things," and "I've heard people talk about them, but never thought I would see one," as they all looked and pointed toward the sky.

Barbara and her mother looked up and saw "a big, huge, round, silver thing moving very slowly and quietly over the top of the building." While she can't remember the exact details of the craft, she does recall "an inner circle with a pattern," meaning it was not just a smooth, featureless exterior. Everyone stood watching in awe as the huge craft silently passed overhead. And while all of the soldiers, and possibly cadets, remained standing there, Barbara's mother said, "Let's get in the car and follow it!"

She remembers "driving by all the cannons" and coming out by the band shell where the craft was moving "real slow over the trees." When it finally went out of view, they decided to hurry home and tell Barbara's father what they had seen. He immediately jumped in the car and took off, and was gone for quite a while.

As they waited for him to return, Barbara's mother called the Military Police, and was told that they had received many calls. The MP also said that this object "had been spotted up and down the Hudson River all day." A startling admission for an MP on duty at West Point!

When Barbara's father finally came home, all he said was that he might have seen "something over the Hudson River," and never spoke about it again. On the other hand, Barbara and her mother continued to speak about their amazing sighting for many years.

Fast forward 51 years to the MUFON conference in Philadelphia, where Barbara came up to me after my lecture to share her story. Her mother has passed away, but her father—a retired Colonel—was still alive. I was hoping to hear his story, as well, and he kindly agreed to speak with me. Prior to my call to him, Barbara spoke to him and was astonished to hear details about his sighting he had never before revealed.

He had driven down to the parade ground, where he indeed saw the huge round craft over the Hudson River. He had a clear look at it, and watched it long enough to know it was "drifting north." When I spoke to him, he confirmed these details of his sighting. I also asked him if he reported it, and he explained that "UFOs were a forbidden subject, so I didn't discuss it." And he was to have more important things to worry about soon after, as he was sent to Vietnam.

Unfortunately, the subject is still taboo in the military, as was evidenced by the MUFON report made by three MPs at West Point in 1993 (see the Casebook chapter). They had decided not to file a report with their superiors of the massive craft they witnessed. UFO sightings don't usually enhance career advancement opportunities.

This case presented a rare opportunity to speak to an Army officer and his daughter about a sighting which took place over one of this country's most historic and revered military institutions. I would love to have other soldiers and their families come forward who may have witnessed this craft in the 1960s over West Point, or at any other time and place, for that matter.

Barbara's father and I spoke for quite a while, and he asked about my research. At the end of our conversation, he said something that got me thinking.

"I hope you find what you're after," he said.

What exactly am I after? I suppose the long answer is that I want to document as many credible eyewitness accounts as possible from the Hudson Valley and the surrounding areas.

The short answer about what I am after is simple.

The truth.

"Frank"
Pine Bush Area
Jan 4, 1971

Army veteran "Frank" was also veteran policeman on January 4, 1971, and living in the Pine Bush area. One night, he had to get up about 2:30am to use the bathroom, and he saw something strange out his bedroom window. There was a pulsating light coming from the field behind his house, and he also heard a faint "whirring" sound. Hurrying to get his glasses, he returned to the window and was stunned at what he saw.

"Oh, Mother of God, what is this!" he exclaimed, as the hair stood up on the back of his neck.

There was a saucer-shaped craft hovering over the field, "a silvery object hovering a few hundred feet from my home. It was approximately 100 feet in diameter, disc-shaped with a row of windows around a domed top."

The most remarkable part was the pulsating glow which went from a "bright scarlet red" to a greenish-blue color, and every time the color changed from red to greenish-blue the *size* of the craft seemed to diminish! Then as it turned red again the apparent size would increase.

Frank watched in awe for quite a while and then decided he would wake up his neighbor who lived on the other side of the field. His neighbor was a military officer stationed at Stewart Airport, and when Frank called him he reluctantly got out of bed and looked out his window. Several minutes passed before the officer got back on the phone.

"Frank, I did see something, but I will swear in a court of law that I didn't see anything and that this conversation never took place."

Clearly, this military man saw something so extraordinary that he didn't want to risk his reputation, or possibly his career, by admitting to it.

Frank continued to watch the pulsating saucer for about forty minutes to an hour, "until all of a sudden it just disappeared."

Several years later, the television show *PM Magazine* interviewed Harry Lebelson about all the activity in Pine Bush. Frank agreed to tell his story for the show, but only if his identity remained anonymous. I do know Frank's real name, as I interviewed his daughter, but I will respect his wishes and keep him anonymous.

When Lebelson had asked Frank about UFO sightings in Pine Bush, Frank replied, "Why, half the police department has seen them and the other half thinks the ones who've seen them are crazy."

Frank's daughter recalled her father's sighting in great detail, and wishes that he had woken her up to also see that amazing pulsating saucer!

Steve
Hollis section of Queens, NY
July 4, 1972

When I was speaking at the MUFON conference in Philadelphia in October of 2016, Steve and two of his brothers were in the audience. The primary focus of my talk was the wave of sightings in the Hudson Valley and Connecticut during the 1980s, where the predominant types of craft sighted were triangles, boomerangs, and V-shaped. However, I also pointed out that large, round UFOs, encircled by lights, had also been seen during that wave, as well as in the previous decades.

As an illustration, I showed the slide of Carol and Christine at Lake Oscawana in New York, holding up sketches they had made of the similar UFOs they had seen 20 years apart. Carol had made an excellent sketch of the craft she had seen from the roof of her apartment building in the Bronx in 1960. One of the prominent features of that craft was the row of rectangular windows around the edge, which emitted a bright light. Little did I realize that the when I showed that image, Steve and his brothers immediately recognized it.

25

It was the 4th of July in 1972, and Steve, along with a brother and sister, were standing in the street, setting off fireworks in the Hollis section of Queens, NY, as were at least a dozen other people up and down the block. His mother and another brother were standing on the front steps of the house. It was about 11pm when they heard people yelling, "What is that?" and saw that everyone was looking up.

It was a large, round craft, with windows around the center that had such a bright, white light coming from within that Steve couldn't tell if there were any lights on the exterior of the craft. It was low enough that Steve could clearly see the windows and he was mesmerized by that white light streaming out of them. He stood staring; trying to see inside of those windows, but the light was just too bright inside.

That night, the news on television reported that a UFO had been seen in the city, so it must have moved over the area. It isn't known how many witnesses there were, but between Steve's five family members, and the dozen or so other people on the street, there were at least 17 just on his block. To this day, 44 years later, the memory is still fresh in the minds of Steve and his family. And when they saw Carol's sketch, they knew they had to share their story of seeing the identical craft.

Using Carol's sketch and description, military aerospace historian Michael Schratt was able to create this amazing image of the circular craft.

26

"Deanna and Lisa"
Norwalk, CT
Summer, c. 1972

"Lisa," her mother, and her sister were driving home from St. Philip Church on France Street in Norwalk one summer evening, when a large, circular craft began following their car. Terrified, her mother continued driving the approximately two miles to their East Rocks Road home, hoping the craft would leave them alone, but it remained just above their car the entire way.

When they got to their house, they all rushed inside to tell Lisa's father. He came running outside, but the craft had gone. He told Lisa to stay home, while he jumped in the car with her mother and drove off toward the local school where he thought he would have a good view to try to locate the craft again.

Several minutes later, "Deanna," who lived just down the street, heard her friend Lisa screaming. Deanna hurried outside to see Lisa running down the street in a panic, yelling, "It's chasing me! It's chasing me!" Sure enough, the craft had returned and Deanna saw a disc-shaped craft "as big as a house" seemingly following Lisa down the middle of the street at no more than 100 feet above the ground!

Deanna's family also came out of the house, as did many families along the street. The craft then stopped and hovered in place for about 30 seconds, tilting slightly a few times. Many parents and their children stood and watched in awe as a band of "different colored lights rotated" around the center of the "charcoal gray metallic" disc. Then something even more bizarre happened.

"It changed shape," Deanna told me. "I know it sounds crazy, but it turned into a barbell shape with rotating ends. Then the whole thing began spinning and it suddenly shrank to a point and disappeared!"

How did the sighting make her feel?

"At first I was fascinated. This was something way more advanced...*way more*. But then I got scared. It kind of felt like they were getting into my head—monitoring us, scoping us out. I got the impression someone was in there, and they weren't friendly. Lisa said she thought she saw figures inside the craft."

While her parents described the same thing Deanna did, to this day she still has a feeling that something is missing—some part of her memory of the event "that was erased." She would like to get more information from Lisa, but her friend refuses to talk about it, as she is still obviously traumatized by the terrifying ordeal even more than 40 years later.

When I asked Deanna if she could describe the craft in more detail, or perhaps make a sketch, she replied that it looked just like the UFO drawing I showed during my presentation at the Danbury UFO Conference—the one drawn by Carol of the craft she saw in the Bronx in 1960. In fact, several people that day told me that it was exactly what they saw, as well.

"When people tell me that they don't believe in UFOs, I just laugh," Deanna said. "I have *no doubt* what I saw, and I will *never* forget."

Newburgh
Meadow Hill Woman Sees Strange Lights
September 27, 1973
by John McNally
The Evening News

TOWN OF NEWBURGH—13-year-old Jimmy Smith of Meadow Hill North development had a corroborating witness for his report of a "flying saucer"—his mother.

Mrs. John Smith said she had seen "a big, bright orange light" go across the sky and come back in the Meadow Hill North area on the following morning, about 3:30am.

Mrs. Smith said she is a cocktail waitress. She immediately added that she never touches alcohol while working (lest doubters think she was seeing things). She had seen the object after she got out of her car.

She went inside the house and tried to wake her husband, Richard, to come look, but he wasn't interested.

She then looked out of her living room window and saw the object returning from an easterly direction. It went behind some trees to the west of the development, the trees lighted up from the glow, and then the lights went off.

Jimmy, who is in the eighth grade at Meadow Hills School, told of his daylight sighting of a saucer-like object while he was on Monarch Drive near his home, last Wednesday, September 17, about 11:00am.

"It was round and white and had a green light out of the bottom and little green lights around the sides," he said.

It wasn't as "big as a house," as one press report described his sighting, but it was the size of a large, luxury type car, he said.

There were also saucer reports that night from police in Monroe and Warwick—an elliptical orange object with green lights.

Mrs. Smith noted her husband, now an executive with a local firm, is a retired Air Force man. She had called ARADCOM, a local army defense unit at Stewart Airport, and spoken with an officer about her son's report. The officer said Jimmy's description matched descriptions of objects cited in Georgia, she said.

"I'm not sure of what I saw, but I know when Jimmy tells me something, he's not playing games," she said.

"John"
Suffern, NY
1976

From a personal perspective, *witnessing* a UFO can have life-altering repercussions, both positive and negative. Unfortunately, *talking* about your UFO sighting generally has negative repercussions that follow you the rest of your life—even if you didn't intend for your story to go public.

Such was the case for an attorney in Rockland County, New York, who I tracked down almost four decades after his 1976 sighting. I had uncovered a *New York Times* article containing his story, and when "John" spoke to me, he revealed how that story came to be printed.

He got a call one evening from a man who was a friend of John's brother, and the man was interested in hearing John's UFO story in his own words. While John was normally reticent about his sighting, he "spoke freely" to this man, as he had been referred by his brother. What this man failed to mention during their conversation was that he was the assistant science editor for the *New York Times*!

At 7:30am the next morning, John got a call from a producer of a popular television show in New York City. The producer asked if he could send a car to bring John down to the studio for a live interview. John thought this was some sort of prank, but when he realized this person was serious, he asked, "What subject do you want me to talk about?"

"Didn't you see the article in the *New York Times* this morning?" the producer asked.

Shocked that his personal story was now in print for all the world to read, he nonetheless decided to do the show, now that the alien cat was out of the bag, so to speak. He was also invited to Washington, D.C. to do a television show there, and that show had a very interesting viewer that day.

"A friend who worked with President Ford called me," John explained, "and she said she was in the room as Ford was watching my interview, and he was enthralled by my story!"

Those were the fun parts of being "outed" for his UFO sighting. The uncomfortable parts were the numerous times in court that judges would call John to the bench and ask, "Have you seen anything lately, counselor?" Or even decades later when someone uncovered the *New York Times* article and circulated it throughout the community in an attempt to discredit him in a high-profile case. Needless to say, when I contacted John at his law firm, he was hesitant to bring this all up again, but with the assurance of anonymity, he agreed to tell me his story.

Under other circumstances, I might not have pursued such a witness, and simply used the information from the article. However, it was because of John's remarkable background that I contacted him—and I don't mean it was only his law degree that made an impression on me. John also has not one, but two engineering degrees. He was also in the military, where he worked on top secret navigation systems, and flew experimental aircraft for three years. So when John had his sighting in 1976, he had literally "seen it all" in terms of what was flying in the skies over America.

As for the details of his sighting, it was about 7:30pm one evening in early September of 1976. John was driving home after work and was exiting the New York State Thruway in Suffern when he spotted two strange craft, and he pulled over to the side of the road to get a better look. For five long minutes he was so "astounded" by what he saw, his "jaw dropped."

The craft were "shaped like two enormous upside-down soup bowls. The red-orange rays of the setting sun glinted from their silvery metallic bodies. One remained motionless above the horizon, while the other slipped gradually and silently from a vertical position into a horizontal one."

After those five amazing minutes, the two craft raced off at an incredible speed to the northwest.

"I definitely looked at them," he was quoted in an article, "and I saw that it was not a natural phenomenon or anything I could explain."

Coming from an engineer and former test pilot with top secret clearance, that is an extraordinary statement!

Although John was somewhat reluctant to reveal other things that had happened over the course of his life, which could only be described as remarkable, one thing I am at liberty to mention was another sighting he had in the 1950s.

"I was sitting in the driveway in my father's 1951 Chrysler New Yorker, waiting for my parents. From the east, I saw this disc that flashed through the sky over the car. I saw it through the front windshield as it approached, and through the back window as it left."

This fits the pattern I have found with so many witnesses who have had intense sightings or experiences—they usually have had sightings as a child, and other family members have also experienced something inexplicable. Naturally, my next question was about his family. While I would not have been surprised if John told me a relative had seen something, I ended up being astounded by what he told me. His brother— the same brother who had directed the editor to John to reveal his experience—had kept silent about his own story, and what a story it was!

His brother was with the Air Force in the 1950s and was stationed in Alaska. One day, he and the base commander received a package containing a manual, some photographs, and pieces of an aircraft. Their instructions were to perform a series of tests on the pieces—pieces that had been obtained from an alien craft!

He was sworn to secrecy for a period of 40 years, an oath he faithfully honored. He didn't tell John about the experience until those 40 years had passed. But that wasn't even the strangest part of the story. According to John's brother, the photographs not only showed the spacecraft, but in the background there were tables with bodies on them. While he couldn't see the features of these bodies, he was able to discern that the figures were *much smaller* than an adult human.

I asked if John's brother was one to make up stories, and he didn't hesitate to respond, "No, *never.*"

"Sally"
Westchester County
c. 1978

I received an email from "Sally" describing a very close sighting involving three witnesses:

"I was driving with two friends from Forest Hills to Tarrytown, NY in 1978 or 1979. When we got off of Route I-87 by the Cross County Shopping Center to get on to the Sprain Brook Parkway we saw what looked like a really bright star as far away as stars appear, but it looked brighter, like a planet or something. We just wondered what it was and kept talking and driving.

"Then it moved in a straight line to the left, very far. We lost sight of it and then when we got onto the Sprain we saw it again. It was changing direction back and forth, up and down. We pulled over on the Sprain on the left hand shoulder. At this part of the Sprain there is an island between the North and South lanes. We got out of the car and it was very close. We walked down onto the island to follow it.

"Then it went from a good distance away but still in sight and moved to right above us, at the height of a tree top. We could see it plainly. It was gigantic, like a football field, pewter colored, matte, not shiny, no lights. It hovered over us and made no noise, there was no wind, the trees were not blowing or anything. We all held onto each other, like our breath was taken away. Then it took off and we found ourselves standing there with our mouths open, holding each other.

"We walked back to the car and another car pulled over, I think it was a plain clothes police car. He asked what we were doing. We asked him if he saw what we saw and he said no, got in his car and drove away. I think that normally a police officer would ask to see license and registration at least, or look in our car, something to cover himself in case we were up to something, but he just drove away."

I asked several questions to get more details on the sighting, and the following is a summary.

- It was summer and about 9pm, so the sky was not completely dark.
- The craft was round.
- "The total sighting from when we first saw it on the Thruway until we saw it up close was maybe 15 minutes. It was up close for a minute or so. But at that point it could have been longer, we were just blown away by what we were seeing so close. I know that as soon as we got back into the car, we looked at the time and told each other to remember it, but after all this time I can't remember."
- "For years after we talked about it and words just could not come close to communicating what we had experienced."

Of the two friends with Sally, one is now her ex-husband and a "well-known professional musician," and the other is a Vice President of a publishing company. Sally is a clinical social worker. I always like to get statements from as many witnesses as possible, but she has been out of touch with her publishing friend for many years, and we joked that no UFO case is worth reconnecting with an ex-husband!

Wayne
Danbury, CT
Winter 1970s or 80s

Wayne did not hear about his parents' sighting from the 1970s or 80s until around 2002. He had no reason to doubt their story, and especially emphasized that his mother wasn't someone who "imagined things."

They were driving one winter's night when they saw a metallic object with bright lights hovering near Route 84 in Danbury. They pulled over and stopped by 93 Lake Avenue, which is now where AAA is located. The craft was only about 100 yards away so they had an excellent view of it, and Wayne was able to create this sketch according to their description.

On top of the craft there were two "butterfly-like antennae" with one blue and one white light. On the underside of the craft were what they described as "ribbon lights." The lights visible in the band of windows

33

around the center "were flashing" in a manner "that made the aircraft look as if it was spinning." [NOTE: This spinning lights effect is something I've heard repeatedly from eyewitnesses of circular craft, spanning several decades of sightings.] Wayne's parents stressed that the "white light was extremely bright" and neither of them ever "saw a light so bright" before.

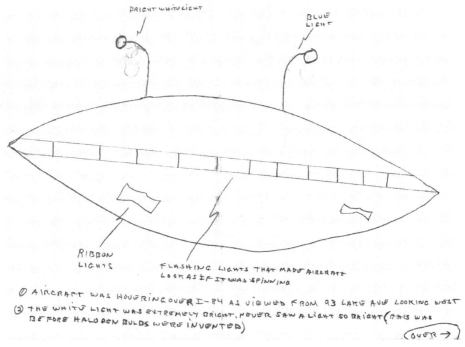

Wayne's sketch from his parents' description.

The craft just hovered in place, and then "had instant acceleration and made no sound" as it shot toward the east. Rather than being frightened, his parents were very excited by what they had just witnessed and actually attempted to follow the object. They headed east on Route 84, and when they were by Exit 7 the craft "flew back over them," perpendicular to the highway. His parents never heard of any other witnesses, and nothing was in the newspapers in the following days. Both of them are now deceased, but Wayne thought people should know about their amazing sighting.

Here's a cautionary tale to always keep your car full of gas and your camera ready during a UFO wave!

"Jack"
Danbury, CT
1983

At about 9pm at their home on Hoyt Street in Danbury, "Jack" and his wife saw a silent, round object just 50-100 feet above the trees, moving east to west.

"It was a full circle of lights, ten to twelve in count," Jack explained. "Each light seemed to have three colors, and they all turned color at the same time. They were red, white, and blue or green. There was a slow crossfade between colors. There weren't any beams of light."

When asked whether or not it was a solid object, Jack gave a thoughtful reply.

"The craft was rotating on its axis," he began. "As to the solidity of the object, I saw nothing between the lights, and can only assume that it was one solid object by the behavior of the rotation of the lights. Theoretically, it could be just a wire frame between the lights, but the way it was slowly rotating and also pitching about a center of axis, indicated to me that it couldn't be ultralights flying in formation. Plus, at the apparent height I would have been easily able to hear any gas engine and prop it there were any."

Jack ran inside to get his camera, but in the minute it took to get back outside, the craft was gone.

"We jumped in the Jeep to chase it, but it was almost out of gas. We drove to a gas station, filled it, and jumped on I-84, heading west towards New York, but too much time had gone by. We saw nothing and turned around over in Brewster, and came home."

Thomas Talarico
Danbury, CT
Fall 1983

Thomas Talarico had picked up his son from a friend's house, and the two were driving on South Kings Street toward their home in Danbury, CT one dark, Fall evening at about 7pm. There was a car directly in front of him, and both drivers slowed because something bright was just "50 to 75 feet from the car."

Both drivers came to a stop when they saw an object hovering above a field at Overlook Farm that was "saucerish-shaped, and a very bright white-silvery" color with it being "brighter in the middle. The dimensions were roughly 100 feet long and 20 feet thick, as indicated in Tom's sketch. And "it made no sound."

Tom watched in awe as this bright craft just appeared to "float" over the field, and this wasn't just a brief glimpse. He estimates the sighting lasted between five and seven minutes. Finally, the object "started moving up," so he and the other driver started driving again. But Tom still had sight of the craft as they headed toward Franklin Street. However, when the apparent size of the craft "could have been covered by my fist," it suddenly "shot to the east" and out of sight.

While Tom felt nothing but curiosity and fascination—that "Wow!" feeling as he described it to C. Burns at the Danbury Conference—his 13-year-old son did not share his father's positive sentiments. After I asked some additional questions, Tom wrote the following, which illustrates how for some people, sightings can inflict lifelong trauma.

"It was probably about 150 feet off the road in a field. About the car in front of me, we both slowed down together and stopped. And we watched it. My son was about 13 years old. All he kept saying was, "Dad let's get out of here." He was trying to hide under the dashboard.

"Yes, we were close and it was large. I never spoke too much about it, because it was so unreal. We talked more about it recently, because my son finally admitted that he saw it. He is now 46 years old. Still, he won't talk much about it. I wanted him to come to the conference, but he said, 'No way.' "

Danbury, CT
July 1984

"We're not alone," says UFO center of light sightings
by Trink Guarino
News-Times
July 14, 1984

Danbury—"We are not alone in this universe."

That is the message from the Center for UFO studies in Evanston, Illinois, according to local residents who reported sighting strange lights in the sky for the past two nights.

Local police said they received calls from about a dozen people who said they saw a strange ring of spotlights hovering low on the horizon. Some said they heard a humming sound. Others reported silence.

The ring is about the size of a football field and has been said to disappear suddenly, then reappear in another part of the sky, according to reports.

The center is calling the reports "one of the most significant series of UFO sightings in recent history."

But more than 500 similar cases in Fairfield County and in New York's Putnam, Westchester and Dutchess Counties have been reported in the past year, said Dr. J Allen Hynek, center director.

About 100 sightings were reported in the last few weeks, said Phillip Imbrogno, an astronomer assigned to the center's investigation.

"The people we have interviewed have Ph.D.s in physics. They are doctors, lawyers, scientists, pilots, people who would not mistake what they have seen."

Poughkeepsie Area
August 27, 1984

Aliens take their cues from UFO conference?
by George Berkin
Kingston Daily Freeman
(Article in August 28 edition)

New Paltz—The aliens it seems, were out in force Monday night, so fast on the heels of the weekend UFO conference in Brewster it seemed possible all the sightings drew from that common source of inspiration.

Even the Poughkeepsie police confirmed some strange phenomenon in the skies. The officers presumed it might have been a squadron of planes from the Stormville Airport. (Killjoys!)

But numerous earthlings in Poughkeepsie's particular corner of the galaxy were convinced that what they saw was from outer space—a multi-colored UFO overhead about 10:00 p.m.

At the same time, another couple driving on the Thruway between Newburgh and New Paltz also witnessed the UFO–but of a pencil-like shape with 14 white lights.

"It was humongous," Gina Francese, 16, of Staatsburg, said of the first object. Shortly after walking out of the South Hills Mall, she and three friends spotted the dish-like craft. "It had multi-colored lights, and it was hovering. It started moving and then it just disappeared," she said.

"It looked like a giant Frisbee with lights on it," added Poughkeepsie resident Rudy Zwezker, 21, who had his close encounter with the extraterrestrial bagel shortly after stepping out of the Dunkin' Donuts, on Route 9, with a bag of crullers.

"It was weird," said Zwezker. "It hovered, started to move, and then it was gone."

"I was more amazed that afraid," said Steve Saba, 17, of Hyde Park. The senior at Roosevelt High School was crossing eastbound over the Mid-Hudson Bridge, and there it was—off to the right, and about 50 feet in the air.

"I thought I was crazy, but other people were slowing down, too," he said.

Did he see any outer space creatures?

"No men, just a lot of lights," said Saba.

"These witnesses and a fourth (illegible line) lights; blue, red, green, yellow and white. And, each of the sightings lasted 5 to 10 minutes.

For Marianne Key, her sighting Monday–above the IBM-Poughkeepsie plant–was an encore.

"I'm not tripping, I don't take drugs, and I don't drink," said Ms. Key, a bit puzzled about her second run-in with the mystifying object.

Ms. Key, 41, had just stepped into the parking lot after finishing a second shift at the IBM cafeteria. "It was like a soup bowl, like a saucer dish: it looked just like *Close Encounters*," she said, referring to the sci-fi movie smash of a few seasons back. About 15 security guards at the plant also saw the UFO, she added.

After she drove to the rear of the building to pursue the wonder, the UFO just disappeared, said Ms. Key. The object emitted an irregular beeping, she reported.

Ms. Francese also heard a beeping sound, but Zwezker said the saucer was silent.

In June, while pulling into her Hyde Park home, she witnessed an identical UFO. "It was the same exact thing, just surrounded by lights. It got so close; I thought it was going to land on the house."

Though a skeptic previously, Ms. Key isn't so sure now. "I don't have the answer, but I'd like to have the answer," she said. "There's no way in my mind that I believe that these were planes."

Now that the UFO is becoming almost a regular occurrence, Ms. Key is getting excited about a third encounter. "I never anticipated seeing it again," she said. "But now I'm hoping to see it again."

Though Richard Bruner and his wife, Virginia, may have seen a different UFO, their experience Monday night, also at 10:00 p.m., was no less spectacular.

While driving north on the Thruway between exit 17 and 18, the West Shokan couple spotted what looked like the UFO.

"It was exhilarating," said Bruner.

Unlike the other reports Monday night, the Bruner's mysterious night flyer resembled "a stubby pencil with a point and a shaft," according to the 58-year-old freelance writer and former Midwest newspaper reporter.

The craft made no noise, and was 500 to 1000 feet above the ground nearly overhead. It was moving very slowly toward the west, and it suddenly disappeared after about 10 minutes.

"I had never seen one before and considered myself very skeptical," said Bruner. But he admitted he's baffled (illegible line) another planet," he said. "And it's possible what we saw tonight was a hoax."

His wife saw it, too—"I'm just incredulous," she said.

And when they related the story to the state police up the road, the trooper said he had seen the UFO also.

What do we make of all this? "There is more in heaven and earth than agrees with your philosophy," said the Bard.

Perhaps Shakespeare was a UFO buff also.

Note: Apart from not being happy whenever someone does not quote Shakespeare properly, one has to wince at the reporter's characterization of the "extraterrestrial bagel." The entire tone of the article is not very serious, but of course, witnesses have been treated far worse than this.

Rodney Bordeau
Danbury, CT
c.1983-85

It was a "calm, clear night" at about 10pm during the late spring or early fall, when Rodney Bordeau, and his brother-in-law were in a Ford station wagon by the Cornell Memorial Home on Homestead Avenue in Danbury, CT. Suddenly, the two men "*felt* a rumbling," although they didn't actually hear anything. They looked up and saw something massive directly above them.

"It filled the entire sky," Rodney said. "It was a round shape, with rotating or pulsating lights circling the edge—and the lights were unconventional colors."

The huge craft—which was very dark in the center—was headed north, and they lost sight of it as it passed over the house next door. The entire sighting lasted somewhere between 10 and 25 seconds. Both men were understandably surprised by the rumbling they felt and the appearance of the enormous, round craft, but while Rodney admitted to being "stunned and then frightened," his brother-in-law really "wasn't

40

fazed" by the experience. However, they did continue to talk about the sighting for weeks.

I would like to point out that Rodney was one of the first witnesses to arrive at the 2016 Danbury UFO Conference that morning, and patiently waited quite a while for his turn to be interviewed by C. Burns. When I emailed him a few days later with an additional question, I apologized for the long wait and said I appreciated his patience. His response emphasized the importance of providing venues for witnesses to tell their stories—even three decades later.

"It was a pleasure to contribute to your work," Rodney wrote. "After all these years, it was a relief to tell someone that was really interested."

Ray Laskowski
Stratford, CT
August 1986

Ray Laskowski, his son Chris, and neighbor, Matt, were on the golf course at the Mill River Country Club in Stratford, CT in August of 1986. The sky was clear at dusk, and there was still "plenty of light" to see the two "very large disc-shaped vehicles" that were "suspended in the sky."

Ray stated that, "The crafts were essentially side by side with one being in the forefront. They were 65 to 75 yards in length, conservatively. Their depth was prominent as well; i.e. their surface from top to bottom. The color of the objects was grayish blue, and there were red and blue blinking lights. There was no sound." (See Ray's sketch below.)

The three of them stood in "amazement" as these craft hovered, until the craft began "very deliberate and silent" movements.

"The objects then moved sharply to our left, then right, in rapid movements one at a time. They disappeared, not fading or drifting away. All three of us remember clearly to this day."

Chris later emailed me with his recollections from that day:

"I remember it like this: out of nowhere, extremely loud, more of a hovering than a very fast take off...bright lights/reddish around the object, not sure if that was the sky color or lights from what we saw...15th hole of Mill River Country Club in Stratford...nothing like a plane flying...more circular/hovering with a fast acceleration...surprisingly somewhat low to the ground."

Interesting, that while the two accounts are almost identical, Ray recalls there being "no sound," while one of the first things Chris mentions was that it was "extremely loud." I have found on several occasions that groups of witnesses can have very different experiences during the same sighting. In any event, this is certainly an impressive daylight sighting of two discs which could not be mistaken as any conventional aircraft!

The following is a refreshingly amusing account! If true, the fact that rocks thrown at the UFO could not be heard hitting it, and the rocks also never fell back to the ground, is nothing short of amazing.

Danbury, CT
c. August 1988

NUFORC Report
I threw rocks at a UFO for about a half an hour
Duration: 45 minutes

What occurred happened in Danbury, Connecticut on Newtown Rd. It was a very dark area with only a couple of city light poles that were on. There were a couple of stores in that area, but they were all closed. There are a lot of hills in this area so it further darkens the area.

I was about eighteen years old at the time. My friend and I were working at a Burger King until about 10 pm. We went outside to wait for a ride and we were talking. We went across the street where there was a pay phone that I was going to use to call to see where our ride was and I noticed that where we just walked from was a seemingly round object just hovering in the air about 30 feet, not very high, no real noise except for humming. I felt and heard a humming just like an electrical substation; there's one in every town. I felt my hairs standing up. The object was about the size of the Burger King, just a little wider. There were about eight, two foot wide bulbs around the object.

My friend and I walked under it at an angle and tried to make out the shape with the stars since it was the only light above, there was no moon and the stars were almost not visible. We first thought it was a hot air balloon with lights on the bottom but with the little stars that were out, we couldn't see how high it exactly was, but we knew it wasn't high like a balloon.

I need to say this, over the years I've read a lot about what other people have written about what they saw, and what's different about mine, is that I think my friend and I are the only dumb asses that threw rocks and tar from the road at it for about a good half an hour. And we didn't even hear the rocks fall back on the ground and we didn't hear them hit the object.

After about half an hour of throwing rocks at it, we watched it slowly rise up then whoosh, it went up fast, in like a couple of seconds it shot up, we saw the lights get closer together, get smaller, and dim, in a matter of two to three seconds.

My take on why it left so abruptly, is that I think they were going to abduct us until they found out they'd have serious problems with the two dumb asses that were throwing rocks at them. Just kidding.

One more thing, there is one more witness, this was a little strange, it was my ride which happened to be my mom. She didn't see it there, but she saw it at her job, which happens to be on the other side of the hill/small mountain, at the Davis and Geck parking lot. We talked about it

43

a few days after it happened, because we ended up walking home. She said she was afraid of it and went back inside to get someone to walk her back to her car. It happened at night, and that is all I know.

"Vic"
Montgomery-Gardiner, NY, c. 1988
Shawangunk Mountains ("The Gunks"), 1993

Often, people are hesitant to provide sketches because they "can't draw," but even the simplest illustration can literally be worth a thousand words. When "Vic" emailed me his sketch, I immediately recognized it as a familiar shape seen in the skies of the Hudson Valley during the 1980s. Our email exchange is below:

Vic: Hi, I had a daytime sighting back in about 1988. I was driving with my friend on Albany Post Rd. between Montgomery, NY and Gardiner on my way to New Paltz. We pulled into a farmer's field, which was on a hill, and watched it for over ten minutes. It was in the direction of Stewart AFB. It was huge!

In 1993, I also had an experience up in the Gunks (illegally camping, which you could get away with back then) out in the middle of nowhere. It was a beautiful night so, last minute, we grabbed our stuff and headed out. We knew it wasn't supposed to rain so we just slept out under the stars as we often did. Suddenly, as we were just sitting there eating and talking, the entire area became brightly lit up from above. Bright as a football stadium! We could see clearly throughout the heavily forested woods surrounding us. After about a minute or so, the light disappeared. No sounds of aircraft of any kind.

I am glad to give you more info if you are interested. Thanks

Zim: Hi, thanks for writing and yes, I would like to get more details. What was the shape of the craft in the 1988 sighting? How did it move? Could you sketch it?

Vic: Thanks for getting back to me. The craft was a circle of bright white lights with a tail of the same lights hanging down. We couldn't see any body to the craft as the lights were so bright and it was far enough away that all the details were not visible. It was light out but getting toward sundown. It didn't move.

It just hung there, not moving as a whole, but some of the lights in the tail were changing places with each other. But so very, very slowly that it was hard to perceive they were moving. From where we sat the UFO was above the tree line at about 30 degrees above the ground. At an arm's length perspective, the craft was about 2-feet wide when viewed between my hands. It was MASSIVE!

It was in the *Times Herald Record* the next day or days after. Lots of people reported seeing it. When I got home I figured out with a topo map that it was in front of, above, or past Stewart (Airport) from where we were sitting.

I remember saying to my friend that if it wasn't from another world - somebody in the Government has conquered gravity, and they have some explaining to do! We watched it for at least 10 minutes, and drove away with it still just sitting there.

Recently, I was watching an old video of that show, *Unsolved Mysteries*, and they were talking about the Hudson Valley UFO sightings. There was a couple on the show that videotaped the craft at night, and the image looked the same as what we saw. A circle of lights with a few lights tailing off it. It was very startling to see what we saw on tape. Have you ever heard of the spotlight I saw being associated with the area?

Thanks very much for letting me tell my story to you.

Zim: Wonderful, thanks so much for the detailed description and sketch, it helps a lot. Love your comment about the government having some explaining to do.

And yes, intense spotlights have been reported quite often, usually over someone or their car.

Vic: Interesting. We were in the middle of the woods at least a mile from RT. 44/55. No roads or trails, leading to where we were. It was the strangest thing I ever experienced. It scared the crap out of my friend.

Pine Bush, NY
August 15, 2015

In September of 2015, I had the privilege of speaking at the MUFON Symposium in Irvine, CA. As the topic of my presentation was the Hudson Valley, the New York state director of MUFON, Sam Falvo, told me about a recent case that had occurred near Pine Bush. But he didn't even need to say the name of the town, as he had my attention the moment he mentioned two words—West Searsville.

I'm not quite sure this a proper analogy, but West Searsville Road is like the Vegas Strip in Hudson Valley ufology—it was where it was all happening in the heyday of the Pine Bush flap in the 1980s and 90s, when cars would line the street every night as eager sky watchers marveled at the incredible displays of lights.

I was further intrigued when Sam said that in the center of a circular impression in the grass, over which the craft had been seen hovering, he measured radiation levels *seven times higher than normal*. I couldn't wait to find out more, visit the site, and perhaps speak with the witnesses themselves. I didn't have to wait long, as a few weeks later I was giving a lecture at the Josephine-Louise Library in Walden, New York, and the owners of the property came to speak to me.

(Before proceeding with their story, I think it's important to bring up the fact that while Pine Bush is referred to as the *UFO Capital of the Northeast*, many of the sightings actually occurred in Walden and Montgomery—including the iconic West Searsville Road, which is actually in the Town of Montgomery. This is not to diminish Pine Bush in any way, but I think it is important to clarify these locations for people not familiar with the area, and give these other places their proper recognition.)

Regardless of modern-day zoning boundaries, this is a remarkable case which illustrates that while activity has greatly diminished in the area since the 1990s, there are still incredible things happening in the same fields today. The following is a summary from my personal interview with a resident of the property who was there on that August 15th night about 8:45pm.

"Jackie" was sitting on the back porch, when her 17-year-old son, "Bill" came running out of the woods at the back of the property. He was shaking and clearly terrified. He said that a circular, metallic craft with red and white lights was hovering just above the tall grass in the adjacent field. However, as scared as he was, he wanted a flashlight to go back through the woods to see if the craft was still there. He begged Jackie to go with him, but she not only had difficulty walking, she had no desire to see a UFO, as the thought frightened her.

Undeterred, Bill ran back to the field. The craft was indeed still there, and then he watched it from a distance of *less than ten feet*. In addition to the incredible sight, Bill felt a strange "humming in his head" that made him "feel sick," and the ground beneath his feet vibrated. He said that all the hair on his arms and back stood up, too.

After several minutes, the craft moved quickly to another location in the field, and then to a third spot, hovering for a while each time, before finally speeding away. The entire sighting lasted between 10 and15 minutes.

Bill was shouting back and forth with Jackie during the entire time, telling her what was happening, and strongly urging her to come and see this amazing object. While Jackie was unable to see the craft through the woods, she did get a minute-by-minute account of the sighting as it was occurring, and her daughter also saw lights hovering high in sky over the field about 20 minutes later.

Bill felt physically ill after the encounter, with pain in his head and stomach. And he was so traumatized by what he witnessed and experienced that he refused to sleep alone for many nights afterward.

The next day, six family members went back into the field and discovered three circular impressions in the grass, about 35 feet in diameter, in the three locations where the craft had hovered. They reported the incident to MUFON, and Sam Falvo investigated, taking samples and measurements. Bill also drew a detailed sketch of the craft. Another MUFON investigator later made two more trips to the site, and during one of them, Bill accompanied him and again experienced the strange humming in his head.

Jackie used her cell phone to take this photo of the broken and bent vegetation in one of the circular impressions.

Fast forward to early November, and Jackie reported that she and her daughter again saw lights in that field, hovering about 30-40 feet above the ground.

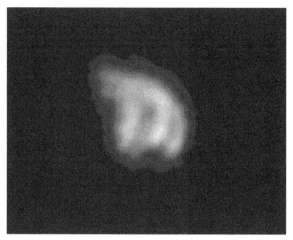

Jackie's daughter took this cell phone photo of the lights over the field. Allowing for some blur from being a hand-held image, it does appear to be multiple lights. Whether or not they were attached to the same object, or multiple objects, isn't clear.

Jackie was kind enough to allow me, my husband, Bob Strong, and Pine Bush researcher and UFO archivist, C. Burns to spend a night sky watching in her yard. Unfortunately, we didn't spot any UFOs, but we were able to get a firsthand sense of just how amazing it must have been to watch the craft over the field directly behind her house.

And one final note: I also received a report from Red Hook, NY, that on August 19, just four days after the initial sighting, a circular craft with a ring of red lights was seen by witnesses.

Activity is alive and well in Pine Bush, and also in the entire Hudson Valley region.

3
Cylinders and Cigars

Milan Pribis
Queens, NY
September 1981

Information from *SBI Report* Issue #36

A former Yugoslav Air Force pilot, aeronautical engineer, and inventor should be familiar with all types of aircraft. However, at about 5:30pm on an early September evening in 1981, Milan Pribis stood near the intersection of Corona Avenue and Broadway in Queens, New York, as a glowing, cylindrical object passed overhead.

"For the first time, I saw an object I couldn't identify," Pribis stated.

At the time, Pribis was listed in "Jane's Who's Who in Aeronautics" as the inventor of "vortex-reducing winglets on airplane wings," and was working as a mechanical designer for Peerless Instruments. He was facing northeast when he saw the landing lights of a plane headed toward him. He recognized that this was a flight path to LaGuardia Airport, so there was nothing unusual about it, but then he saw a "brighter, yellow light to the right of the airplane at about 600 yards away from it."

The plane continued to his left toward LaGuardia, while the yellow light stayed on a path to pass right over his position. As he watched, Pribis quickly realized that the yellow light could not be a conventional airplane, as it turned an orange color and made absolutely no sound. But then things got really strange.

"It seemed to metamorphose to a cylinder with a domed top and lines of a deeper shade down its surface, and it seemed to undulate like a jellyfish."

The object was not metallic and was "somewhat indistinct" as it passed directly overhead. He lost sight of it behind some trees, but while it was above him, the object "appeared as big as his thumb held at arm's length." Pribis observed this bizarre craft for about four minutes, and the entire time he was at "a complete loss" as to what he was witnessing. He stated that he was familiar with everything from weather balloons, to

50

satellites, to all types of aircraft in between, but this was beyond anything he knew.

Pribis tried to report the sighting to LaGuardia Airport, as he was fairly certain that the pilot of the aircraft on approach for landing must have seen the cylindrical object, but no one ever answered the phone. He didn't decide to speak to a reporter until a couple of weeks later, when he read an article about another sighting in the area which occurred on September 5 at 10pm, which may have been the same night of his sighting. The September 5 sighting involved ten witnesses who saw a UFO which beamed a bright light onto a girl watching from her window.

Was this the same object on the same night, or were multiple UFOs visiting Queens in September of 1981?

**

I have to say that this is my favorite case in this book, due to the extraordinary credentials of the witness, the remarkable description of the craft, and the reaction by the military. Intimidation and cover ups were alive and well in 1983…and probably still are.

Victoria Lamas
Chappaqua, New York, c.1983

Victoria is not your average UFO witness. For several years, she was an FAA trained plane spotter at LaGuardia Airport. Working the night shift, her job was to identify incoming planes by their configuration of lights, and then visually identify and record the tail numbers.

Even though planes have transponders that identify these numbers, on numerous occasions the numbers Victoria were seeing did not match what the transponders were saying. The reason for this was simple—people (usually drug dealers) stole the planes, altered the numbers, and then were stupid enough to fly into a major New York airport thinking that no one would notice the difference.

She later worked at Westchester County Airport, where her duties also included filing flight plans, fuel calculations, and dealing with the unexpected, which at an airport could be just about anything. It was while she was employed at this airport that she and her mother encountered something very unexpected as they were returning from grocery shopping to her home on King Street in Chappaqua.

"I was near my house when I looked up and said, 'Holy Mackerel! Look, mom, it's a UFO!'"

A car was already stopped by the side of the road, and Victoria pulled up behind it. A third car stopped behind her.

"I got out of the car and my mother freaked out and started screaming for me to get back in. The car behind me had a woman and her kids, and they were all screaming. The man in front of me was yelling, 'Look at that!' and was literally jumping up and down."

What were they all seeing that elicited such reactions?

"The craft was so huge I couldn't see the edges. There was a line of pine trees about 50-feet-tall, and they were on a ten-foot hill. The craft was directly above the trees, so it was about 60 feet above the ground. I looked for markings, like 'United States Air Force,' but there was nothing. And there were no seams, it was completely smooth. It was silvery metallic, but I couldn't see any seams. It just wasn't anything I recognized."

That is a powerful statement coming from someone who identified commercial, civilian, and military aircraft for a living!

Victoria went on to describe the two "lines of lights," one red and one white, running the length of the craft. The lights dimmed and brightened, and when the white lights were at their brightest, they illuminated the entire underside of the craft.

"There was no sound, but there was a rhythmic, low bass that you could feel. And the tree tops vibrated in unison with this rhythm, waving back and forth."

Even though her "mother was terrified," Victoria wanted to get even closer to the object. She thought by driving up the hill of Bear Ridge Road she would be able to see the craft at eye level.

"For some reason, though, I couldn't see it, which was strange because it was so huge. So I quickly drove back down the hill to King Street and turned into my driveway. I ran into the kitchen because from there I had a good view of it again, and it was within 50 feet or so of the enormous water tank that was on my property."

That tank had once held water for the town of Chappaqua, and while it was very large, this craft was much larger. As her house was on a hill, she now had a better view of the object, and estimated it was about 300 feet long, although it was still hard to determine the shape, as she was looking at it edge-on.

"The best I can describe it, was looking at the front of a cigar-shaped object. Perhaps if it had tilted to one side I would have been able to get a better idea of the shape, but honestly, the shape wasn't my biggest concern at that moment."

Victoria decided to call a friend in the tower at Westchester County Airport, and she described the object and its location.

"We have it! We have it on the screen!" the man said, indicating the object was on radar. "I can't tell you what it is, as there's no transponder, but there's something big there!"

A few minutes later, the phone rang. It was her husband's friend, Bob, who lived nearby, and he was also in a state of great excitement.

"You have a UFO by your water tank!" he declared. When Victoria told him she saw it, he continued. "Oh my god! I am watching it through the binoculars!"

They both watched it for several minutes, and just as they were saying that they couldn't believe it was staying there for so long, "it zoomed off so fast it was like a bullet." It headed west, toward the town of Pleasantville.

Later that night, Victoria also spoke to a friend, Linda, in Bedford, which was to the north. Linda was outside talking to a friend, when an object slowly came overhead; an object "so huge it obscured the entire sky." They were also unable to determine the shape.

The next morning, Victoria drove to the airport, anxious to speak with the radar man in the tower. He was waiting for her in the parking lot and came running over to her car the moment he saw her pull in.

"Whatever you do," he said in a highly agitated state, "do not say you saw it if you want to keep your job!"

Victoria asked him what he was talking about, and the man explained that right after they spoke, "military men burst through the door with their guns drawn," knocking over a table and knocking over other things. She would have thought he was kidding, but she could see he was obviously "scared half to death."

The men threatened him, and told him he would lose his job if he said a word to anyone. And if anyone asked him about what he saw on radar, he was to reply that "it was only a flock of birds."

Victoria was stunned and perplexed by all this, and when she got to her office, she was immediately told the boss wanted to see her. When she went to see him, he also "looked terrified."

"If you want to stay at your job, you didn't see anything!" he blurted it.

"How did you know I saw it" she asked.

"Word got out," he replied. "Jobs are at stake here. You didn't see anything. It was a flock of birds."

While her boss refused to say who had threatened him, and what they had said, she later found out that the military men had come from the Air National Guard base at the airport. When she asked the radar man if it could have been a secret military project, he assured her that the ANG had also seen it on their radar, and it "wasn't military." It certainly wasn't a flock of birds, either!

From that point on, everyone at the airport was paranoid of losing their jobs, and of repercussions from the military if they broke their silence. But many others in town had seen the huge craft, often describing it as being triangular in shape, and they weren't keeping quiet. There were some articles in the newspaper speculating as to what people saw, and a group of witnesses got together at the local library and demanded answers from the government, but, of course, there were no answers.

There was also a story from that night that never made it to the newspaper. Two Pleasantville cops followed the object to the baseball field. They got out of their car and started running towards it, when "a beam of light stunned them, and knocked them senseless." Victoria couldn't personally vouch for this story, but enough reliable people in the area were certain of the authenticity of the report.

Victoria had never seen anything like this before, and nothing like it in the 30 years since that night. She was "not at all" scared by the massive object, "just curious." She admits she listens more closely now to other people's accounts of UFOs.

While Victoria can't say what it was she saw, "I know what I *wasn't* looking at. I was trained to identify helicopters, jets, and small planes— commercial, civilian, and military. I *know* something is out there."

Note: Westchester County Airport was built in 1942 so the Air National Guard could protect New York City's water supply system. In May 1983, the Guard unit was transferred to Stewart International Airport, so Victoria's sighting had to have taken place before then.

"Michael"
Carmel, NY
c. 1983

After speaking to a Connecticut MUFON group in April of 2015, I received the following information. Not only is this an excellent, multi-witness sighting, but Michael also saw the hoaxing pilots who didn't fool him for one second.

My name is "Michael." My mother attended your presentation yesterday at St. Catherine's Church in Greenwich, CT. She gave me a copy of your book, which I have only briefly skimmed as of this writing. I grew up in Lake Carmel, N.Y. and I witnessed a UFO several times during the early-to-mid 1980s. I wrote a detailed description of my experiences in a letter to a gentleman who was doing some research on this topic about twenty or so years ago. Sadly, I do not believe I saved a copy of the letter, nor do I recall the name of the gentleman I sent it to. But I can still recall the experiences, if you're interested in hearing about them. Here is a brief summary:

I was in high school at the time, perhaps in my senior year (1983). A group of friends and I were helping another friend move. This friend lived down the hill from the Kent Elementary school, off Farmer's Mill Road. I believe the name of the road is Meadow Court. There is an expansive wooded area, which remains to this day, off to the west toward Whangtown Road and Kentwood Lake. I believe it was on a Friday or Saturday evening in September or October.

It was dark and I recall seeing an incredible bright white light off in the distance to the west, up on a hill. My initial thought was that it was a spotlight from a house. Upon closer examination, I realized the light was shining down on the ground. After about ten seconds, the light went off. A massive object moved in my direction, pausing in the valley. It was silent and it had a single red light at one end. Several of my friends witnessed it as well. I recall feeling befuddled, intrigued, excited, but not at all frightened. Mostly, I was curious to understand what my eyes were witnessing.

We watched the object for maybe fifteen minutes or so when the red light separated from the massive object and started moving slowly about the area, although it never came near us. It was quite a show! The red light then began to move to the north, out of our field of vision, and a short while later, the massive object followed. Both appeared to move to the north and west toward White Pond. My friend and I jumped in his car and started following it down Farmers Mill Road. I used to hang out at White Pond frequently (it was a local party place for high school kids) and some of my other friends happened to be there when I arrived.

I recall a few of the girls were absolutely freaked out because the massive object hovered over White Pond with the same white light shining down toward the water that I initially witnessed. I recall hearing that an abduction involving some fisherman in a rowboat occurred that evening on White Pond. The object was gone by the time we arrived at White Pond.

It had continued moving to the north toward Fishkill. Many people reported seeing this object on the same night, but I think I had a closer view of it than most people, other than my friends at White Pond. It was literally right in front of me, close enough that I could see the object in complete darkness, simply by the contrast between it and the night sky. It was much wider than it was high. I've heard it described as being cigar shaped. Perhaps it was. Up close, it just looked massive.

By the way, I also saw the imposter ultralights some months later, which in no way could be mistaken for the massive object I saw, which I believe to this day to be a UFO. The ultralights flew right over me while I was traveling on Route 52 near Stormville Mountain. They were continuously moving in a "V" formation and made more noise than a landscape crew mowing and blowing someone's yard. If they were trying to appear UFO-like, they were a complete fraud.

There was another sighting by me and a few friends in the same wooded area behind the Kent Elementary school, near Kentwood Lake, months later, but it was farther off in the distance. This second experience wasn't nearly as memorable as the first, but exciting nonetheless. In my opinion, what I witnessed each time was not of this world. I believe in

UFOs because of my personal experiences, much like people who have had a spiritual experience believe in God. I know what I saw, and I will never forget it.

Thanks for your efforts to raise awareness of this phenomenon.

Suffern, NY
Fall 2012

This account came from a friend of "Jay," a man whose sighting I wrote about in a previous book, and Jay's wife referred this witness to me. Was it a secret military vehicle, or an alien spacecraft? While we can't jump to the conclusion of the latter, it would be comforting to believe that the government isn't testing cruise missiles over heavily-traveled, major New York highways!

Hi Linda, I was speaking with Jay at work and brought up the topic of "have you ever seen a UFO?" I guess I did this because it always stays in my mind—what we (me and my wife) saw. It's not the topic of conversation anyone would normally talk about, but I know Jay well enough for that. He told me of his sighting and then I told him of mine.

It has been a while (4+ years) since we saw it. I did not record the date, but the memory is just as vivid as if it happened yesterday. Before this email, I spoke with my wife about it. We agreed that it was in the fall (probably November).

Here is the sighting: We were on our way from Pearl River to the Woodbury Commons Outlets. The time was approx. 1PM. The day was dry, clear sky, good sun. We were travelling West/North along I-287. We were just past the Airmont exit. I saw the object first, and could not believe what I was seeing. I then had my wife look out the passenger side window where she was sitting to confirm the object. She saw it as well. I had her put window down; no noise other than wind from the road.

The object was totally tan in color, except for a small black triangle in the midsection, with the triangle pointing to the direction it was heading. The direction it was heading was exactly along I-287,westbound. It was travelling probably in the neighborhood of 100 to 150 miles per hour. It was about 300 feet from the highway as it moved. It was about 100 feet above treetops.

As it moved along the highway, I sped up, because it appeared to be something you could follow. As I did, it accelerated a little more. The road started to curve to the left around a small mountain near Suffern. The object went to the right of the small mountain peak and over the mountain, and kept going straight into the distance and out of view.

The objects shape: torpedo with perfectly rounded ends

Size: Approx. 40 feet long

Color: light 'cardboard' tan

Markings: small black triangle in center, oriented in the direction it traveled

Movements: only forward movement, no rotation

Appearance: the texture of the tan surfaces seemed slightly bumpy or grainy. Flat to semi-gloss sheen on tan surfaces, deep flat black on triangle. Triangle seemed to be painted on tan surface (no fin, or control mechanism).

As the object accelerated ahead of us, we saw more of the backside of it, confirming it was torpedo in shape. This was happening in broad daylight with many other motorists travelling down the same road. Maybe we were the only ones to see it, because it was pretty close to the treetops and slightly off the highway. This all happened in a matter of seconds.

We chalked it up to some new military cruise missile. Nevertheless, it stands in our book as a UFO.

And in my book, too!

4
The Hoaxing Pilots

It's unfortunate that I have to continue to devote time and effort to the issue of the hoaxing Cessna and ultralights pilots who thought it was so funny to pretend to be UFOs, while frightened and distracted motorists below were driving off the road. I covered the ultralight topic in depth in my first UFO book, *In the Night Sky*, going so far as to go for a flight in an ultralight so I could better understand their capabilities and characteristics.

At the Danbury UFO conference in October 2016, one man told me that his father had been acquainted with two of the ultralight pilots, each of whom were ex-military, and at the time, were both commercial pilots. As flying at night and turning off the lights on their aircraft were illegal, these reckless and foolish men were repeatedly risking losing their pilot's licenses and livelihoods for the sake of a stupid joke.

When the *News Times* article appeared about our Danbury UFO Conference, two of the online readers posted the following comments:

- DD430

I saw it while living in New Milford one night. It turned out to be a bunch of ultralight aircraft that had taken off from Stormville, NY and it was a pretty impressive sight.

- Sashatree

Hate to burst bubbles, but DD430 hit the nail on the head. My father and his friends all owned ultralights and absolutely DELIGHTED in pulling off UFO hoaxes like these. He was part of the group responsible for all of the "UFO sightings" during the early 80s. They all had radio headsets on to speak with one another so they could coordinate lights, positions, "going dark" to make it seem like they disappeared, etc. Of course, flying ultralights at night is completely against FAA laws (especially b/c they didn't have regulation lighting on them and are so slow!) so everyone involved (and their families) were sworn to secrecy so the guys wouldn't lose their pilot's licenses. My dad passed in 1997 and after reading so many stories from people absolutely convinced they'd seen UFO's in the area, I decided that the truth must come out. Just a bunch of men acting like teenagers and laughing their butts off when the stories and videos surfaced about them. I'm not saying UFOs don't exist. I'm saying that the ones in the Hudson Valley and Danbury area are all guys from Stormville Airport pulling pranks.

- DD430
The guys did a great job of it too! It was fun to watch.

- Sashatree
Thanks. They were really a bunch of older men that were practical jokers at heart. A lot of planning went into their "performances"... radio headsets to communicate with one another, ground training for formations, installing special lights they could remotely control (go off and on all at the same time to make it look like the "ufo " simply "disappeared"), studies in how the human brain works, specifically that if you have a lighted perimeter against a dark sky, the human brain "blocks out" the middle of the circle and fools people into thinking they're looking at solid object, installing special mufflers on the ultralights to make them as quiet as possible, etc. They were all very smart, as well as fun-loving.

What these people consider "smart" and "fun-loving," I find to be moronic, childish, irresponsible, and cruel, considering how many people were terrified and had car accidents because of their idiotic "pranks." What angers me even more, however, is the brainless and ignorant statement that these hoaxers were "responsible for all of the 'UFO sightings' during the early 80s." The sad part is that the casual, uniformed reader might actually believe that.

A former fireman, Paul McAllister, who attended the Danbury UFO Conference provided the following account of his experience with the ultralights in February of 1983 at about 8pm:

"At the time I was a member of the Germantown VFD-Danbury. We were doing training at the boat ramp, when someone saw the lights in the sky. We saw five or seven lights moving slowly from west to east. The lights appeared blueish white.

"I then told the driver to turn on the truck's red lights. When this happened, the lights, which were slightly to the north, veered toward our location. We had heard about people seeing lights in the sky prior to this. As the lights approached our location, I had two firemen get on the truck and man the floodlights, which were off at the time. As the lights got closer, about 1,000 feet, I had them turn on the floodlights and aim them at the lights.

"At this point we saw 5-7 ultralight craft caught in the beams. They immediately began to break the 'V' pattern, turning left and right and turning off their lights. We tried to follow some with the floodlights, but they were soon out of our sight.

"At the time the sky was clear, no clouds. I was the truck officer at the time. Also note that I was also a police officer. I checked around and the rumor at the time was a group of individuals was using the old Stormville Airport in NY to fly ultralights doing this."

Too bad these pilots were not followed and arrested, as it would have saved a lot of confusion and disinformation. I have spoken with several police officers from New York and Connecticut who were under orders that no matter what people reported seeing, the official response was to tell witnesses they saw ultralights.

Unfortunately, the infamous Stormville Flyers[1] also included a group of pilots flying small Cessna planes. Those pilots and their families were also sworn to secrecy, and they also all managed to escape arrest, even though at least one was identified by the tail number on his plane when he landed, and his name was made public at the time in an *APRO Bulletin*[2]— Ivan P. Hersh, of Stormville, NY.

Thirty years later when I found this information in the APRO article, I tracked Mr. Hersh to his retirement home in New Mexico. I wrote him a letter stating that it was time to come clean and set the record straight with flight logs of when—and more importantly—when they *didn't*, fly in formation pretending to be UFOs. Unfortunately, however, I was just a little too late, as the post office returned my unopened letter and had marked it "DECEASED." (Not having corresponded directly with Mr. Hersh, I can't state for certain he was one of the Stormville Flyers, and can only say that the APRO investigators saw him land after flying in

---

[1] In newspaper articles, the spelling of this term varied from Flyers to Fliers, but as the former appeared to be used the most, that is the spelling I chose.

[2] In *APRO Bulletin* Vol. 11 No. 6, a detailed article by Dick Ruhl and Richie Petracca, "The Westchester Sightings," describes their contentious encounter with the Stormville Flyers after they watched them land one night in June, 1984, and tried to take photographs. Ruhl took a picture of Hersh's Cessna's tail number, N-76106, before the pilot turned bright lights on him to prevent more photos. Another pilot threatened to take Ruhl's camera, fly it into the air, and drop it—which the pilot claimed they had done to another person who tried to photograph them. In Ruhl's opinion, 90% of the sightings during 1983-84 were the result of these hoaxing pilots, who he said were extremely adept at flying in tight formations, had painted their planes black, and had most likely installed special mufflers.

formation and photographed his Cessna plane's tail number, which indicated he was a co-owner of that plane.)

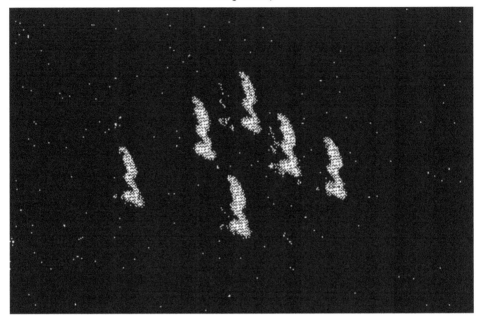

APRO's Dick Ruhl took this photograph of the Stormville Flyers. Note they are not in a uniform pattern and stars can clearly be seen between the planes.

A local magazine also recently printed a letter from a man who spoke to one of the Cessna pilots a few years ago. I contacted this man asking him to get me in touch with the pilot, but so far this pilot has not responded to my request. To date, none of the hoaxing ultralight or Cessna pilots has had the guts to give their name and go on the record.

Such was the case in an interview with one of the Stormville Flyers' Cessna pilots conducted by a reporter with the *Poughkeepsie Journal*, and published in the February 8, 1984 edition. The following are some excerpts:

The pilots said they never wanted people to think they were UFOs. They just enjoy flying at night. Together. But then people started looking up. And so began the trouble.

At first these pilots, all local men, thought the UFO stuff was kinda funny. Then it got out of hand. Drivers almost got in accidents looking at them. UFO buffs went bananas over it. The national press picked up the story.

And now the pilots wish to remain anonymous—even though this kind of flying is legal. They just don't want any hassles. "One thing we've never wanted is publicity. And now it's been blown so out of proportion, it scares us," said one of the pilots, a Dutchess County man who agreed to speak for the pilots only if he wasn't identified by name. "We're afraid if we're identified now, the FAA (Federal Aviation Administration) will hassle us with an investigation and put our certification in jeopardy," he said

The UFOs were generally seen on Thursday nights.

"Most of these accounts could describe the sight created by formation flyers," said the Dutchess County pilot, adding that Thursday was the most convenient flight time for the pilots. "I'm not saying I don't believe in UFOs. But I've never seen one," the pilot said. "And I do think people are ignorant about flying—and allow imagination to make up for a lot of things."

The pilot said the single engine planes—sometimes Cessna one fifties—fly in a V-shaped or diamond formation as close as a wingspan apart. Each aircraft has required red, green and white navigation lights, as well as bright, white landing lights.

At least one of these pilots—usually near the rear of the formation—uses a rotating beacon that warns nearby aircraft. He said the formations travel faster than 100 miles per hour, but often appear motionless because it is so wide and can be seen from long distances.

"If someone's on the ground and we're moving toward or away from him, it might appear we're not moving at all."

The pilots usually take off separately, then slowly move into formation one by one until a crude V-shape is formed with as many as five planes. They fly together for miles, making constant adjustments along the way.

"The guy in the lead—the tip of the V—has the easiest job. He just flies ahead and tells everyone his next move before he makes it."

The flier said the pilots communicate with each other by radio and sometimes with hand signals. He said the pilots usually stick to the well-known path over the Taconic Parkway, and have traveled as far south as Westchester.

The pilots last flew together on New Year's Eve, circling separately over Westchester while glancing at distant fireworks in New York City's Central Park.

The pilot did acknowledge that few fliers risk these types of nighttime formations. But he insisted it is safe for well-trained pilots, adding he has about 3000 hours of flight experience in more than 15 years.

"It's beautiful. Enjoyable. It's only dangerous if you don't know what you're doing," he said, adding the pilots avoid fatigue by never flying in formation for much more than an hour.

A spokesman for the FAA confirmed that it is not illegal to fly planes in formation at night. But he questioned its safety.

"Unless you were really good, it's risky at night," said Louis Architoff, Manager of Public Affairs for the agency that regulates commercial flight. "Not only are you looking for each other, you have to watch out for other aircraft in the area. Actually, I think it's kind of foolhardy."

J. Allen Hynek, perhaps the country's leading UFO researcher, has devoted much of the last year studying the reports about boomerang–shaped objects. Hynek, Director of the Center of UFO studies in Evanston, Illinois, had a cameo role as a scientist in the hit movie 'Close Encounters of the Third Kind.' He, too, finds it hard to believe that single-engine planes could account for reports that the UFO made 90-degree turns and hovered over witnesses. Hynek said he wanted to talk to the pilots to find the truth.

"We would like to see their flight logs, conduct a scientific inquiry," Hynek said. "Until some of these pilots stand up and are counted, the testimony of cops and witnesses—an IBM executive, a meteorologist— still suggested something else. Something spectacular."

But the pilot said he and his fellow fliers have no plans to go public.

"This is our private enjoyment," he said. "We don't want to stop, but we don't want to be hounded either. And if somebody tags me—asks me if I'm one of the fliers—I'll deny it. And then I'll stop."

So this was one of the typical Stormville Flyers, claiming it was all in good fun and acting innocent, when he knew damn well that many local residents were terrified, and local police were furious that their phones were tied up and their manpower diverted every time the Stormville Flyers flew. After causing so much trouble, this pilot even had the nerve to whine that he didn't want to be hounded!

The following opinion piece by columnist Jean Yanarella appeared in the Evening News on October 8, 1984, and voiced the frustration experienced by the average resident who saw that officials were doing nothing to stop this potential public danger:

Close Encounters of the Worst Kind

You can't go into a crowded theater, yell "fire!" and not be subject to arrest, law enforcement officials tell me.

Why is it then, that six bozos can go up in planes, imitate a UFO, scare the wits out of thousands, and not be punished?

I've not received a satisfactory answer to that question yet.

Thank goodness the pilots have decided to cut down on their antics, at least for now.

Hopefully, they won't decide to start up again after being featured in the November issue of the national science magazine *Discover*. According to the author, the pilots, who call themselves the Martians, and their allies, are worried.

Discover reports the pilots think it has all been fun and games, but they are afraid of losing their Federal Aviation Administration licenses for infractions, such as turning off navigation lights during a night flight. I don't know why they're worried; the FAA has been telling me all along that the pilots, who apparently fly out of Stormville Airport in Dutchess County, haven't been breaking any rules.

Discover also said the pilots are afraid of being charged with breaking some local criminal nuisance law. It would be about time.

Another fear that has rid the skies of these fliers is the possibility of liability. The pilots sometimes would fly slowly with their landing lights on over a busy road, like the Taconic State Parkway, alarming motorists who see a giant "UFO" suspended over them. A pregnant woman nearly drove off the road in the Hudson Valley after being scared by the pilots' show in the sky.

It would happen sooner or later that some innocent person or the pilots would get hurt. The injured pedestrian—or the survivors—most hopefully would be smart enough to sue the pants off the good ole boys who get their jollies by freaking out people on the ground.

Let's hope the pilots have finally come to their senses. If they haven't, let's hope federal, state and local officials will come to realize that the skies are an inappropriate place for child's play.

With law enforcement officials having looked the other way when it comes to the antics, it appears some members of the public are taking matters into their own hands. Suspected members of the Martians have been getting mysterious telephone calls from strangers. One report is of receiving an outright threat. This is a sign the public has lost faith in the appropriate authorities doing their job.

Let's hope it won't take a tragedy to make the pilots decide to do better things with their planes.

So as we can see, this was not all fun and games as the pilots claimed, and once they realized that they might be inconvenienced or get into serious trouble, they stopped. Over the span of two to three years, at least five of the pilots were identified by reporters, police, or UFO researchers, who would follow their formation back to Stormville and wait for them to exit their planes. However, even having been caught red-handed, they would deny everything—even to the point of denying they had just been in the air, even though the witnesses just watched them land and get out of their planes! Two of the planes were also identified as being owned by someone in Stormville, and a third had been registered to a company in Kansas.

I would dearly like to finally be able to stick a fork in the Stormville Flyers issue, but unfortunately, they have inextricably woven themselves into the Hudson Valley wave of sightings in the early 1980s. If just one of the original flyers or their family members would step up and come clean, and make their flight logs public, it would go far to separate the genuine from the hoaxed sightings.

However, as it stands, the Stormville Flyers were all foolish, irresponsible cowards in the 1980s, and remain foolish, irresponsible cowards 35 years later—with several of them literally taking their secrets to the grave.

Yet we can't let these ignorant men cloud the truth of the sightings that came before and after them. While the Stormville Flyers have forever muddied these waters, any rational individual who studies the 1980s has no doubt that not *every* UFO sighting was the result of "six bozos" in their planes.

This is an example of the type of Cessna plane at least one of the hoaxing pilots was using. Reports were that the planes were painted black to help avoid detection.

5
Triangles, Boomerangs, and Vs

While popular culture continues to use the term Flying Saucers as a blanket term for UFOs, they come in a wide variety of shapes and sizes. There are many examples of very early triangle sightings, but they really burst onto the scene with boomerangs and Vs in the early 1980s in the Hudson Valley and western Connecticut. It's no surprise, then, that this chapter is so large, as witnesses from the 1980s continue to come forward, and triangular craft continue to be seen today.

However, as so much criticism and negativity has clouded the 1980s wave due to the hoaxing pilots—the Stormville Flyers—flying in formation (see previous chapter), I thought I would start this chapter with a story so far removed in time and distance, that it sets a clear and distinct precedence for such angular craft.

Winifred Chapin
Twin Spits, Washington
September 3, 1956

An interesting letter—mainly because of the sketches provided—was sent to APRO in regard to a sighting which occurred on September 3, 1956, in Twin Spits, Washington, which is on the Puget Sound about 30 miles northwest of Seattle.

Winifred Chapin wrote that on a "clear moonless night" a V-shaped craft came "from the west over the water" and "it seemed to be flying low for such an aircraft." She noted that its lights were a steady "<u>brilliant</u> red," which was unusual as "there was no blinking of wing lights such as one observes on transport planes." Also, it was the unusual "streamers of lights" coming out of the rear of the aircraft which first "caught her eye."

What adds credibility to her account is the fact that she was quite familiar with aircraft, as Naval Air Station Whidbey Island was just several miles across the sound to the northeast. Chapin wrote that she would "see jets maneuvering all over daily," but was adamant that she had "<u>never</u> seen anything similar."

If accurate, her sketches are remarkable depictions of a V-shaped craft, with steady red lights along the leading edge, and streamers of light exiting from the trailing edge. She says that she never heard the sounds of any motors or engines, but confesses she wouldn't trust her hearing. At no point in her letter does she exaggerate or try to embellish the details of her sighting; she just reports the facts as she observed them.

Was this a very early example of the V-shaped craft that would be seen over the Hudson Valley decades later, or was the military experimenting with a flying wing-type aircraft on Whidbey Island? In any event, something unusual was in the sky that night, and all V-shaped craft throughout history were not the result of the Stormville Flyers!

***

Not only is this a daylight sighting of a triangular craft, it occurred in 1965!

Poughkeepsie, NY
Fall 1965, 5pm

NUFORC Report
Early evening encounter at intersection near Arlington High School with object hovering above intersection, and then quickly disappearing.
Duration: 5 minutes

Was driving to Arlington High School for a basketball game (therefore probably a Friday night). It was still daylight (getting near dusk, so the date of Dec. is uncertain as it has been a long time).

As I approached an intersection with Route 55 (?) from a rural road just east of the high school, I saw a very distinct object hovering at very low altitude above the intersection as I approached. I stopped and had a visual sighting for several minutes (there was no other traffic on this back road I was on.) I believe the object was triangular in shape, but it did have what I remember to be 3 blinking lights on its perimeter. They were different colors. Then as the lights changed colors, the object quickly and silently took off in a westerly direction.

***

While this witness claimed the triangular object was seen all the way from Virginia to New York on this date, I searched both the MUFON and NICAP databases for December 9 in 1976-1980 and could not find additional reports.

In any event, this account is typical of so many black triangle sightings, including the center hatch.

Ringwood, NJ
c. December 9, 1978, 7pm

NUFORC Case
Triangular aircraft sighted from Virginia to NY State in '78
Duration: 3 minutes

I remember the date because it was my birthday, but the year may be off by a year or two. It can be checked because it was reported from Virginia to New York State in the newspapers and evening news on TV.

My mother, father, brother and I were watching the NY Rangers on TV when my brother noticed lights coming towards our house. At first, we all thought they were just planes in formation. But, Mom, my brother and I all ran outside to take a look.

As we stood on our sidewalk, this UFO slowly, silently, flew just above the trees. It was going so slow for such a huge object that it was hard to believe it could stay in the air. The three of us just stared up at this object as it ever so slowly flew right over us. It really looked like it was just missing the treetops, it was so low.

70

It was black underneath, triangular in shape with, as I remember, 5 lights. One in the front, and two on each side. It also looked like there was some sort of round opening in the middle that was closed shut. It couldn't have been more than 100 feet directly above us.

That night, it was reported on the news.

Glens Falls, NY
November 12, 1981

In the northern reaches of the Hudson River, about an hour north of Albany, is the town of Glens Falls. On November 12, 1981, there was a series of sightings of a large triangle in the Glens Falls area. This case is of great importance for a number of reasons. First, it predates the lower Hudson Valley wave of sightings. Also, the appearance of this craft, which one witness so aptly described as being "damn big," seems to have disrupted both the telephone and electrical service.

Finally, this was a case that was immediately investigated by the SBI, the Scientific Bureau of Investigation, which was an organization composed predominantly of police officers who had the skills and experience to conduct excellent investigations. The following article was written by SBI's co-founder, New York City Police Detective Pete Mazzola, who was also the editor and publisher of the organization's publication, *The SBI Report*. I want to thank John Schuessler for generously providing me with copies of *The SBI Report*.

UFO cause eyed in upstate N.Y. telephone cutoff
Phones quit as huge UFO hovers
by Pete Mazzola
The SBI Report, Issue #35

Second in a four part series

The following is a statement which was broadcast over WWSC-radio, in Glens Falls, New York on Friday November 13, 1981; "A number of persons from throughout the Glens Falls-Queensbury area reported sighting an unusual object in the sky last night. A spokesman from Warren County Airport told us he had received calls from several individuals claiming to have seen a large triangular shape object with lights as big—if not bigger—than the Goodyear blimp. An airport official said the object wasn't anything from the airport and he wasn't sure what it might have been. Most of the persons sighting the object said it moved very slowly, approximately 1000 feet above the ground, having orange, yellow and white lights and made no noise."

May have disrupted phones

Chief investigator for SBI (Scientific Bureau of Investigation) in New York, David Waters, claims that his investigation leads him to believe the UFO observed by numerous people may have caused the interruption of telephone service for three hours and sporadic power failures in the area. Waters states that it is not unheard of to have power and phone failures in areas where UFOs are sighted.

Thanks to Waters and independent researcher Paul Bartholomew, through a cooperative feedback procedure, we were able to clearly define the events of November 12, 1981 to our readers. This type of cooperation should be a model for all other UFO researchers to follow, indicating that harmony, respect, and an exchange of information can be achieved in the field of ufology.

The first person to report the sighting to station WWSC was Mr. Bartholomew's brother, Robert, who was taking phone calls from witnesses and relaying the messages to his brother for further investigation. And although the sighting primarily transpired in Glens Falls, it is by no means confined to this area or time (around 6:40pm EST). UFO reports were also received from Saratoga Springs, Hampton, Granville, Whitehall, and Richford, and several other states.

One witness, William Barrett of Glens Falls, stated, "I looked out of the window about 6:40pm and this thing came out of the eastern sky…coming from the east for a period of time and then turned south. It had several lights…white lights…shaped like a triangle with the sides not quite as long as its base. The object was relatively low flying and some of the seven lights on it were flashing while others remained stationary. But what got me is it was damn big."

The interview continued with Mr. Bartholomew asking question after question in reference to the sighting. Barrett further commented, "The object wasn't making any audible noise…not like a jet, private aircraft, or helicopter. This thing was noiseless!" During the sighting, Barrett had time to call his neighbor next door. Hence, Mr. and Mrs. Roger Hamman viewed the strange object as well.

Wide as a football field

Mr. Hamman claims, "I ran out on the lawn with my wife and there was this object in the sky…large, very large…triangular-shaped. The best way to describe it would be to relate it to ducks flying in formation. I heard absolutely no noise being emitted from this object and observed several lights around its edges. To relate just how large this thing was I'll say that it appeared to be as wide as a football field…low to the ground. I don't know whether or not I believe in UFOs, all I know is that I saw this thing, my wife saw it and my neighbor saw it and I have no idea what it was."

Next came Mr. Francis Baker of Hampton, who also reported the object. Baker states, "The object was triangular in shape, like a hang glider…since it was noiseless…and tremendous in size. My wife also observed the object with me sometime between 6 and 7pm for approximately half an hour. The object was circling toward the east." The Bakers were on their way to a Grand Union supermarket and when they arrived, Mrs. Baker pointed the object out to a woman outside the store and she observed the object, too.

At about 7:15pm Paul Henderes of Saratoga Springs claimed he saw the object along with two friends. "I only saw the lights…it was really clear. It was scary watching it for about five minutes…you know the phones were out, and lights were going out all over the place…truly scary!"

Of course, more sighting reports were received (see the UFO Supplement, September 4 and 11 issues) throughout the day. Dave Waters called numerous city and government agencies in order to determine if the object was conventional in nature—explainable. In an article appearing in the Schenectady Gazette (November 1981), staff reporter Michael Sorensen interviewed New York Telephone's spokesman Carmine Angelotti in reference to Waters' allegation that UFOs caused the phone interruption over the area. Angelotti, naturally being the district staff manager of public relations, claimed the malfunction was possibly due to a minicomputer failure. However, Angelotti gracefully stated, "I found Waters' telephone call to me refreshing, a delight to think that UFOs could have been the cause of the problem. Our technicians thought the call was very interesting when I told them about it." Angelotti went to a lot of trouble for someone who was near positive a computer failure caused the malfunction of telephone service. He called AT&T to see if any studies had been done in the Bell system about UFOs and their effect on phone service. "They have never been asked that question before," he said.

Needless to say, the phone company's position was that there was a mechanical malfunction, and UFOs had no connection to the phone disorders of that evening. "It's a rare occurrence that computers go down. The switching system is the most complex system on this planet. However, this is not to say Mr. Waters is not correct," Angelotti concluded.

Mohawk Valley a UFO hotbed

Waters said he could not prove cause and effect of the UFO sighting with the phone disorder. Yet, Waters commented, "This is not the first sighting of a UFO in this area of New York. UFOs are often reported along earthquake fault lines, and a fault line exists from Lake Champlain south to Schenectady and continues on to Manhattan." Waters added, "Not many people know this, but the Mohawk Valley is a hotbed for UFO activity."

"Dottie"
Fairfield, CT
c.1980s

The following is a story related by "Dottie" about a sighting that occurred with her boyfriend:

"I was at the commuter parking lot on Jefferson Street in Fairfield which is near the GE headquarters. I honestly can't remember either the time of year or the year itself. I do remember there wasn't any snow on the ground, and I don't remember it being really hot or really cold, so my guess is fall or spring, as there were leaves on the trees.

"We were sitting in my car (we were actually arguing about something) and I saw this formation of big white lights in the shape of a boomerang in the sky coming from the area of the headquarters. It seemed to move very slowly. We were both confused and amazed at what we were seeing. We watched it slowly come towards the corner of Jefferson Street and Stratfield Road and it started going past the bunch of trees on the corner.

"I pulled the car up to the entrance of the lot to get a closer look. It seemed to be in front of us, but not by much. I remember thinking it was about the size of Brookside shopping center or at least a football field, it was huge. It hardly made any noise, if anything it was more of a slight vibration. It's hard to describe.

"While we were watching it, it slowly moved away, then it stopped; the lights seemed to move inward, and then it pivoted and headed back the way it came, which was slightly in our direction. I remember putting the car in park to get out and get a better look, and when I got out of the car it rolled back a little and I screamed, since I thought we were being sucked up with the car!

"It continued to move very slowly towards the gas station on the Merritt Pkwy. So I drove in that direction and my boyfriend was watching where it was going. It went beyond the trees off of Congress Street, so I turned on the first street off of Congress, which was a hill. In the seconds it took to get beyond the trees so we could see it, it was gone. Nowhere to be seen.

"We drove up and around to a point where we could see at some distance and there was no sign of it. We went back down to the lot and looked all around, went up Jefferson Street to get a good look for distance and nothing. But within minutes there were several small aircraft in the area, I want to say at least 3-5.

"We went back to his parents' house and were telling them about what we saw and carrying on about it and put on the radio. People were calling in to WICC to say they saw bright lights in the sky. It is something I will always remember and am glad I experienced it, as scary as it was. I am a believer. I was in my early 20s at the time."

Two things of note in Dottie's story: First, the way the lights stopped, moved inward, and then the entire thing "pivoted," which does not sound like the way any conventional aircraft banks and turns. Also, it is interesting to note that several aircraft were then seen—and they had no question that they were regular "small aircraft," as opposed to what they had just witnessed.

Michael Gilroy
New Fairfield, CT
Early 1980s

Michael Gilroy was driving from Putnam Lake on Fairfield Drive in New Fairfield, CT one clear night when he saw something "the size of a football field, moving low and slow. It had bright lights that 'V'ed' out somewhat like a boomerang. And I remember seeing one light at the end of the object. It made no sound. I'll never forget it!"

After some additional questions, Michael responded with the following:

"When I saw the UFO it was incredibly slow. I could not see the structure; however, I witnessed it for what seemed like 15 minutes. It moved incredibly slow and was very low in the sky right above the tree line. The time of night was between 8:30 and 9:30 p.m.

"I saw what seemed to be 8 to 10 very bright lights on the craft. There was a blinking light I saw very far back, and I couldn't tell if it was part of the same craft or not. All the lights seemed to be moving at the same speed.

"In my mind I know it could not have been something from this world the way it moved."

One feature to note in this case is the blinking light "very far back." This is a feature that has been described in numerous cases of both V-shaped, triangular, and boomerang craft, as well as with some discs. Often, this light seems to be part of one enormous structure, while at other times, it appears to be a separate craft, as it moves independently.

There have also been many reports of a red light exiting the center or back of a triangular craft, disappearing for some period of time, and then returning to the inside of the craft.

Ann
Danbury, CT
1983

The following is an excellent example of the fact that the massive, silent triangles of the Hudson Valley wave of the 1980s were also seen across western Connecticut—particularly in the Danbury area.

"I just wanted to let you know my story about the UFO I saw when I was 13 in 1983. I was outside on the back deck of my mother's house, feeding the stray cat that was hanging around our house some cheese and I remember it being a cool and clear night. I was looking up at the stars and then I looked back down at the cat to give it more cheese, and then when I looked up to my left hand side there was a huge triangle-shaped object hovering above the tree line—no noise and a lot of lights. It just sat there.

"I ran back in the house to get my parents who were already in bed. I was yelling, 'There is a huge UFO outside.' Of course, they did not believe me, but I said it again and I said, 'I'm serious, come!' and then they jumped up out of bed and came, and so did my brother and sister because they heard all the yelling.

"We went back out on the deck and it was still there in the same place. So we were all looking at it and amazed. Then it started moving very slowly towards the deck and my parents yelled at us to get back in the house. And we all did. But as it was moving we did not hear any noise from it.

"We were still watching it from the kitchen window and the dining room window. It moved very slowly right over our house. Then my parents went to the living room window and so did we. It went to the front yard, then over to our neighbors' house. It hovered over their house for a few minutes, and then slowly was moving until we could not see it any more.

"I never felt afraid; I was more amazed and excited. The next day in the newspaper they said it was a group of low-flying aircraft flying in formation. While I don't know what it was that I saw, I know it was not a group of aircraft flying in formation. It was one object."

I asked Ann a few questions, and the following is her response:

"It was black and it had different color lights. It was truly amazing! I would say it was about the size of a 747 airplane wing tip to wing tip, maybe a little bit bigger. I know a lot of people saw it that night. I wish I could see it again."

Harer Family
Montrose, NY
March 24, 1983

It was a typical evening in the Harer home in Montrose, New York on March 24, 1983. Suddenly it became anything but typical when a neighbor called and told them to run outside and look up in the sky. Ron, Shirley, and daughters Tina and Audrey ran outside and couldn't believe—or understand—what they were seeing.

"It was HUGE!" Audrey told me. "It was a boomerang shape with hundreds of colored lights. *Hundreds and hundreds.*"

They all watched in awe as the immense object glided slowly through the air with a barely perceptible, low hum.

"I kept asking my father what it was and he was speechless. My dad always had answers, and for the first time he didn't have answers. It was just 'that look' on his face!" Audrey explained as she tried to convey the shock and puzzlement they were all feeling.

Tina ran inside to get a camera while the others watched transfixed. Unfortunately, by the time she returned the craft had passed out of view over the tree line. At the time, Ron was a lieutenant in the Mt. Kisco police department, and he ran inside to call headquarters. The officer who answered said they were "flooded with calls" as the craft had just passed overhead.

This brings up another puzzle—Mt. Kisco is fifteen miles from Montrose. At the slow speed the craft was traveling, how could it possibly be overhead in both towns almost simultaneously? Was there more than one craft in the sky that night? Also, people stopped along the Taconic Parkway from Millwood to north of Yorktown Heights and were reportedly watching the craft hovering above them at treetop level for as long as twenty minutes at one point (see Triangles Chapter in *In the Night Sky*). Perhaps if it was possible to obtain police records from that night, a timeline could be constructed of the sightings to determine if just one craft could be responsible for all of the sightings.

Speaking of the Taconic Parkway, Audrey immediately called her best friend to see if she had also witnessed the enormous craft, but no one was home, so she left a message on her answering machine. About two

78

hours later her friend called back—she and her family had been stuck in traffic on the Taconic Parkway because everyone had stopped their cars to get out to watch the brightly lit boomerang overhead.

Whenever I investigate a case, I always like to speak to as many witnesses as possible, and I was fortunate enough to also be able to interview Ron. It is important to note, that in addition to being a police officer, Ron was a bombardier on antisubmarine aircraft in the Navy. He served on no fewer than five aircraft carriers over the course of his career.

"I know aircraft," he stated plainly. "What I saw that night was not a formation of ultralights or any other planes. The lights were steady and moved as one unit. This was a single object. At first I thought it might be a dirigible like the Goodyear blimp, but this was bigger."

Ron was very familiar with both dirigibles and ultralight aircraft, as he had seen them while in the Navy.

"And I used to watch the ultralights fly out of Stormville Airport," he said. They would fly in formation, but that formation would "quiver" as these super light planes were unable to maintain a tight pattern for any distance.

Ron described the hundreds of lights on the craft in the same manner as Audrey had, but added another interesting detail I hadn't heard before.

"There was a silvery-white glow in the center."

When asked how he felt at the time, he said he was in awe, but never felt fear, and didn't want to show any sense of alarm in front of his kids so they wouldn't worry. I also asked how his fellow officers reacted to his sighting.

"One of the guys was a real comedian and he made up a certificate for me that said I was a 'UFO Observer,' but it was all in fun. A female police officer from New Castle also saw it, so I wasn't the only one."

In another interesting note, the neighbors who had alerted the Harers to the craft had two previous sightings. About seven years earlier, c.1976, they were building a house about five miles away and had two separate *daylight* sightings of "Frisbee-shaped objects which seemed to be spinning." Both were glimpsed for a short time and then took off at high speed.

Finally, when Audrey told her niece, "Nancy," about the Danbury UFO Conference, and the fact that I had spoken about Pine Bush, Nancy surprised her by relating her own UFO story, which occurred in Montgomery, near Pine Bush, and is in the Casebook chapter.

"Jake"
Ridgefield, CT, Summer 1983
Ridgefield, CT and Peach Lake, NY, c.1987
Danbury, CT, Summer 1989

When a friend sent "Jake" the *Danbury News Times* article about our Danbury UFO Conference, he told me it "was like a weight was lifted from his shoulders" as he felt that he would finally be able to speak to someone who understood what he experienced. We spoke at length in October of 2016 and I very much appreciated both the details and the way he expressed his feelings about his three remarkable encounters.

In all other regards, Jake is a typical family man living in Connecticut, having raised five successful children. However, in regards to what he has seen, he is now a member of that somewhat exclusive club of those whose lives have been changed forever by things that defy explanation.

Jake's first experience occurred during the summer of 1983, when he was attending Ridgefield High School. He was with his girlfriend, "Pam," and another girl, "Jill." It was about 10:30 or 11pm on a warm summer's night, and off in the distance towards Danbury, they saw an unusual set of lights. Taking a closer look, they realized "it was gigantic, the size of a city filled with white lights. Thousands of white lights."

Jill was nothing short of hysterical at the sight of this massive object, which would suddenly disappear, and then instantly reappear a great distance away. "It was *there* and then it was gone. Then it was over *there* and then it was gone," Jake told me.

Far from sharing Jill's fear, Jake and Pam were "mesmerized" by the remarkable sight of this angular "city of lights." He knew they were seeing something amazing—something most decidedly *not* of *this* world. Glimpsing something this incredible for just a few moments can be life-altering, but the three friends stood there watching for an astonishing 20 minutes. Finally the craft disappeared and did not return.

"I was mad when it was gone," Jake told me. "I wanted so much to see it again. It's hard to describe how drawn to it I felt."

They drove the still-hysterical Jill home, and then headed for Pam's house. On the way home, something frightening occurred.

"This doesn't have anything to do with the sighting," Jake told me, "But it was kind of weird that it happened right after."

Out of nowhere, two bright lights came up behind their car within two feet of the back bumper. They naturally assumed they were headlights, but they couldn't see the vehicle, and the bright lights were definitely right behind them, "chasing" them. Frightened by their pursuers on the dark and winding back roads, Jake sped up to 60 or 70 miles an hour trying to lose them, but still the lights stuck with them through all the dangerous twists and turns. Then just as suddenly as the lights appeared, they made a sharp left off the road, kicking up a cloud of dust as they departed.

Was it just some local kids playing a prank on an isolated car on a dark, country road? Of course, that is the simplest and most likely explanation. However, given the extraordinary nature of the previous events of that night, and the fact that they never actually saw the vehicle, the author in me can't help but imagine a more unearthly scenario!

Both Jake and Pam had told their parents what they had seen, but of course it is a difficult story to believe. To be honest, Jake couldn't blame his parents for being skeptical about what they had seen, as it certainly sounded like it was a story from the realm of science fiction. However, he was greatly relieved when a day or two later, the *Danbury News Times* and the *Ridgefield Times* both ran articles about sightings, and their parents were able to see that their kids were not making up the story. According to one newspaper account, the object was seen over a local prison, and the terrified inmates were begging to be let out their cells.

Unfortunately, Jake's relief at the articles was short-lived, as the newspapers later reported that the mystery of the massive city of lights in the sky, which could appear and reappear in a flash, was nothing more than a weather balloon! This "stupid excuse" made Jake angry, as it no doubt did to the other hundreds of witnesses from that night.

The next sighting took place a few years later, most likely in 1987. Jake and his girlfriend were driving from Ridgefield, CT on Route 116 to go to a liquor store in Peach Lake, NY. They hadn't yet had anything to drink, and they were once again alone on a very dark road.

"I can still picture it so clearly as I was driving my Volkswagen along the road," Jake told me. "Suddenly the sky was blacked out, and above us was a dark triangle with a light in each corner. It kept pace with us for miles, remaining in the same place over the car. We were both really scared and my girlfriend was crying. She had mascara all over her face from crying, and she kept telling me to pull over."

This time, there was more than just the sighting of a craft.

"I know this is going to sound strange, but I felt like we were being scanned. It was like the scan started at the front of the car, moved across the hood, *through us,* and out the back. I felt really bad, weird. There was this slight tingling feeling, and the feeling that I had no control over the situation. I didn't like it."

The black triangle was at least the size of a football field, there was absolutely no sound, and it was no more than a few hundred feet above the tree tops. The bad feeling continued as the massive craft kept pace with Jake as he drove between 35 and 40 miles an hour along the dark road. Over the border in New York, there was a French restaurant, so Jake pulled into the parking lot, as his girlfriend was still crying and terrified.

"The restaurant had closed," Jake explained, "but I ran in the back into the kitchen. The kitchen staff was still there, and I was yelling at them to come outside and look up at the sky. When we got outside, the craft had gone. They all laughed and asked what I was smoking."

Before relating his third experience, Jake told me about something that had happened to him in Clearwater Beach, Florida. A school of dolphins was sighted about 150 yards offshore, prompting most of the locals to get out of the water. Jake did just the opposite, and started heading out toward them. Before he could get very far, the dolphins swam in to him and began circling around him. Some even jumped over his head!

"It was an incredible experience," Jake said. "Almost spiritual. It was wonderful being so close and interacting with these dolphins."

I think this feeling of intimacy with another species was what Jake wanted to convey to me, to keep in mind as he described the encounter he and his girlfriend, "Emma," now his wife, shared together in the summer of 1989. They were traveling from Ridgefield to their home on Mill Plain Road in Danbury one night. At the time, near the ramp to Route 84, was a Hilton hotel.

"Do you see those lights?" Jake asked Emma, as he saw some unusual lights above the hotel.

"What lights?" Emma replied, as she peered out the window.

Jake turned down a dead-end road and drove about 200 yards to get a better view of the lights, and Emma was finally able to see them. Their view became even better as the lights then seemed to move *straight toward* them. Jake then turned around and went back to the main road.

"It was weird, but it seemed to know we were there and came right over the car! I went to get out to look at it, but Emma kept telling me not to. But I *had* to get out. I didn't even care if it was going to take me. It was just so amazing…a spiritual thing."

At this point in our conversation, Jake actually broke into tears and became very emotional. It continues to amaze me that no matter how many decades have passed, these remarkable events still have the power to move eyewitnesses on the deepest and most intimate levels.

Once again, the craft was a massive, football field-sized, solid, black triangle that "blacked out the sky. There was a white light in each corner, and maybe a reddish light."

"The lights were not blinking or flashing like on a plane, but they were soft…pulsating alternately on and off. It was very soothing."

Jake said the best way to describe the pulsations was to make a sound, which was like a slow, deep *vroomp*. Despite the explanation with the sound, Jake stressed this huge craft above them was absolutely silent. Emma found the courage to get out of the car, too, and they stood there in complete awe for at least five minutes.

"Then another car was coming up the ramp," Jake stated. "I ran over waving my arms, yelling at the driver to stop."

"What's the matter," the man asked, getting out of his car.

Jake told him to look up, and the man's reaction was priceless.

"*Holy shit!*" the man yelled. "That ain't no ultralights!"

"No it isn't, and you'll never see anything else like it again," Jake told him.

"I'm leaving!" the man replied, clearly unnerved by the huge black triangle hovering silently above them.

The man jumped back in his car and took off, and Jake and Emma continued to stand there and stare at the craft for at least another five minutes. Then the craft began to slowly move.

"I remember every detail. I can still picture it clearly," Jake explained. "It nudged backward just slightly, and then started to move forward at no more than five miles an hour. It was so peaceful and quiet the way it moved.

"We continued on to our home on Mill Plain Road, and even though it took us about 10 minutes to get there, from our deck we could still see the craft! We continue to watch it for another 30 to 45 minutes! Even though it was now about 1:30am, since it was moving towards Ridgefield, we both called our parents and woke them up and told them to go outside to look for the craft, but they didn't see it. And the next day, there was nothing on the news or in the papers."

So how does Jake feel after having three remarkable experiences?

"I am *so* lucky! To see something so extraordinary not once, but three times, I am just so lucky. They were so real; I just had to tell someone about them. And to me they aren't UFOs, but they are IFOs—Identified Flying Objects, and by that I mean I saw them, I experienced them, and I know they're not of this world. They saw me. They knew me. And it was such a weight off my shoulders to be able to tell you about them.

"I know what I saw, and no one can ever tell me different. I have *no* doubt."

It was a very long, emotional conversation I shared with Jake that day, and his story really reinforced why I do what I do. To have complete strangers open up and tell me things that have struck such deep chords within them is both an honor and a privilege. And perhaps all of us who have experienced such things are not strangers after all. We are a "unique Band of Brothers," someone had just told me a day earlier at the MUFON conference in Philadelphia.

In many ways the UFO community is a family—a dysfunctional family to be sure!—but a family nonetheless. Jake's experiences, and his willingness and relief in sharing them with me, does create a bond that only those who have witnessed something similar can appreciate. And hopefully by continuing to tell these stories, it will help others to deal with things they can never fully explain, nor ever expect to fully understand.

Putnam Valley, NY and Mt. Kisco, NY
1980s

The following is a series of email messages from a couple concerning two sightings from the 1980s. One was a V-shaped craft, which is why it appears in this chapter. However, the other was so low and massive there was no way to determine its shape.

"In the late 1980s in Putnam Valley, New York, my husband was working on his car—a Chevy Chevette. He was removing an engine and was under the hood of his vehicle in the back yard of his home. It was a beautiful sunny day, not a cloud in the sky; it was around 5:00 in the afternoon. All of a sudden as he was looking down at his engine, a dark shadow appeared over his head. It made him look up, and when he did there was a huge craft hovering overhead right above the tree line. It was barely moving and was huge. It made a very low humming sound.

"It was a flat black and bigger than a football field, heading north toward Fahnestock State Park. It moved very slowly. When he saw the craft he dropped his wrench, knowing it was something from another world…with a feeling that he may be sucked up inside. He was scared to death, running inside his house, almost unable to speak, and told his mother and grandmother what was outside.

"His mother went out onto the deck and saw it too. His grandmother actually chased after it down the road on foot. She was astonished to see such a thing, and had the urge to follow it.

"This took place one mile south of Oscawana Lake, up the road from the police station. To date there is nothing to compare to what he and his family saw. Something he will never forget…"

I asked if he could see the shape of the craft and if there were any lights. Her response:

"I did ask him about the shape. He said it was massive, took up the whole sky, and it did not have lights that he would have been able to see because it was still light outside. There were many sightings in the 1980s in the area. I lived in Mt. Kisco, NY and I also saw a UFO while driving in town with my sister and aunt. It was a summer evening, maybe '84 or '85, because I was not driving myself yet, but we saw something different. It was a V-shaped object with lights, I think 3 on each side. Many people in town saw it that night. There were people pointing up at the sky while we drove around town that night."

Her husband then replied with more details of his sighting.

"It took up the whole sky, because it was right over the top of the tree line, barely moving. The hairs on my arms stood up. I was scared to death it was going to take me. No way this craft was from this planet. It was so huge and it was barely moving. It just floated over the tree line and had a low pitch hum. To date I have never heard a sound like it. It's been many years and it is an old memory and I still remember it like it was yesterday. I remember the exact place, the car, my position, the feelings I felt, when it hovered above me. It was a perfectly clear day. I was looking down, removing the engine from the car. I saw a dark shadow moving over me on both sides with my peripheral vision. Before I looked up I thought I would see a dark thunder cloud moving over head blocking the sun. When I looked up I was shocked and scared to death. I didn't look for long because I ran for my life into the house. I will never forget that day."

And that, ladies and gentleman, is a perfect example of the impact a sighting can have on a person, and how those feelings can last for the rest of their lives.

Linda Benedict
Danbury, CT
1980s

Linda Benedict was driving when she saw a black boomerang "the size of a jet liner," but moving "impossibly slowly." The following is in response to some questions I had for her after she submitted a report form on her sighting:

"I don't know the date - too long ago. But I do remember talking to people about it - they saw what I did.

"Yes, it was light enough to see the structure. I believe it was around dusk. I think I was going home from work because there was a lot of traffic. I remember continuing on my way, passing under the craft and losing sight of it behind me. I only could see the bottom because it was almost directly overhead. It was boomerang-shaped. I've been thinking about it and I think it did have lights. They were constant - not moving

86

around, and small - about what you might expect to see on an airplane. The craft was black. It wasn't emitting any beams. I saw no windows or doors. It was in the vicinity of Rt. 6 and Eagle Rd. It was moving slowly - seemed to be following Newtown Rd (Rt. 6) in an eastward direction. I remember thinking that it was way, *way* too low and slow to be a regular airplane."

Katonah, NY
Winter/Spring 1983

Some people who attended the Danbury Conference and filled out witness report forms wrote highly-detailed accounts. This witness, M.G., however, kept it short and sweet. The sighting occurred during the early evening by the intersection of Routes 35 and 684 in Katonah, NY.

no Sound
lights
felt awed

"Joe and Bill"
Danbury, CT
Spring 1983

"Joe" and "Bill" were next door neighbors who were up very early one cool, clear spring morning in 1983. The two men were getting ready to leave for a car show in Pennsylvania at about 5am, when they saw a "huge V-shaped thing in the sky," Joe, a contractor in the aerospace industry for many years, said. "It made no sound and had many lights on it. It moved very slowly to the north then reversed for a bit. Then it turned north again until we could no longer see it." The entire sighting lasted an impressive 20 minutes.

Bill, a member of the Civil Air Patrol, described the V-shaped object as being, "about the size of a B-52 at 1,500 feet, coming silently and slowly from the south (Bethel, CT) up Route 302 and South Street. It continued going north toward the Danbury Hospital area, with a detour slightly over the Shelter Rock area. It returned to its original course and continued north. It was silent, dark, with several dull lights."

"As I remember, the lights were red, and possibly one white one in the front of the huge V," Joe added. "We were just amazed by the size."

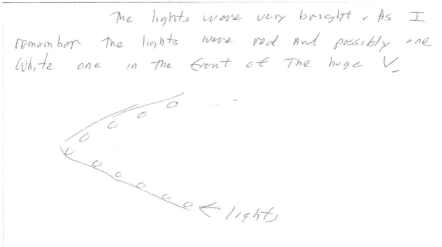

The "detour" the massive craft took was over some electrical "transmission lines," which is often a common theme with UFOs.

As the craft passed ever so slowly overhead, just at treetop level, Bill asked, "Should I shine a light on it?"

"No!" came Joe's emphatic reply.

No sense looking for trouble!

I asked for some clarification about the way the craft "reversed" and turned, and both men agreed it was unlike any conventional dirigible or airplane.

"It turned on its axis," Joe said. "It did not appear to bank as a plane would."

Both men also described how black the craft was, clearly indicating it was one, solid object. Joe also divulged that a close relative of his, a police officer, also saw the V-shaped craft. However, Joe also learned that the police were instructed to use the standard excuse that all sightings were the result of a formation of ultralights. The Danbury *News-Times* ran an article the next day repeating the ultralight explanation for the early morning sightings throughout the area.

88

However, on another occasion, Joe and Bill also saw the ultralights trying to look like a UFO, and like most witnesses, knew there was no comparison between the wobbly hoaxers, and the silent, massive, solid black craft that they witnessed.

Warren and Judy Flagg
Tappan, NY
and two observers in Wallkill, NY
November 23, 1983

In 2014, I received the following email from Warren Flagg about a sighting which involved him and his wife—two of the most credible people I've ever interviewed:

I'm a retired FBI agent who lived in Tappan, NY from 1976-2000.

On the evening of I believe November 22 or 23, 1983, I was playing indoor softball at Rockland Community College. After the game, I drove my Volvo down the NYS thruway toward my home in Tappan just off the Palisades Parkway exit 5.

As I turned onto the Palisades Parkway from the Thruway, I noticed 5 bright lights hovering across the entire northbound and southbound lanes of the Parkway. The 5 lights were in the shape of a V and they were only several hundred feet above the Parkway, not moving. I immediately pulled off the Parkway onto the grass to the right and got out of my car. I wanted to hear if there were any engines running. As I exited the car, I noticed that all the northbound cars and southbound cars also pulled off onto the grass on each side of the Parkway. I could hear no engines. My wife, who was in the Volvo with me, got out of the vehicle as well, and we all observed these lights. The lights were at least 5 feet in diameter and lit up the entire Parkway on both sides of the road.

The lights lasted about 5 minutes and then banked towards Tarrytown, NY and vanished.

I turned to the man in the vehicle immediately behind me and asked him, "What do you think?"

He stated, "That was not man-made."

I agreed.

When I got home I called the police and reported what I had observed.

The next morning the *Journal News* listed the sighting as a hang glider.

I'm sure that was not a hang glider!

I spoke to Warren about his sighting to get a few more details, and mentioned that I appreciated speaking with someone from the FBI, as that certainly boosted the credibility factor.

"We don't lie," he stated plainly.

The sighting occurred somewhere between 9-9:30pm, and he stressed that it was "stationary and silent." He also mentioned that the police officer who took his report was laughing at him, which is the main reason most witnesses don't bother to report their sightings.

I also spoke with his wife, Judy, who was a medivac flight nurse who "had spent a lot of time in the air." She described the lights as being "huge," V-shaped, and part "of one unit," definitely not separate aircraft. Judy also said that no one who was standing outside of their cars looking at the object was speaking—it was like they couldn't talk because of the almost hypnotic effect of this massive, silent craft.

One of the most amazing parts of the sighting was the way the craft departed. As it began to move away, "It went straight up and was gone!" Judy said. "The way it disappeared so incredibly fast, I was in awe. There was no sense of fear; I was never scared."

Judy had another sighting in the summer of 1987 at a softball game at the Deer Head Inn on Western Highway in West Nyack, NY. If you grew up in Rockland County, as I did, you knew that the Deer Head was synonymous was softball, and the sight of the bright spotlights around the field was a common sight on a summer night. Only this particular night there were some additional lights.

"There were strange, red-orange colored lights just above the tree line," Judy told me. When the object departed, it did so "outrageously fast."

Perhaps this craft had been attracted by the field lights?

Getting back to the November 1983 sighting, I found an account posted on Ufoevidence.org which describes the same 5-light craft seen by a father and son in Wallkill, NY (about 50 miles to the northeast of

Tappan) on the night of November 23, just about 30-60 minutes after the Flagg sighting:

Summary: Watched triangular-shaped ship follow Hudson River Northbound. Then turn West. Then turn South for a landing in the back forty swamp.

Sighting Time: 10:00 PM ?

No. of Witnesses: 50 [Note: The witness explained that this number came from a subsequent newspaper article about the sighting.]

Duration: 20-30 minutes

Size of Object(s): 250 ft wide?

Full Description & Details

I was twenty-one just before Thanksgiving 1983. Was at an old farmhouse in Wallkill NY, went out with my Dad at night to look for deer in the field. We had a flashlight taped to the barrel of a .22 rifle. Noticed lights moving among the stars as we went out to the field. After spending some time in the field we walked back to the farmhouse and saw the lights again so I asked my Dad what it was. We watched the lights follow the Hudson River North then turn West, then turn South and come right at us. The ship had 5 lights (guessing) in a triangle shape. The ship was completely silent as it made its approach to land in our swamp. My Dad said we were walking out there to meet it. I told him I was going to get my 12 gauge. He then said the words he would regret the rest of his life. "Signal it's safe to come in." I pointed the .22 at the ship (all I could see were the lights) and turned the flashlight on and off. The ship stopped 50 - 100 feet above the ground, and the lights that were pointing down on the ground pivoted up toward us. We were standing in a different kind of illumination. Then the ship reversed direction and went straight up in total silence. After getting 200 (?) ft altitude we watched the ship take off out of sight travelling at a speed impossible for human technology and in total silence.

This witness, now a postmaster, describes the same silent hovering, and then rapid vertical ascent, as the craft the Flaggs saw—only he and his father got more than they bargained for by "signaling" the craft with the flashlight. Apparently, the old adage applies to UFOs as well: Be careful what you ask for!

I think that the multiple, credible eyewitnesses, spread out at a distance of at least 50 miles, each describing the same type of lights and flight characteristics, makes this case one the most important and compelling during the Hudson Valley UFO wave of the 1980s.

Maria
Danbury, CT
Fall 1983

Maria had just dropped off her daughter at the roller rink one Friday night about 7pm, and was driving on Hayestown Road near Glen Hills Road, headed toward Danbury Hospital. Two or three cars were pulled over on the side of the road, and Maria stopped, as well, because something large was in the sky just a few hundred feet above her.

"It covered the sky," she said. "It was football field-sized, silent," and was so low "it looked like it could drop out of the sky. It was boomerang-shaped with white and red lights."

It hovered above the cars for "several minutes at least" before slowly starting to move at a "creeping" pace. The craft headed east, and Maria slowly lost sight of it over the trees. She called the Danbury police, and they indicated they had received many calls. Maria was specifically asked if she had heard a noise, as apparently other witnesses reported hearing a humming sound, but she told them she hadn't heard a sound.

This is just another incredible example of a massive, silent object, hovering motionless over witnesses for several minutes. Just imagine what that must have been like!

"Mary"
Danbury, CT
1984

One evening in 1984, "Mary" was driving on Route 84 from New York to the North Street shopping center in Danbury, when she saw a V-shaped craft "flying low." It was about "30 yards at the widest point" and there was "no noise."

As she slowed down to turn into the shopping center parking lot, her car "lost the brakes" for a couple of seconds, but then the brakes returned and she was able to safely stop. I asked if she ever had problems with the brakes before or after, and she replied, "Never."

In the parking lot, there were approximately 20 other people watching the craft. There were lights on it, but Mary specifically said that "the lights were on the inside of the V," as opposed to the leading edge. Mary can't say what it is that she saw, but she knows what it wasn't.

"The Danbury *News-Times* reported it was ultralights. I don't think so."

A /\ Shape

Mary's illustration of the lights on the trailing edge of the craft.

Chappaqua
June 11, 1984

While a UFO sighting in the middle of a Town Board meeting might make front page headlines today, this was actually a regular occurrence in the Hudson Valley in the 1980s. If you weren't a local resident and didn't live through that incredible wave, it's hard to convey the depth and length of the experiences of those years.

UFO Disrupts Town Board meeting;
no vote taken in possible identity
by Royston Wood
Chappaqua Journal
Wednesday, June 13, 1984

What with one thing and another, the June 11 Town Board work session, doubling with a Board of Ethics meeting in another part of Town Hall, was far from placid. Members of the press were up and down like yoyos as first one board, then the other, went into executive session (a total of four executive sessions were recorded between the Boards during the evening). And right in the middle of a weighty discussion of the Town Leash Law, a police officer rushed in and announced that the UFOs various people had been reporting, could be seen in the sky outside Town Hall.

It would be an overstatement to say that people were killed in the rush, but some twenty honest citizens, led by their elected representatives, streamed out into the balmy night and, sure enough, there were the lights. Exactly as it has been reported on other occasions, a V-shaped formation of five or six white lights was moving slowly away to the north. The lights looked as if they belonged to nothing more than a high-flying, delta-winged aircraft; there was no noise, and the lights faded as they drew rapidly away.

Town Supervisor Lois Mitchell opined that the lights were indeed that of a high-flying military aircraft. Then someone else pointed out that it seemed illogical for an aircraft which was not showing the usual warning strobe lights to show a series of very bright white lights to its rear.

Stewart UFO Theory Scoffed
The Evening News
August 27, 1984

Brewster – The thought of one woman that the government might be flying UFOs from Stewart Airport, New Windsor, in secret experiments was discounted by Dr. J Allen Hynek of the Center for UFO Studies at a conference here Saturday.

There have been no leaks of such a thing taking place, he said.

Besides, he said, it wouldn't be very irresponsible of the government because the phenomenon could cause large traffic crashes as people stopped to watch the objects.

Then, as an afterthought, he quipped the government isn't always overly responsible.

"Jerry and Matt"

Danbury, CT
c. 1984

It was around midnight when "Jerry" and his friend, "Matt" were driving from Danbury Hospital toward Brewster, NY on Route 84. The sky was overcast, but not completely dark, due to the sky glow from all the street and building lights. Had it been a clear night, the two friends may not have seen the incredible silent object they witnessed, silhouetted against the clouds.

"It was a solid, black triangle," Jerry said. "No lights that I can recall."

While the exact date is not clear, Jerry was able to describe more details of their sighting:

"If I had to guess, I would say '84 or '85 but can't be sure. What I can tell you is that it was at the same time that the reports of ultralights flying out of Stormville were around, as I had read that in the Danbury *News-Times* shortly before the sighting. This, however, was most definitely *not* a formation of ultralights.

"It was a large, solid, black triangle with no visible sign of propulsion. No exhaust, no propellers. It was low enough that the altitude itself was notable and striking as it appeared to be very low relative to the highway for such a large craft. In terms of speed, I would say somewhere around 80 miles an hour. I am guessing that because we were driving on I-84 and the craft stayed ahead of us during the time we were on the highway, but was not pulling away at great speed. There were no lights that I recall and the craft was a triangle, not the V-shape that I know some others have seen. It would have been travelling at well below stall speed for any conventional aircraft of its size.

"We pulled off the highway at Exit 4 (west bound) and pulled into what I believe was an empty lot where a McDonald's now exists. There was another motorist who had pulled off for the same reason. He was standing outside his car when we pulled in and we spoke briefly. The three of us; my friend, the other motorist and myself, all watched the craft head toward Ridgefield (I think we could still see it after pulling off, but that too is fuzzy). The time was likely around midnight, but I don't know the exact time. It was after 10:00 PM because I called the tower at Danbury

Airport the next day to see if they had any idea what it was. They said the tower closed at 10:00 so they had no information at all to offer.

"The driver of the car I was in is one of my best friends, so I have at least one eyewitness who can corroborate what we saw. Neither he nor I have discussed it in this level of detail so I don't know if his recollections would differ in any way from mine.

"I make no assumptions as to whether the craft was terrestrial or extra-terrestrial in origin. All I can tell you is that it was not a conventional aircraft, civilian or military, NATO or Warsaw Pact. I am not an expert, but I can identify many aircraft and this was most definitely something well out of the ordinary."

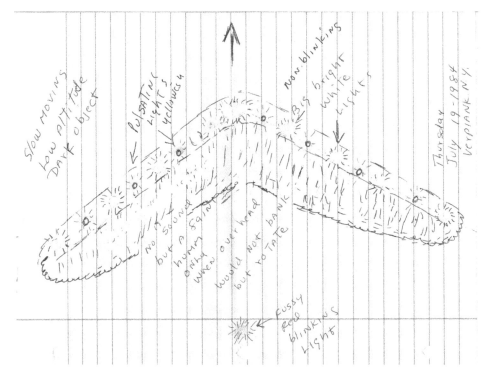

Cesar Padilla witnessed the famous boomerang on July 19, 1984 in the town of Verplanck, NY and his story is in *In the Night Sky*. After the book was published, Cesar attended one of my lectures to bring me a sketch of the craft. Note that he saw a solid structure—these were *not* separate planes—and there was a red light trailing the object, which many other witnesses have observed with other UFOs. Also, he clearly states that this boomerang "would not bank" into turns, "but rotate."

96

Mr. G, Part 1
Monsey, NY
1984

Mr. G's story is split into two parts. The first part, about his V-shaped craft sighting is here, and the second part is in the Abduction chapter. This may be a case that illustrates that the more interest you show in *them*, the more interest *they* have in you.

"In 1984, my wife and I lived in Monsey, NY, in Rockland County. In the evening, after food shopping at the Pathmark on Rt. 59, as we arrived home at the Blueberry Hill Town Houses, we saw six lights in a V-shape to the east of us, somewhat over the Spring Valley airport that used to be there.

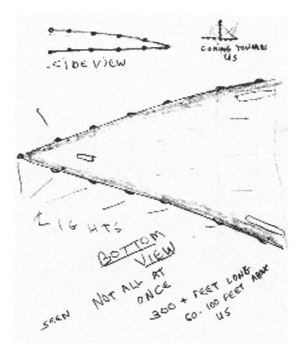

"We threw the groceries in the townhouse and decided to go up to the top of the hill there for a better view. We were in my car watching the lights as they headed south, at about our eye level, then it made a flat turn

97

towards us showing six lights on each edge of the 'V,' and also a line of six lights going up the center of the ship.

"It headed directly towards us and finally went overhead just above the telephone poles very slowly. It was made up of metal panels and covered the sky about the size of a football field. As it passed, I decided to follow this up Rt. 306 till the end of it and was unable to follow further.

"Days later we experienced beings in the apartment. This occurred many times after that."

Irene Lunn
Mahopac Falls, NY
August 20, 1984

Multiple Sightings in New York
The APRO Bulletin
Vol. 32 No. 11

In *The APRO Bulletin*, volume 32, issue number 6, field investigator Dick Ruhl and his team of New York investigators, described their stake-out of the Stormville, New York Airport and subsequent identification of the "Stormville Pilots" who had been flying in the Westchester area and creating a sensation. Mr. Ruhl is convinced, as Headquarters personnel are, that a very small fraction of the reported cases in New York in the last two years are unidentified, and that a substantial number of the overall cases were actually misidentifications of the Cessna flights.

Mrs. Irene Lunn, the wife of a policeman, who lives in Mahopac Falls, New York, has had several sightings of UFOs in her area, and has seen the "Stormville Pilots" as well. Field investigator Gerry Arena interviewed Mrs. Lunn, and the following report in Mrs. Lunn's own words, with illustrations by Norah Bazzurro, based on Mrs. Lunn's own drawings, comprised a very startling case.

"On August 20, 1984 at 9p.m., daylight savings time, my daughter Erica and I were driving home from the store. As we approached Deer Trail Drive, I looked to my west and saw a large object directly over the pond at the Circle A Farm on Austin Road in Mahopac. I stopped the car at the corner and noted the time. The object was triangle-shaped with an L-shaped tail piece with one red light, one green light and eight white lights (see drawing). The object was traveling south, when suddenly it made a 90-degree left turn and came slowly towards us. I drove home (around the corner) and parked at the top of my driveway. The objects stayed with us, however, and I had approximately 25-30 seconds to run into the house and get the binoculars. As I ran out, the object was clearing the end of my house and was directly over my driveway. I looked through the binoculars (10 x 50) and saw it appeared solid and appeared to be metal which was a very dark gray to almost black in color. It maneuvered left again and went across the street over my neighbor's house and hovered for 3 minutes just before her tree line. I would say it hovered over her backyard.

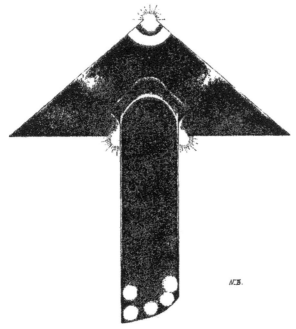

"About one minute after it started hovering, another UFO came out of the west over my driveway. It traveled slowly and was rectangular in shape with four white lights in each corner. I looked through the binoculars and verified in my mind that it, too, was solid with the same coloring as the UFO (A). It traveled from west to east toward UFO (A) and as it got closer it blocked (A) from my view for approximately 5 seconds. Then UFO (B) just vanished from sight and UFO (A) was still hovering.

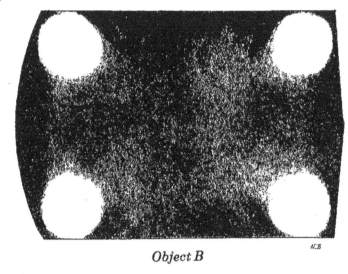

Object B

"Neither UFO made noise—in fact, you could hear the crickets. However, I noticed they seemed to be quieter as this incident took place. In fact, everything seemed to be quieter, like there was nothing else except Erica, me and these two objects. After 3 minutes of hovering the UFO came back. Before it started to move, however, all its lights went from green to red—to the original pattern.

"It came back over the driveway traveling east and as it approached I observed through the binoculars a windshield similar to an airplane except you couldn't see in. As it came closer, I was totally permeated with this feeling that it was letting me know that it knew I was watching it. As it passed over the trees, my daughter went totally hysterical and ran into the house. About 30 seconds later it came back over the trees from the west and made another 90-degree turn right and proceeded south out of my sight. I remained motionless, going over in my mind the whole incident and then I came in the house and immediately called Peter Gersten[1] at approximately 9:20 p.m. to report what had happened.

---

[1] Peter Gersten was a local attorney and UFO researcher. He had offered a $1,000 reward for the identities of the Stormville Flyers.

"I just want to say that while this incident took place, I was anxious but at the same time peaceful. The rest of the night I was very elated, but for three days following the incident I was very depressed and 'down' and couldn't stop thinking about the whole thing. In fact, as of the writing of this report (September 3, 1984), I still find myself constantly thinking about it and constantly looking into the sky. I would also like to mention that on August 8, 20 and 27, my two-year-old daughter was extremely restless in bed and very awake although she was asleep."

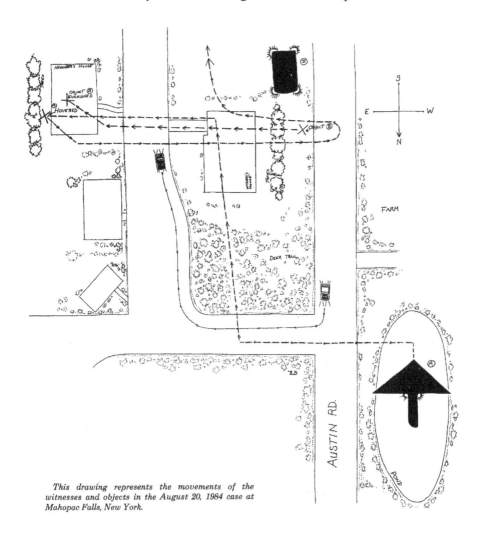

This drawing represents the movements of the witnesses and objects in the August 20, 1984 case at Mahopac Falls, New York.

Mrs. Lunn was interviewed by several newspapers in the 1980s, and was a staunch advocate for having the Stormville Flyers stopped, as they were clearly a public nuisance. In her experience, there was no mistaking the hoaxing pilots for the real UFOs, and she was quoted as making the following statement:

"It's not the pilots, because I've seen them. The pilots are the pilots. The object is the object."

Janice Laughlin
Hawthorne, NY
Summer, c.1984/85

It was a clear summer night in 1984 or 1985, at about 10pm when Janice and her mother saw something strange.

"It was a boomerang, not huge," she explained. "It hovered right above the trees on my road in Hawthorne, NY. It was summer, the windows were open, and there was no sound. It had white lights."

After hovering, the craft "slowly moved up to the next road over the trees and out of sight. The trees did not move," as the craft passed over them. And Janice once again emphasized that there was, "NO sound!" The entire sighting lasted several minutes.

Janice also had two other sightings of circular craft.

"I should also say in the early 90s we were living in Yonkers, NY and we were traveling down Broadway, which is a couple miles from the Hudson River. It was around 10:00 at night, and I distinctly saw a craft right over a house. I want to say it was circular with lights all around. I turned my head to get my husband's attention, turned back, and it was gone, in a split second. But I know I saw it!

"Also about 3 years ago [c.2013], it was around 6 pm on a winter night. We were walking in our church parking lot, on Quaker Hill in Pawling, NY. We would do this almost every Wednesday night for an hour, waiting for our daughter practicing in church. Anyway, we are always looking up; there are always a lot of planes. But one night my husband said, "What is that bright white light?"

It was almost like a very close star, a perfect circle, and another one adjacent to it. We stared for a few minutes, and then it just simply faded, as did the other one a few seconds later. Don't know what that was. Just had to add that!"

Donald Barber
Poughkeepsie and Beacon, NY, Fall 1987-93

In the fall of 1987, Donald Barber was an engineer for IBM in East Fishkill. He was recently named manager of the second shift, so his "lunch hour" was at 8:00pm. He headed over to the South Hills Mall in the Poughkeepsie, and when he got out of his car he noticed there were a lot of people standing in the parking lot. He couldn't understand what was going on, and then he realized they were all looking in the same direction, toward the southeast and the Hudson River.

Turning to look, Donald saw a huge "wedge-shaped" craft with several white lights. The craft was absolutely silent and was hovering, or moving so slow from the southeast to the southwest that it appeared to be motionless.

"It must be those ultralights the *Poughkeepsie Journal* keeps writing about," Donald thought to himself, and then went inside to get something to eat.

For about a month before this sighting, numerous articles about formations of ultralights pretending to be UFOs had filled the pages of the *Poughkeepsie Journal*, so Donald just naturally assumed this is what people had been seeing. Even so, there were a couple of things about these supposed "ultralights" that didn't make sense, especially to an engineer.

"The lights always stayed equidistant, even when the wedge turned on its axis ninety degrees," he stated. "I was joking that the pilots must be holding onto ropes to stay in formation. Also, as I watched for 15 or 20 minutes, the movement appeared much too slow to be any kind of an airplane."

When he came back out to his car after about 15 minutes, the strange craft was gone, but there were still about a dozen people near his car talking about it. I asked whether these people were excited, frightened, or just curious.

"Curious, and dismissive," Donald replied.

"Dismissive?" I said with some surprise.

"Yes, they were all dismissive, because they had also read all of the articles about the ultralights, so they didn't think this was anything out of the ordinary.

A second sighting occurred on Thanksgiving of that year. Donald was living in a house in Beacon, New York. From the front he could see the Hudson River, while the view from the back deck was of Mount Beacon and the three or four very tall antennas at its peak. There were five friends and family members present, and as they stood there looking toward the mountain, they noticed a white light moving up and down and back and forth through the antennas.

"Oh, that must be those ultralights again," Donald told everyone.

#1 –   Silent, slowly rotating & hovering ; No sound.

#2   mt Beacon

However, once again, there were things that just didn't make sense in the context of conventional aircraft. First of all, there was the up and down movement, and the fact that this light was going in and out between the antennas, passing *extremely* close. As they watched this apparently incredibly reckless pilot, other white lights also appeared and began the same strange movement. These lights were always white, and never flashing, and completely uncharacteristic of standard aircraft lights.

"The other thing was that we never saw these lights moving towards the antenna," he explained. "When we saw them, *they were already there.* We never saw the lights moving towards the antennae or moving away. They were just there and then they weren't."

Donald lived in this Beacon house from 1987 to 1993, and he periodically would see these strange white lights moving around the antennas on top of Mount Beacon.

"I can't say that it was as regular as every week, but it certainly was not uncommon," he told me.

I was particularly intrigued with his accounts of the strange lights over Mount Beacon, as in my *Hudson Valley UFOs* book, I first wrote about the mysterious airship wave of 1909, when residents of Newburgh, New York, stood in the streets to watch strange lights moving up and down over Mount Beacon! Has this been a hot spot for over a century?

What also makes Donald Barber's accounts compelling is that never at any point during his sightings did he think he was looking at a UFO. It wasn't until just a couple of years ago that he learned about the Hudson Valley wave of sightings in the 1980s when he was watching a show on television. He always thought he was looking at the reckless antics of ultralight pilots. Now that he realizes so many other people during that time saw similar things, he is looking at his sightings differently. Perhaps these craft did not behave like ultralights, because they were something *very* different.

Phil
Upper Nyack, NY
Early 1988

It was early 1988 when "Phil" was outside his boarding school in Upper Nyack, New York, and saw some strange lights in the night sky.

"It was a widely opened V-shape and there were too many lights to count, at least 50. The lights were all white and equally sized. It passed overhead very slowly and there was absolutely no sound. I couldn't see any structure, just the lights."

A friend also saw the V-shape lights and told one of the dorm heads, who called the police. The police told him it was nothing to worry about, as it was simply pilots flying in formation—the same old excuse that was used for many years in the Hudson Valley.

"I wasn't at all frightened as I watched it," Phil explained, "because it didn't fit any conception of a flying saucer, like I had seen on TV or in the movies. It was so unfamiliar it didn't trigger anything. Had I seen a classic flying saucer, I would have been scared."

The sighting made the student newsletter, but no investigation was launched, as it was dismissed as a formation of ultralights. Phil can't say exactly what he saw, but he has come to believe that there are "non-earth" craft, and that we possibly have some "reverse-engineering" to make our own remarkable craft.

Rhinebeck, NY
1989

This NUFORC (National UFO Reporting Center) case illustrates the fact that enormous, silent, black craft of various shapes were still seen by many witnesses in the Hudson Valley as late as 1989. This is also important as a solid, dark structure was clearly seen, not just a pattern of lights.

In my opinion, the duration and extent of such reports also weakens the secret military project explanation, as this object was chevron-shaped. While one can imagine the government experimenting with a couple of designs for stealth craft, and then somehow managing to keep them all secret, could they really produce massive craft in all the many shapes of chevrons, boomerangs, V-shapes, and triangles of numerous sizes and configurations, both smooth and textured, with a wide variety of light patterns, all in the span of a few years, all of which were tested over the Hudson Valley, but never seen to land or take off, and not one scrap of evidence of their existence has been uncovered in over 30 years? And where did they store this huge fleet of dozens of football field-sized craft?

While I can't say for certain these were extraterrestrial craft, I also have not seen any evidence to say they were manmade.

NUFORC Report: Late one afternoon of 1989, I was on my way home from work. I had an approximately 45 minute ride which took me through the town of Rhinebeck, NY. Lots of traffic, as it was rush hour and many people were on their way home.

Traffic started to slow and it became dark. As I looked out my window, I realized that the sky had gotten very dark very fast, and people were stopping their cars, pulling off to the side of the road. I looked up and was surprised at the sight I saw. Hovering above us was a huge, very dark, almost black, object, chevron-shaped, very large and covering not only the road, but buildings on both sides of the road. The sky was completely blocked out, it was that large an object and although I am not sure exactly how high up it was, nothing could be seen around it. Dark gray/black underneath...silent, not a sound did I hear from it, and moving extremely slowly. There were some lights underneath, but I did not count them or take note of any color. To me they were just bright, but small lights.

People were pointing up, and some were out of their cars or nearly stopped in the roadway. This object continued moving forward slowly along Route 9 East, heading towards the Route 9G intersection, east. It sped up a bit, but never any sound could be heard and it disappeared heading towards the town of Red Hook. I later heard reports of it being sighted on the Taconic State Parkway heading south.

Lauren
Yonkers, NY
c.1992

The following is an exchange of emails in 2015 between the witness, Lauren, and myself, regarding a sighting of two black triangles along the Hudson River in a very populated area, just a few miles north of Manhattan. What really makes this sighting stand out is that the witnesses were *looking down onto the tops of the crafts!*

107

Lauren: Hi Linda, I missed your presentation on Thursday at the Warner Library. But I wanted to report something I, and two friends, witnessed somewhere between 1990-1994. We were standing on a balcony overlooking the Hudson in Yonkers (building on Warburton Avenue) on the top floor. It was Thanksgiving night. We saw, coming from the north, a very large black flying triangle (not boomerang) that moved stealthily (so silent you could still hear the din of the river) that was low-flying and that hugged the Yonkers shoreline. We could see the top of it. As soon as this craft passed, another one came along. I looked into the cockpit (rounded glass) and saw a light and some entity but couldn't see the whole figure. We all were flabbergasted. We wondered, either way - aliens or the military - what do they think they're doing flying down the Hudson, close to shore, - and where do they intend to go once they get down to Spuyten Duyvil or the George Washington Bridge? It has been a mystery and very haunting. It was definitely c.1992-93, not in the 1980s. What do you think? Best wishes, Lauren

Z: Fascinating, and I love your comment--*What do they think they're doing?* I have often wondered that myself. Could you give me the approximate size and altitude, as I would like to include this sighting in my next book. Are you still in contact with either of those friends, as I would like their input, as well. Thanks!

Lauren: I'm not good at judging altitude, but we were on the 6th floor (the top floor) of this apartment building. I did a little research and found the site for Untermeyer Park which is not far and found the following:
"Train: The Greystone Metro-North station is on the Hudson line and is less than a mile away from the gardens. The gardens are a 20 minute uphill walk from the station: walk uphill from the station to find the stairs on the left to Warburton Avenue. Climb the stairs. Cross Warburton Avenue and go up Odell Avenue until it ends at North Broadway. Turn right on North Broadway and walk to 945 N. Broadway, which is on the right. Caution: this is a significant uphill walk of more than 200 ft in elevation."
If we were 200 feet above the shore, and then we add the height of the six-storied building, that's how far above the river we were. The "aircrafts" were so low, again, that we got a good view of the tops of the

aircrafts. It's almost impossible for me to know how far above the Hudson they were, but they were flying very low. There is nothing from the Metro North tracks going up that hill but trees, until you get up to Warburton Avenue. So if anyone saw this, they'd have to be up at the same elevation, up on Warburton where all the housing is.

I have lost touch with the two friends (I did reach out to one of them in 2007, but he never responded to the card I sent; I might try again.) As far as the size of the crafts is concerned, the cockpit was tiny compared to the rest of the craft.

I don't know if this helps, but it's what I can come up with at the moment. I wish I was better at judging size from a distance.

Z: This helps a lot, thanks for looking up the info on the elevation. This is an amazing story, and as you say, military or alien, that was very bold of them to fly so low like that. It's like they wanted to be seen.

Lauren: Imagine being on a train, looking out the window, and seeing one of those fly by? Someone on Metro-North, either engineer or passengers, may have seen it. It was around 11 pm, not sure if I mentioned it.

So if the building Lauren and her friends were in was 200 feet above the river, and they were on the balcony of a six story building, which would be about 60 feet high, then she was observing from a height of 260 feet. Given the fact that they were *looking down* to the top of the black triangles, then these craft must have been flying at an altitude of no more than 200 feet!

The following is from a document designed to identify and report low flying aircraft that are violating the law. As you can see, the craft Lauren saw should have been at least 500 feet above the river, or if it was flying over any structures in this heavily-populated neighborhood of Yonkers, at least "1,000 feet above the highest obstacle." If these were military aircraft, they were clearly violating the law in a big way. If they were not our military, well, there's not much we can do about it!

New York Flight Standards District Office (FSDO)
Low Flying Aircraft

This document was prepared by the Eastern Region FAASTeam to provide guidance on low flying aircraft.

The Federal Aviation Administration (FAA) is the government agency responsible for aviation safety. We welcome information from citizens that will enable us to take corrective measures including legal enforcement action against individuals violating Federal Aviation Regulations (FAR). It is FAA policy to investigate citizen complaints of low-flying aircraft operated in violation of the FAR that might endanger persons or property.

*(b) **Over congested areas** -Over any congested area of a city, town, or settlement, or over any open-air assembly of persons, an altitude of 1,000 feet above the highest obstacle within a horizontal radius of 2,000 feet of the aircraft.*

*(c) **Over other than congested areas** - An altitude of 500 feet above the surface except over open water or sparsely populated areas. In that case, the aircraft may not be operated closer than 500 feet to any person, vessel, vehicle, or structure.*

Earl Laughlin
Ardsley-Dobbs Ferry, NY
Spring/Summer 1993

Earl thought his story was "very vanilla" and probably not of much interest, but on the contrary, post-1980s wave sightings are quite important. For starters, the Stormville Flyers were long gone, so the small plane and ultralight excuses can't be used. Also, for all those who believe that UFO activity in the Hudson Valley ended with that wave, this case illustrates that the massive "Vs" were still flying our skies years later.

The following is Earl's account in his own words:

Saw Mill Parkway, 3:30am
"While driving northbound on the Saw Mill Parkway at Livingston Ave., I almost hit cars who were stopped in the road. I did not understand why they were stopped. Then I looked up.

"There was a large, black, V-shaped wing moving very slow north. All the cars exited the road at the Dobbs Ferry exit. I chased the object. The faster I drove, the faster it moved.

110

"It finally departed the roadway in Irvington near the I-87 exit. It made no noise and traveled at treetop level."

John
Putnam County, NY
2002

I spoke to John at an event in 2015, and he gave me a brief description of a close sighting he had in 2002. He later sent the following full account, with sketches he added to photos to illustrate just what he saw.

"In the spring of 2002—end of March beginning of April—I went outside at just after 9pm to get firewood, as it was still cold at night. As I was bringing the wood back to the house, movement in the sky caught my attention. I looked towards the north, and approaching from the horizon, I saw an object getting closer. I thought at first it was an aircraft of some kind, but began to notice that it had no green (starboard) or red (port) wing lights. The object seemed too slow, to almost hover, just above the tree line approximately 50-60 feet away. There was no sound. I can only describe the 'sound' as though it was 'disturbing' the air.

"The night was starry and crystal clear. I was stunned by the apparent size...the object covered the stars as I held out my arms at shoulder width. The color was a non-reflective, gun metal gray. By the outline, the object was wedge-shaped. I noticed that the object had 4 opaque 'lights' on each leading edge of the craft. They appeared to be oriented at a slight downward angle, yet no light was projected or emanated from them. (As would a car's headlights or a spot light.)

"After hovering for about 60 seconds, the object began to 'drift' up the hill along the tree line without a sound. Definitely not an 'air breather.' As the object reached the top of the hill, it gained altitude. (It appeared now to be about the size of a quarter.) At this point, the object was surrounded by many multi-colored 'hula-hoop' lights. The object (now in the western sky) began to bank towards the east and accelerate over the I-84 corridor which I can see from my property.

"My house is approximately 875 feet above sea level and approximately 400-500 yards above the I-84 corridor. It disappeared over the hills on the westbound side of I-84. The distance from my property to where the object faded from sight is approximately 2-3 miles. The entire sighting lasted 2-3 minutes. I called the Putnam Co. sheriff's office to report the incident. They had no other reports, but said they would send a deputy. I advised them the object was no longer in sight. I called Stewart AFB and was told they knew nothing about an object as described in the vicinity."

I responded with: "Thanks so much for this very clear account. Looking forward to the drawings. One question, when you say 'air breather,' do you mean an aircraft with exhaust?"

John's answer: "Correct. No exhaust sound, no prop sounds. No whoop of a helicopter rotor, just a low frequency 'rumble' as though the air around it was being disturbed as it moved."

Note: This is not the first time I have heard of "hula hoops of light" around a craft. In *In the Night Sky*, I wrote about Hank Vanderbeck's 1953 sighting in Saugerties, NY of a cigar-shaped object encircled by four alternating hula hoops of red and green light.

Frank Z.
Bridgewater, CT
May 19, 2012

Frank Z. provided the following description and sketch of a sighting of a boomerang-shaped object flying "at the height of a small prop plane," that he and four or five other people observed in Bridgewater, CT on May 19, 2012:

"We were hanging outside at a wedding reception drinking, talking, and smoking. I was not drunk and wasn't smoking as it was still fairly early. As we were talking, we saw "something" in the sky above us that flew overhead. It was a series of shaped lights. The best I can describe the lights is that they looked like balls of flame, blueish-white, soft and not overly bright. We were all trying to figure out what the heck it was.

"It flew overhead and kept going for a bit, and just disappeared midway toward the horizon. I remember checking Twitter to see if anyone else saw it. I think there were one or two posts, but not a lot. I meant to listen to the radio later but I think I forgot. Also, whatever it was made no sound at all. We all noted that."

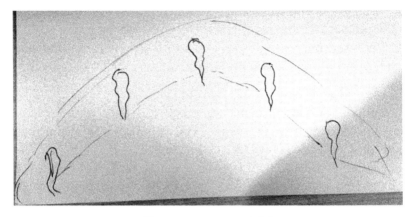

Germantown, NY
November 6, 2012

After some previous communications with this witness, I received the following comprehensive account of a very lengthy and close-up triangle sighting. If people think that triangular craft are a thing of the past in the Hudson Valley, this should convince them otherwise.

Hi Linda, I'm sorry I haven't been able to get back to you right away. I've had a lot going on in the past week. Anyway, we decided it was time to tell someone about what we had seen that night in 2012. It was the presidential election night in 2012. I think it was the 5th or 6th of November. My husband and I had gotten out of work and had just picked up our daughter, who was 10 at the time.

We live in Germantown, NY in southern Columbia County. We had taken Round Top Road from Woods Road in Germantown on our way home. It was just becoming dusk and we were almost to where Round Top meets Church Ave. when all three of us noticed a blue ball in the sky to the right of our truck, just falling out of the sky. It looked like a neon blue to me. Looked silverish-blue to my husband. I told my husband that we should go look for it. He said there was no guarantee that we would even find it. That it may have looked close to us but in fact it could have been miles away.

So we then crossed Church Ave. to get to the other side of Round Top where we live. It took us maybe 2-3 minutes to get home after that. We pull into the driveway in the front of our house. My daughter and I head for the back of the house as we don't have a key to the front door and always use the back. As we get to the back of the house we both notice a huge bright light low on the south of our field. My husband was getting tools from the truck before coming in the house and I called for him to come look at this.

It was moving very slow and low and bright. He had no idea what this could be. None of us wanted to go into the house. We wanted to see what this was. At this point it was starting to get dark out. I would have to say it took about 15-20 minutes for it to get to where we were. As it went past us moving about 10mph (at least that's what it seemed) it made no noise and was as big as a house. It was at or just above tree level. It was triangular-shaped with 3 lights on each angle tip that looked to be gold. There was a bright red light in the middle underside of the object. The front of the triangle looked almost circular shaped. This is where the bright white light was coming from. Except it looked as if it was an inner light glowing out.

It passed by us and went north. My husband continued to watch it until it disappeared, but my daughter and I went in the house since I was cold standing out there for so long. After we were in the house for about 10-15 minutes we heard a loud noise outside the house. I looked out our bedroom window and saw two large helicopters with red lights flying low on our property going towards where we saw the object come from. They were only there for about 10 minutes and then they left going in the same direction of the object we saw.

I told my husband at the time that they seemed to be military helicopters as I had the opportunity in high school to see a Black Hawk helicopter up close one day on our football field. He agreed that they were definitely larger than a regular helicopter. I'm not sure where the closest base is but we haven't seen them since.

I feel that everything we witnessed that night was connected. I can't say whether it was a UFO we saw or a new military vehicle being tested. What I do know is that all three of us witnessed the same thing. We weren't scared at all. We were all in complete awe. Two things that I can't get past are the facts that it could move without noise and it didn't have wings. We live out in the country and I can tell you that it was completely

115

quiet that night. If we weren't looking at this thing flying over us, we wouldn't have even known it was there.

Thanks for letting me share our story with you.

Manchester, CT
November 14, 2015

MUFON Case #73426

This is another MUFON case for which I have to thank Mike Panicello. As my father was a Marine, I may be favorably biased toward the testimony of any Marine, but Mike did assess this witness as appearing to be "open and honest." While this sighting occurred in central Connecticut, about 60 miles from Danbury, and since Mike also categorized this sighting as the "best case" he had ever worked, that was good enough for me to include!

"I am a former Marine Corps scout sniper and highly trained/experienced in observation. I was dropping off my dad following a road trip back from a wedding. I was driving my vehicle southbound on Main Street in Manchester. Just before (~250 feet) the on-ramp to I-384 East, I noticed what I initially thought was an airplane flying over my position northbound directly above Main Street. It seemed to be EXTREMELY low to the ground for an airplane, considering the lack of proximity to an airport, and was flying VERY slowly. The speed-altitude abnormality and strangely positioned lights prompted me to stop my car in the middle of the road and get out (the road was devoid of other vehicles). I looked up at the 'airplane' in awe for 1-2 minutes. It was hovering/flying in a constant path at a constant speed and altitude in COMPLETE SILENCE. Upon closer observation, there was a triangle-shaped, completely blacked-out craft with three yellow-white lights equidistant apart from each other close to the corners of the triangle. Directly underneath the triangular craft was the image of a 747 (I believe) airplane. It appeared to be a real object except for how low and slowly it was flying. It remained directly below the triangle-shaped craft and did not waver at all from this position as if they were moving in complete unison or even attached to one another... Based on the perceived size of the image of the airplane, I would guess that the aircraft was at approximately 500 feet altitude. Based on that altitude, I would guess that it was flying at

116

approximately 25 knots (~30mph). If the craft was larger than I perceived it, it may have been much higher in altitude and faster in speed, but the image of the airplane would have been WAY out of scale if that was the case. I stood in awe and just watched the craft pass overhead on the same trajectory, trying to make sense of what I was looking at. I would have filmed the whole event but my cell phone was dead at the time from the long road trip. I served 8 years in the Marine Corps as a scout sniper, 2 years of which I served as a combat instructor with the Air Force. I served on three combat tours and am EXTENSIVELY trained and experienced working with different types of aircraft from many different countries and I have NEVER IN MY LIFE seen anything like this."

Where do I begin to discuss this case? Taking this highly-trained, ex-Marine Corps sniper at his word, what are we to make of this image of a conventional 747 aircraft being directly beneath a most decidedly unconventional black triangle? Was this 747 some sort of a holographic projection; an illusion designed to provide camouflage for the triangular craft? If so, was it a secret military project, or something extraterrestrial?

I could speculate all day about the ramifications of this sighting, but suffice it to say that *someone* possesses technology far beyond what we use in ordinary daily life.

New Milford, CT
November 17, 2016, 8:45pm

This is yet another sighting which occurred in the area on the busy night of November 17, 2016. The following is the description posted for it as MUFON Case #80488. I want to thank Mike Panicello, Connecticut State Director of MUFON, for bringing this case to my attention.

"Driving home on a clear night, approaching a stop sign in rural area, noted brightly lit craft flying very slowly directly towards me at low altitude. The white spotlights were VERY bright and spaced widely apart, making a helicopter unlikely so I stopped at the intersection to observe what seemed like a strange phenomenon. It took about three minutes to reach me, traveling less than a mile. As it got closer I saw a blinking red light on the nose and thought "plane." But it was so slow, low and silent. Moments before it would have been overhead, it made a perfect ninety degree turn. At that point I could see its underbelly clearly. It was a perfect black triangle, slightly wider at the back than the sides (triangle tip facing forward for flight) with white and red line of lights along the back flashing in a sequence back and forth. Shortly after it turned it traveled behind the tree line and I continued on my way home."

So on this single night, there were three very different sightings and encounters on a roughly 45-mile straight line going east from Montgomery, NY, through Pawling, NY and on to New Milford, CT. Even more intriguing is that each case was very different—a rectangle and entity sighting, a boomerang, and a black triangle. The MUFON database lists several other sightings which occurred that night across the country.

Mini-waves of sightings such as those that took place on November 17, 2016 should make ufologists sit up and take notice. As extraordinary as it would have been if a single type of craft had been seen across the region that night, this wide variety of sightings is quite rare—and much more difficult for skeptics to dismiss with a single excuse!

6
Indian Point Nuclear Power Plant

Now called the Indian Point Energy Center in Buchanan, NY, this nuclear power plant was built on the site of an old amusement park in the 1950s, and began operation in 1962. It has been the target of UFOs on several occasions documented in the book *Night Siege*, as well as in my first UFO book, *In the Night Sky*. At the Pine Bush UFO Festival in 2015, a man, "Joe," who had been a security guard at Indian Point, related an incident that occurred there in late 1985.

While on duty one night, Joe got a call from his supervisor.

"They're back!" the supervisor said.

"Who's back?" Joe asked, having no clue what his boss was talking about.

"The UFO!"

Joe had not been working at the plant when the first major sighting occurred over one of the reactors on July 24, 1984, but he had certainly heard stories of the huge craft which had caused the security and alarm systems to malfunction. Running outside, he saw a massive, V-shaped craft at least the size of a football field, with enormous lights.

"It certainly wasn't trying to hide," Joe told me.

Unlike most sightings of this type where witnesses describe the eerie silence of the craft, this one made a bizarre and unnerving sound.

"It was like an aluminum canoe bending and creaking," he said.

After the craft moved away, the staff was told "not to speak to the media" about what they saw. And even though thirty years has passed, Joe did not want his identity revealed for fear of possible repercussions.

At the Danbury UFO Conference in October 2016, C. Burns interviewed a woman who grew up near Indian Point and had numerous sightings of UFOs over the power plant. I spoke with her a few days later and was surprised to hear that "it was the thing to do" for area residents, to get in the car and find a good spot to watch UFOs over Indian Point!

"It didn't happen every night," she explained, "but it happened regularly enough that it was the thing to do."

I admit I had no idea that there had been so many sightings over Indian Point during the 1980s, especially to the point where it became a favorite pastime of area residents! Yet no public investigations were ever carried out, and press coverage was at a minimum.

However, it should be noted that UFO activity over these nuclear reactors did not begin in the 1980s. An article which appeared in *The Spokeman-Review* from Spokane, Washington on October 14, 1976 entitled *Numerous UFO 'Sightings' Made Near Nuclear Plants* at least pushes the timeline back several years. The following is an excerpt from that article:

Several UFOs have been reported over Stony Point, just across the Hudson River from the Indian Point nuclear reactors. Others have been spotted over plants in Tomkins Cove and Haverstraw.

[It should be noted that the power plants in Tomkins Cove and Haverstraw were not nuclear plants.]

The article goes on to say that there had been over 100 reports to local police during a three-week period that August. Several sightings were also witnessed by the police, and one involved as many as 25 witnesses at the same location.

A MUFON report may push back that timeline even further, to 1969:

June 1969
Saw yellowish, round, lighted object, silent, circle the Indian Point atomic power plant in Peekskill, New York on the Hudson River

I left work around midnight and headed south on Route 9W. As I came around the top of Buckberg Mountain (Tomkins Cove, NY) I saw a light over the atomic power plant. At the bottom of the mountain, I pulled over by the river and got out to watch it. It circled slowly at a low altitude. It made no sound at all. It was very quiet and dark where I was.

I am a pilot with well over 500 hours in my 1943 Stearman biplane and am very familiar with aircraft of all types. After watching for a while,

I went south and observed the light still near the power plant, but now to my northeast. It then seemed that the light went out and I didn't see it again. It didn't make any sound and circled in a non-wobbly way at a low altitude around the power plant.

Clearly, the wave of Indian Point sightings began long before the publicized event of 1984. And as further proof that these sightings did not occur just two or three times, here are two additional cases which were reported to NUFORC, one of which also mentions helicopter involvement, as had been seen on other occasions.

Peekskill, NY on July 5, 1985
Duration: 8 minutes

Description: Triangle-shaped, orange-colored, translucent object hovered near Indian Point Nuclear Power Plant emitting a loud whooshing sound. I was lying on my living room sofa and my three friends were sitting on my front porch (high on a cliff), overlooking the Hudson River. All of a sudden, my one friend started to call out my name. I was starting to doze off and ignored his calls at first, until the tone of his voice went frantic. I jumped up and ran outside. The object was clearly visible between my house and the Indian Point Nuclear Power Plant. The object was an orange-colored, translucent triangle. It almost seemed to be stuck or frozen. It was emitting a high pitched whooshing sound. My one young friend started to jump up and down and yell "take me, take me," at which point the object seemed to come closer. I distinctly felt menaced and started to cower toward the house. The object then made a 360 degree circle out over the river and then disappeared over the tree line to the east.

Buchanan, NY in August 1988
UFO over nuclear reactor- 14 helicopters around it

4 people, driving north on Route 9, saw a large rotating circle of lights flying over the area of Indian Point Nuclear Reactor (restricted airspace) on the Hudson River. I counted 14 helicopters flying around it. Cars were stopped all along the road to watch the incident, but we didn't stop, for

121

some reason. This definitely happened in August of 1988, but I can't remember the exact date or time (evening).

The following MUFON case is of particular interest as the witness was a local police Detective Sergeant on a boat in the Hudson River by Indian Point:

At or about 2300 hours during the summer of 1987 or 1986, I was on my boat, anchored at Haverstraw Bay, just south of the Indian Point Power Plant in New York. I noticed an object in the sky, moving south at a very slow rate of speed. It displayed four spotlights evenly spaced along the front of the object. The object was silhouetted against the night sky. What amazed and puzzled me, is that based on its rate of travel and its altitude, it should have fallen out of the sky into the water. What puzzled me further was that it made no noise. It reached a point which was almost directly overhead, when it stopped forward movement, turned, and proceeded back in the direction from which it came, finally disappearing from sight. At the time of this sighting, I was a Detective Sergeant with the Ossining New York Police Department.

There's something else noteworthy which I came across during my newspaper archive searches. In the Triangle Chapter, there is the story of the multiple sightings on November 23, 1983, across a 50 mile stretch of the lower Hudson Valley. Just the day before, there was some trouble at Indian Point. Perhaps it was a coincidence, or perhaps there had been some UFO activity again?

Indian Point 2 out of Service
Buchanan, NY (AP)
Journal News
Thursday, November 24, 1983

Consolidated Edison's Indian Point 2 nuclear power reactor shutdown automatically Wednesday and will be out of service for several days, a company spokesman said.

Spokesman Bowin Lindgren said that the nuclear reactor, located 30 miles north of Manhattan, shut down when an instrument showed a possible problem with a pump bearing in the non-nuclear part of the plant.

The utility will check to see if the instrument reading—which showed the bearing to have moved slightly–was correct and if so, it will fix or replace the bearing, Lindgren said.

If not, it will fix or replace the instrument that gave the incorrect reading, he added.

While the plant is out of service, maintenance service will be performed on a hydraulic system associated with the turbine, the spokesman said.

Note: A subsequent article stated that there actually wasn't any problem with the pump bearing, and that the shutdown must have been the result of a faulty reading.

In January of 2017, New York Governor Andrew Cuomo announced that one of Indian Point's nuclear reactors will cease operations by April 2020, and the other will shut down a year later. The question remains: Once Indian Point is closed for good and the nuclear material is removed, will the UFO activity in this area also cease?

7
Rectangles

Based upon some UFO reporting sites statistics, rectangular-shaped craft constitute only about one to two percent of the total reported sightings over the last several decades. However, in the Hudson Valley region, enormous rectangles have been making quite an impression on witnesses in recent years. Are rectangles the new triangles?

While this following account is maddeningly short on details, it does provide yet an early rectangle sighting in the Hudson Valley, so perhaps rectangular craft have been with us all along, but are now becoming more numerous.

Athens, NY
c. June, 1969

NUFORC Report
Rectangle shaped object was huge, dark colored, with some white lights.
Oddly quiet and fast.
Duration: 3 minutes

We saw a huge, dark, rectangle-shaped object silently hovering over our car. Parked on Leeds Athens Road in Athens, N.Y.
Around 10pm near dirt parking area by NYS Thruway bridge.

This next case is interesting for a couple of reasons. First, it is another relatively early rectangle sighting. Also, I find it rather curious that the witness happened to end up moving to this location! Also, the fact that another sighting occurred here would indicate this area had a particular draw to UFOs for some purpose.

Avon, CT
August 30, 1978, 1am

NUFORC Case
Driving early AM in Avon Ct., I spotted an object fifty feet in the air as large as a house.
Duration: 10 minutes

I was driving back to where I was staying that night after dropping off a friend. I was driving up a road in Avon CT when I saw a bright light up ahead; I thought this was unusual for this time of night. I proceeded up the road and when I got to where the light basically was coming from, there was no light present. I looked around in curiosity and discovered an object the size of a house hovering about fifty feet in the air. There was basically a half moon and visibility was good, this object was very dark and large, there were no lights on and it made no noise whatsoever.

I parked my car in the middle of the road and left it running with the lights, on hoping someone would come down the road to witness this as well. I stood still in one spot staring at this object for about 5 minutes, fearing what it would be capable of doing. I looked around and saw a house that had its lights on, so I ran over to it and knocked on the door. I waited for a couple of minutes, but nobody answered.

I ran back to where my car was and the object was still there. I became so scared I jumped in my car and drove off quickly. As I went to the stop sign at the end of the road, I looked up and the object had followed me all the way down the road. I turned to the left and saw the object was still following me, so I floored the gas and never looked back again.

It took me over a month to tell anyone else, but eventually I told my parents. We ended up moving to an area basically right where this event occurred, and a neighbor saw the same thing almost one year to the date later. She described the exact same event I witnessed.

This next NUFORC case an early northern New Jersey rectangle sighting, just several miles from the Hudson River. (And you have to love those "unimaginative" witnesses!)

Emerson, NJ
c. November 10, 1979, 1am

NUFORC Case
Duration: 2 minutes

In the fall or winter of 1979, my parents had a UFO encounter in Bergen County, New Jersey. These are blue-collar, relatively unimaginative people who had absolutely no interest in, or knowledge of,

125

UFOs. My father was a house painter with a sixth-grade education, and mother was a secretary.

Anyway, they lived in a little town called Emerson, which is perhaps 25 miles from New York City.

On this night, around midnight or perhaps 1 a.m., they were coming home from a bingo game or similar small-town event, when they saw a large, brightly lit and low-flying rectangular object near a major thoroughfare, Kinderkamack Road.

It was so large and well-defined that they first thought it was a billboard, and they remarked something like: "Gee, why would the town put up a big billboard like that?" Then they noticed that it was moving slowly and silently over the town. It just moved away, over some treetops, and that was the end of the encounter. They never reported it to law enforcement, and they never heard of anyone else in town seeing this object.

Tomkins Cove, NY
November 19, 1983, 8:55pm,
Reports of UFOs
by Robert Gribble, Dir. of UFO Reporting Center
SBI, Col. 6, #42, 1984

A square-shaped object—estimated to be 40 feet across and showing four brilliant white lights –was observed in a stationary position over high voltage electric transmission lines. The three witnesses were riding in a car and reported that the object followed their vehicle and approached to within 200 feet of their car. The witnesses fled to a neighbor's house and observed the object until it moved away.

From inside the house they could hear a humming sound. They had the object under observation for about 6 minutes.

Note: In *In the Night Sky*, I reported on another sighting of a craft over power lines in Tomkins Cove in the 1980s. The following night, the power lines were sparking where this craft had been seen. From this location, the Indian Point nuclear power plant is visible just across the Hudson River.

It never ceases to amaze me that witnesses who have the most incredible experiences sometimes hesitate to tell their stories, as they don't think they are of much value. Read the following stunning account and judge for yourself if it is "worth much."

New Fairield, CT
February, 1984

Not sure my story is worth much. I was 23 at the time. A friend and I drove in my car to pick up a half gallon of ice cream on a cold February evening in 1984 (we had a craving). We stopped at the stop sign on the crest of a hill near St. Edwards Church in New Fairfield, CT. We looked up and were surprised to see a craft flying over us for about 15-30 seconds. It appeared to be descending maybe 50 feet above us.

It flew right over our car, and was the size of two football fields. It wasn't speeding by, nor was it hovering. It moved at a steady rate, but it was coming down. It had colored lights (not blinking) around the front of the ship. Though the front was rounded, the ship was rectangular in shape. What impressed me most, and what I haven't forgotten to this day, was its massive size, yet it was completely silent. The silence of something that large was amazing. After flying over our car, it continued down behind a mountain top nearby and we literally braced for a crash, but heard nothing. That was it.

It happened so fast. We didn't even mention it when we returned home (with our ice cream in February...). But the next night when we saw the story on the news, we told my friend's family.

The experience hasn't changed me in any way. I never felt afraid or in any danger. I thought, and still think, that seeing this craft was an absolutely amazing experience. I don't know what it was. I had never seen anything like it before and haven't seen anything like it since. It was a really stunning sight!

Sonya Sartori
Dover and Wingdale, NY and New Milford, CT
1984-2010

Sonya Sartori, her husband, and two kids, were driving on Route 22 in Dover sometime in the 1990s, when they spotted something over a cow pasture across from the high school. Sonya described a square object "at least the size of a house, if not bigger" which had four white lights, one in each corner. It was silent and right at treetop level. They all watched in amazement as the object hovered and floated, "but then it had the strangest motion of bobbing up and down." It eventually rose up slowly, and gradually moved away, following the power line towers.

Sonya stressed that to all the family members the memory is still very vivid. As if to confirm that, she emailed me the following the day after we spoke.

"I called my son about the UFO that we saw across from the Dover High School on Rt. 22, and he remembered so much about that night like it was yesterday. He said it was October 1993 at around 8:00 pm. He also remembered the object as square-shaped with more than 4 lights on it. He also verified that it hovered over the power lines and bobbed up and down while doing that."

On another occasion in 1990s, Sonya was about to let out their dogs one night at their home in Wingdale, when she looked up and saw "a massive black, chevron-shaped" object, that was "bigger than a football field filling the sky." The object was completely silent and had no lights, but it was easy to see as it "blotted out" the bright, starry sky. Yelling for her kids, they ran outside, but the object had just moved out of sight to the south by the time they got out there.

Sonya and her husband had another sighting from their home back in November of 1984, although her husband steadfastly refuses to believe there are such things as UFOs. They were just returning from grocery shopping, when they saw a large triangle of white lights coming from the east.

"Oh, it's those airplanes," her husband said dismissing the object, as he referred to the pilots who had been trying to pretend to be UFOs.

"No, there's no motor sound," Sonya pointed out.

128

"Don't even bother looking at it," her husband continued. "Let's just get the groceries inside."

"There's absolutely no sound, and the lights are in a perfect formation," Sonya observed, realizing it was clearly one object. "Those *aren't* airplanes."

However, despite all the evidence to the contrary, to this day her husband still believes it was a group of airplanes flying in formation, because that was what the police and media kept telling everyone.

Sonya's most dramatic sighting was also her most recent. It was June of 2010, around midnight, and she was in a New Milford, Connecticut hospital after having some surgery.

"I know people are going to think I was drugged up or asleep, but I was not on anything, and I was wide awake watching TV," she stressed emphatically. "At first I thought there was a forest fire, but then it got brighter and moved up into the air. It was like the burning sun, pulsating orange and yellow and changing color. I actually slapped myself in the face to make sure I wasn't dreaming. This huge ball of fire started coming right toward me and I was afraid it was going to crash into the building. I actually thought that this would be the end; that I was going to die.

"I was so scared, I looked away for a moment and crossed myself. When I looked back, it had stopped. It was tremendously huge, bigger than a football field. It was shaped like a half Moon, and by that I mean it was round and the top half was light but the bottom half was dark. But then it shifted its shape to something like a diamond, and then shifted again to a completely bright ball with what looked like fire all along its rim. It started to move again and headed north, away from the hospital. The next day, when my husband came to visit, I told him the story and he insisted that I was hallucinating. I told him I wasn't on anything, and was wide awake, but he didn't believe me."

I asked if she had checked the MUFON website or any other UFO reporting sites for that night, and she said that she had. A witness had reported seeing the same ball of fire in New Preston, Connecticut that same night. New Preston is just eight miles north of New Milford, which was in line with the direction of where Sonya had seen the object move off. This was a critical piece of information, to once and for all put to rest the idea that her sighting had been the result of a drug-induced hallucination.

This is not the only strange objects seen in this area of Connecticut. Sonya sent me an article from 2012 which involved a bright green light "the size of a whale" that was seen falling out of the sky in nearby Bantam Lake. A witness reported the sighting, which was corroborated by a state trooper who had called in the sighting to his dispatcher. Local firemen took a boat out on the lake, but despite an extensive search, no debris or trace of the object was ever found.

To the average individual living outside of the Hudson Valley/Tristate area, this may all sound like a lot of sightings for one family. However, for those of us who have lived our whole lives here, it really isn't unusual for someone to have multiple sightings spanning many decades. While I can't explain why that is, I have no doubt that we live in one of the most active UFO regions of the country, if not the world.

***

This is not the only UFO to be described as being like a "building lying on its side." See the Casebook Chapter, Ellenville, 1989.

Waterbury, CT
c. August 1, 1996, 11pm

NUFORC Case
HUGE rectangular object over downtown Waterbury in 1996/1997
Duration: 5-10 minutes

I was leaving an evening class at an area high school when I noticed what I thought was an airplane at first, off in the distance over some homes.

I was walking to my car across a parking lot, and it kept getting bigger as it came closer. By the time I got to my car, it was across the street, over some houses and I couldn't believe what I was seeing. It was big then, with "windows" and lights along the sides (blue, white, green, red). The lights blinked in a type of sequence.

I continued to get into my car and drive home, taking a left out of the parking lot and heading to a stop light, where I just stared and couldn't take my eyes off of it. It was on my right side at this point, so I couldn't see much of it because it was so huge.

I drove down the street to get on the highway and it was on my left side now. It looked like a building lying on its side.

I drove to my mom's home to get my kids so fast that night that I don't even remember getting there. I told her, but she thought I was crazy.

I didn't sleep for a long time after that. I never heard of anyone seeing it over the city and I can't understand how nobody else saw it. It was huge.

I really just want to know if there is anyone that may have seen it too. I never heard any sounds coming from it, either.

Pine Bush, NY
c. 2004

A man related a story to me about his mother and sister. His mother's lawyer, who lives in Pine Bush, told her that she should go there and look for UFOs. This bizarre suggestion was out of the blue and he didn't explain why she should go, but it sounded like an interesting thing to do.

So about 4pm one day his mother and sister were driving around Pine Bush, when all of a sudden, a massive rectangle the size of a football field rose up out of the trees. The craft "resonated with harmonic vibrations" that the two women heard and felt.

Stunned by what she had witnessed, his mother relayed their experience to the lawyer and asked why he had made the suggestion in the first place. The lawyer said he had recently encountered a gray alien in his backyard in Pine Bush. It addition to the shocking sight, the lawyer said the 'gray' smelled really bad.

As I did not speak directly to the man's mother or her lawyer, I can only relay this as secondhand information. However, rectangular craft have been making appearances in the area for several years, and Pine Bush is famous for things rising up from the ground—as well as a variety of entities.

Hunter, NY
January 20, 2012, 5pm

NUFORC Case
A massive rectangular craft in between two mountains hovered for a minute and disappeared
Duration: 1 minute

131

A large rectangular craft with 2 green lights running the whole length of the craft.

[Yes, that is the entire report!]

Jim
Napanoch, NY
August 8, 2015

This is another excellent example of the massive rectangles which have been appearing in the Pine Bush region over the last several years.

"It was 10:30pm, and it was sitting above the tree tops maybe 200 feet off the ground on Route 55 in Napanoch in a wooded area," Jim told me. "It was rectangular in shape, with two red lights on each end. I could only see the one side, since the trees blocked some of it. It was about 175-200 feet in length, and I watched it for maybe one or two minutes. I pulled over to watch it before it disappeared over the mountain slowly, going towards the west. It was very quiet, and made no noise."

"It made me feel nervous and excited to see it. Every night, now, I go out about the same time to look for it. It shook me up for days after I saw it, but I would like to see it again.

"I came home and woke up my wife to go out and look for it. We drove up to the lake to see if we could find it, but didn't see it."

His wife added, "He still looks for it, and he still says it made him feel weird! Wish I saw it too!! I will never forget that night and the look on his face."

8
Cops

Police officers see it all. When everyone else is sleeping peacefully in their warm beds, cops are out at all hours in all kinds of weather dealing with drunks, thieves, and worse. It is also not uncommon for them to encounter other things in the dead of night—strange lights in the sky and flying craft. Sometimes they try to pursue these craft, and sometimes they are pursued.

The following is a collection of cases which illustrate that if you really want to know what's going on with UFOs in your hometown, ask a cop.

Port Jervis, NY Area
September-October 1965

For several weeks in 1965, strange things were going on in the skies over Port Jervis, as well as the surrounding area. Thanks to Sgt. Michael Worden of the Port Jervis Police Department, I have the actual police blotter reports written at the time of the events. In addition to the eyewitness reports of discs and lights by police officers and civilians, there is the curious report of a possible powerful sonic boom or explosion—the result of which one angry resident wanted compensation for a mirror that broke. My favorite entry is from a major at Stewart Air Force Base, basically wanting to know what on earth was going on—although I imagine his language may have been more colorful, as he had been "swamped" with UFO reports.

Presented next are some newspaper articles which appeared locally during this time, followed by two Project Blue Book cases. Naturally, one of the cases was dismissed as a balloon. However, the second case was dismissed because the male witness was much too interested in the subject of UFOs, so he was deemed to be unreliable—even though his wife also saw the object, but apparently wives' testimony didn't carry the same weight!

With reports of UFOs flooding the area, *The Evening News* couldn't possibly take the journalistic high road in regard to the phenomena. Instead, they made fun of all the witnesses by printing the following photo of a tossed garbage can lid on the *front page* on October 1, 1965, with the caption reading:

Saucy Saucer – Miss Christine Lupinski, a stenographer in the Orange County Clerk's office at Goshen, takes a surprised (?) look at an unidentified flying object from top of county office building. Any resemblance of the craft to a garbage can cover is a feature the Martians have not yet revealed.

Port Jervis Police Blotter Entries (printed as entered)

Wednesday, September 22, 1965

9:56pm—Answered call to Paul Hess, Hess store, Kingston Ave who said that he seen a circular object in the sky with yellow, red and green lights pointed it out to me in the North by Northeastern section of the sky, below stars was a bright white star, with red and green lights, circling same, very bright in colors when seen through binoculars. Could not make out what it was, but seem to be traveling N-N-E to S-S-W very slowly.

Saturday, September 25, 1965

1:25pm—Ronald Velton, Tri County filter center at Fosterdale, N.Y. will stop at Headquarters later today for info on unidentified flying objects.

9:04pm—Officer Masanotti reports he observes the same object with green, red and white lights in the northern sky that he saw Wed. night.

9:26pm—Walter Rau E. Main St. reports he saw a flying saucer with red and green lights in the sky by High Point [New Jersey] and wants to go to observe it from Point Peter. Told him O.K. Officer Masanotti reports a plane went by at that time.

Monday, September 27, 1965

8:37pm—Gene Smith and Danny Murduck of Butler Trailer park report a disc shaped object with rotating red lights traveling at great speed-low-and no sound seen by them—these were two separate calls at about same time.

10:45pm—Major Work—Stewart Air Force Base phoned and inquired about flying objects, claims he is swamped by phone calls from people in Port Jervis – Middletown and Goshen – reporting all kinds of objects in the sky – I informed him we had several calls reporting objects in the sky, but I myself had not seen any.

Wednesday, September 29, 1965

4:45pm—Monica Kozykowski, Franklin and Church Street reports an explosion some distance off jarred her house causing a $69.00 mirror to fall and break and wants someone to pay for it. Advised her it could possibly be a sonic boom and would be almost impossible to determine liability.

Tuesday, October 5, 1965

2:20am—Answered call to Mrs. Cooper, Fowler St, who reported that she could see a light going on and off up towards Ridge Ave, could not find no wires arcing could be street lights she seen with trees blowing back and forth giving an illusion of a light going on and off.

Newspaper Articles

'Saucers' Seen At Port Jervis
The Evening News, September 27, 1965

PORT JERVIS – Police here said today that they had received a number of calls from residents saying they had seen flying objects in the sky Wednesday and Thursday evening.

The objects were described as circular colored lights said to be red, green and white spinning and hovering in a circular pattern over the city.

Witnesses called them "flying saucers," police said.

UFO Reported At Maybrook
The Evening News, September 28, 1965

MAYBROOK –Many Town of Montgomery residents Monday night spotted what they thought was a "flying saucer."

Carmen Panero, Jr., a youngster, told *The Evening News* the unidentified flying object circled Maybrook three times between 8 and 9pm.

The object spotted had a white glow and resembled a star, but at times it blinked a red light. However, no noise of any engines was heard at as the object flew through the sky.

At 8:45pm, a number of persons in Maybrook saw the white object fly through the sky just north of the village, then towards Middletown as it started a red light blinking.

Seen at Otisville
The Evening News, October 7, 1965

OTISVILLE—A display of colored lights in the night sky over Otisville has been reported by village residents who witnessed them.

Robert C. Wilson, 17, of 15 School St., said he has seen white lights every night since Saturday. He feels there's a logical explanation for them, he added.

Mrs. Clifford Korth 15 Orchard St., has also seen the lights and was frightened by them on one occasion. Driving home on the Mount Hope Road at 11:05pm, Tuesday, she noted "a very bright light." When she stopped the car, she said the light seem to be going in circles. "I got out of there fast," she said.

Dr. Walter Gard, associate professor of chemistry at Orange Community College, said of the lights, "I can't be responsible for what others see that I don't see."

However, he said that recently he identified two flashing lights over Middletown as the specific stars, Arcturus and Cappella.

They are among the ten brightest stars in the solar system, he explained, and displayed vivid red, green and white lights during certain weather conditions. They are "fairly common phenomenon" and are seen at different places in the sky.

He said he has not seen the northern light display this season, but would not discount the possibility that others have seen them.

Mr. Wilson, a high school sophomore, who was home today with a cold, said he has seen the lights between 7:30 and 10pm and at 11pm. They seemed to spiral slowly across the sky. Near the horizon, they flashed like a bright red ball and disappeared, he said.

He was inclined to believe that they are connected with some government projects, because he has seen airplanes in the sky at the times he noticed these objects. The planes seemed to come close to the lights without making direct contact. On cloudy nights, the lights are lower than the clouds, he said.

Mrs. Korth said she has seen two lights in the sky one time. They seemed to stand still a while and then flashed red and white colors.

Project Blue Book Reports

September 27, 1965, 2:40pm, Swan Lake, NY (about 32 miles north of Port Jervis)

Stuart H. Cooper, a student from Brooklyn College who was deemed to be a "quite reliable" witness by the Project Blue Book reporting officer, "watched a white disc make a shallow dive and then proceed into a climbing turn. The object was just like a bright light to the naked eye; it is uncertain what azimuth the object was spotted because the road is quite winding."

Cooper observed the disc for about one minute, and was able to take four photos with his box camera before the object moved quickly out of sight.

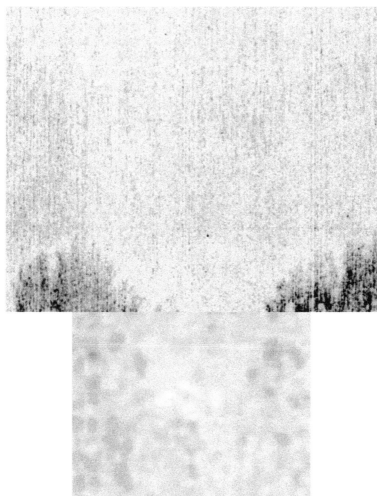

This grainy copy of one of Cooper's photos was in the PBB file. Cropping and enhancing the object in the upper left portion of the image does bring out some interesting details, but doesn't solve the mystery.

The official Project Blue Book conclusion for Cooper's case: "Description and photos are consistent with that of a balloon sighting."

September 27, 1965, Goshen, NY
(Note: This sighting actually occurred in the town of Chester.)

Photo of the water tower at the former Camp LaGuardia as seen from Route 17 in Chester in 2017.

Observer and his wife saw "Circular object with a conical top." Its apparent size was "quite large—basketball diameter," and it was on "Route 17...between light of Camp LaGuardia and water tower." The object had a "row of steady red lights on circumference. Green lights on top left. Low whistling sound associated with object." The object was in sight for about ten minutes, during which time it "hovered, turned (with right angles) North and South. Moved West, backed up then passed out of sight to East."

Official Conclusion: "Witness regarded as UNRELIABLE." The reason? The witness "has several books on the subject" and "has a hobby of UFOs."

Kingston, NY
February 26, 1968
The Evening News

"Invaders" in Ulster? UFOs Seen

Kingston, NY—Two state troopers early today reported seeing four unidentified flying objects –UFOs –southwest of this Ulster County city.

The troopers, identified as Carl Van Wagner and John Colan, reported sighting one object at 12:00am in the vicinity of Hurley Heights. At 1:07am, they said they saw three more objects–all with "pulsating red and green lights," over the community of Krumville.

The object disappeared from the sky about 3:00am. It was a clear, starlit night in the area.

Saugerties
Light Seen in Ulster
September 18, 1973
The Evening News

SAUGERTIES, N.Y. (AP) – Two town policemen on night patrol reported seeing a huge, shimmering light hovering over the New York State Thruway today.

"It lasted maybe 15 seconds, and then disappeared," Peter Karashay said. The town policeman estimated the light to have a radius of about 100 miles.

No other reports were received from Ulster County residents of the sighting, but Karashay and Howard Ostrander said they were sure of what they saw.

"They were pretty shook up about the whole thing when they got back," the police dispatcher told a newsman.

Note: The article did state the radius of the light was 100 miles, but that is doubtful as it was characterized as "a shimmering light hovering over the New York State Thruway," which implies something much smaller. In any event, it was shocking enough to shake up two police officers.

Capital District, Albany, NY Area
August 20, 1974

The following is a fascinating case involving "innumerable sightings of flying objects" by both military and Civil Air Patrol pilots, six air traffic controllers and airport radar, numerous State Police, local police and sheriff's department deputies, radio broadcasters, newspaper reporters, and hundreds of witnesses lining the streets. One of the objects was tracked on radar traveling at an astonishing one mile per second, while others were able to stop and hover—one of which hovered directly over the patrol car of a State Trooper at an altitude of just 200 feet.

The objects were primarily seen in the Capital District just north of Albany, including the State Police of the Loudonville barracks, to Malta, about 20 miles to the north, and Schenectady about 12 miles to the west. Perhaps of greatest interest that night were the objects seen in the Schenectady area—over the Knolls Atomic Research Laboratory, which designs and builds power plants for nuclear-powered warships.

Despite the wealth of radar and eyewitness data, the official stance of this mass-sighting quickly devolved to it all being the result of a single, small plane, or in the case of the radar, possibly "the weather."

Below is the APRO article which appeared in the July-August 1974 issue of the *Bulletin*, and newspaper articles which appeared in the days after the sighting.

New York Police See UFO
APRO Bulletin
July-August, 1974

State Police from two upstate barracks, that at Loudonville and at Malta, N.Y. observed an unidentified flying object on the evening of

August 20, 1974, as did the crew of a passing Army training plane. Both the police and the Army personnel were in repeated communication with the control tower at the Albany Airport. The latter dispatched aircraft to the scene of one of the sightings, and got the radar returns which seemed to indicate the passage of an object moving at about 1 mile per second.

According to state police, the first report came from the crew of a T-29 military trainer, which reported a fast-moving, high-altitude object of strange configuration. Later the Loudonville barracks noted an unknown at lower altitude, and a red object hovered directly over the car of a trooper from the Malta sub-station who was posted near Clifton Knolls, N.Y., and who was subjected to a prolonged debriefing by officers of the state police units in the capital district. Trooper Thomas Cole, like the CAA officials at the airport, freely answered some of the questions submitted by the press and private investigators.

These sightings were near the Knolls Atomic Research center of General Electric and the adjacent AEC atomic center. The so-called capital district consists of Albany, Schenectady and Troy, along with numerous suburbs and villages. During 1971, there were a few UFO reports coming from the southern fringes of the district, but in 1973 and again in 1974, the principle focal points seemed to be north of the center of the loose-knit metro area, which is itself located between the Catskill Mountains to the south and the Adirondacks to the north. One of the largest wilderness areas in the USA, it is protected by the Adirondack State Forest Preserve Authority.

Current reports are being further investigated by Robert E. Creegan, faculty member at SUNY Albany, and APRO consultant. Some students from his course, Borders of Science, are assisting. Attempts to extend and deepen the initial information have run into difficulties which some people associated with the University characterize as "official opposition."

Information officers of the New York State Police (State Troopers) now state that on one occasion an airplane-like sound was associated with one of the objects reported in southern Saratoga County, just north of Albany. In most cases the object or objects were reported to be completely silent, but officials now prefer to accept the aircraft explanation. Information officers say that the police are now interested in pilots who may have been flying without navigation or other lights at dusk and into the night. No attempt has been made to explain several police and civilian reports that the objects would come to a near stop at times, and then move up and away with incredible speed. The fact that one object flew above and faster than a military trainer plane also throws some doubt on the mischievous cub plane theory now advanced officially.

The control tower people at the Albany County Airport now assert that the radar return they were getting on the evening of August 20 might have been from a small aircraft or from "the weather." No differences between those two, nor of the real-time reports that at times the object was moving at speeds up to Mach 5, that is, about one mile per second.

As a result of official disclaimers, it has become more difficult to get additional statements from civilian witnesses, who now seem to fear ridicule, or worse. This now seems to be one of those UFO cases which the late Dr. E. U. Condon characterized as "dead-end streets." But not for the reasons he gave. The cul-de-sac nature of these studies seems to be a function of at least two factors: intrinsically difficult features of the objects, such as extreme changes of pace, and silence or obfuscation on the part of officials concerned with reducing public demands for explanation and in some cases for protection. As for the State Troopers, it is now stated that men from three barracks observed unknowns on August 20, and none of the initial reports coming from civilians or from the police or from the airport suggested anything remotely like a cub plane in configuration or behavior.

Comic in the Albany *Times Union* newspaper.

'Something' visits Capitaland— something fast

By GERARD BRAY

Something was in the skies over Clifton Knolls Tuesday night, something that stood still 200 feet above a State Police car for a while, something that passed over a military training plane coming through the area at 8,000 feet, something that the Albany Airport control tower clocked at more than 3,600 miles per hour, something that a State Trooper from Loudonville saw puttering along at about 100 miles an hour.

With every detail according to on-duty troopers, this is what that something did during its brief Capitaland sojourn.

At approximately 9:30 p.m. in clear skies somewhere over the Round Lake-Clifton Knolls area, it passed over a T-29 military trainer travelling at 8,000 feet. According to what the entire flight crew attested to the Albany control tower and tower officials told State Police, it was moving at great speed and at a greater altitude by far than the military plane.

Shortly thereafter a State Trooper from the Malta barracks was sitting on Raylinsky Road, Country Knolls, keeping watch in his patrol car. Something red hovered 200 feet overhead for a brief time, then left. By 11 p.m. the trooper was telling colleagues he had seen a fixed wing aircraft. Colleagues were pointing out that fixed wing aircraft cannot remain stationary.

Two small planes were sent to the area from Albany. The Albany tower fixed them on its radar, but could not locate the something while the light planes werre in the area. Shortly after the light planes left, however, something moving at a great rate of speed was picked up. A tower official told a State Police officer he didn't know of any planes that moved that fast. That fast was 17 miles in 16 seconds, approximately Mach 5, he said.

Trooper Thomas Cole spent 45 minutes with the trooper who saw the something stop in mid-air.

Times Union article.

145

Twinkle, Twinkle, Little?—How We Wonder What You Are
The Post-Star, Glens Falls, NY
August 22, 1974

A crowd of several hundred persons gathered on Dix Avenue late Tuesday and early Wednesday to watch several objects in the sky.

The unidentified flying objects were seen over a large portion of the Northeast on a brilliantly clear night.

Casting off color changes, the objects were seen to hover in the air as well as move in various directions at high rates of speed.

First reports came in from persons in the Malta and Round Lake areas of Saratoga County.

State Police reported "innumerable sightings of flying objects in the air over Saratoga County."

The Civil Air Patrol at Albany sent units into the air to investigate. The pilot of one airplane said he was flying over Albany at 8,000 feet when a silent object flew over his craft at a tremendous rate of speed.

When the objects were first seen in the Glens Falls area, over West Mountain, radio station WWSC began getting telephone calls from listeners asking about the strange colored objects in the night sky.

Michael Jetter, host of "The Talk Show" was flooded with calls about the objects, so newsman Norman Mjaalvedt went outdoors to broadcast descriptions of the objects.

As their outdoor broadcast continued, a crowd started to collect around the radio station and in a large parking lot across the street.

The station received calls from persons throughout the area reporting sightings of the objects in Fort Ann, Stony Creek, Lake George, Argyle, and several other locations.

By midnight the crowd had grown to more than 100 persons, at least two had brought large telescopes mounted on tripods to the scene and Glens Falls police were directing traffic.

The crowd continued to grow in size, and as the cars and spectators filled the street, Glens Falls police, who had now been joined by units of the State Police, asked the crowd to the move to East Field on Dix Avenue.

Within an hour hundreds of persons had gathered from as far away as Granville in East Field to watch the movements of the unknown objects

146

through telescopes, binoculars and to listen to the reports of those fortunate enough to have the high-powered lenses.

Efforts to determine what the strange objects were resulted in no definitive answers. There were as many theories as people at East Field.

State Police were involved at Loudonville, Saratoga and Glens Falls, in answering calls and trying to check on the objects. Glens Falls police, Warren, Washington and Saratoga County sheriff departments and other law enforcement agencies, all said they had no information on what the object might be.

The office of public information at Plattsburgh Air Force Base said they had no information on what the objects might be and had no sightings in the area of the large airbase.

At one point during the evening, two staff members of *The Post Star* were outside the newspaper plant trying to see the objects and went onto the porch of a nearby building for a better view.

Within moments they were accosted by a Glens Falls police officer sent when they had unknowingly triggered a silent burglar alarm. They told the astonished policeman they were "reporters looking for objects in the sky," which, they noted, he didn't seem to believe. The pair was identified and hurried back inside the newspaper office.

Even local car dealers jumped on the UFO bandwagon.

Six astonished traffic controllers track UFO on radar— at 3600 miles an hour
By John M. Webb and Denis D'Antonio
(Note: Someone sent me this clipping and the newspaper name and date were missing.)

A UFO streaking through the night sky was tracked on radar traveling at an incredible 3,600 miles an hour—and then vanished from the screen before the astonished eyes of six air traffic controllers at New York's Albany Airport.

The mysterious speeding object shot past an Air Force jet, startling the pilot, and was also observed from the ground by police and area residents.

"I've never seen anything move so fast," said 32-year-old Jim Maturo, one of the Albany Air traffic controllers.

The UFO was one of several brilliant but slower-moving objects that appeared over the farming community of Round Lake, 12 miles north of Albany, about 8:00 p.m. last August 20.

Residents spotting the UFOs called police, who observed the objects and contacted the Federal Aviation Administration control tower at Albany Airport.

'We've received all kinds of UFO reports here over the years, but this was the only time we were able to detect anything on radar. It was just an amazing experience," recalled Maturo.

"We were as mystified as the police and about what it was up there.

"It was uncanny that policemen were watching what seemed to be the same object that appeared as a blip on our radar screens.

"I watched it split into two separate targets. Later, it split into as many as four. About an hour after we'd been watching these objects, I made contact with an Air Force pilot on a training flight about 20 miles north of Albany."

"He reported he could see some lights to the south which were stationary. But shortly after that, he suddenly reported seeing an object that moved across his path from north to south in a blaze of orange, traveling so fast he was shouting out with excitement on the radio.

"I picked up the object on radar south of the military aircraft and coming toward the airport at an estimated 3,600 miles per hour. When it got to the airport, it vanished."

Said air traffic controller John Guzy, 33: "It came straight for the airport at an unbelievable speed. I was watching my radar screen and just couldn't believe my eyes. There was no explanation for what happened next. The objects seemed to be heading right for our control tower. But once it seemed to get above us, it just vanished."

Air traffic controller Tom Lawson, 29, who also tracked the fast-moving UFO, said: "The military pilot was really excited. He said he'd never seen anything that moved so quickly in his life—and neither have I."

Robert King, 54, was the supervisor in the control tower the night of the sightings. He recalled: "The objects were visible on all four radar screens, and we observed them for more than two hours."

Said state trooper Warren Johnson: "I just couldn't believe my eyes. I saw one object hovering in the sky. Then I saw another come out of the north at a hell of a speed. It was red or orange. And it flashed right overhead.

"I don't know of any aircraft that could travel that fast, and it sure wasn't a meteor."

Trooper Michael Morgan recalled: "I saw three or four objects moving at heights between 500 and 1,500 feet. At times they moved slowly and at other times they were real fast. It was strange. I've never seen anything like it."

Additional Information

The following occurred on the same night:

August 20, 1974, 10pm, Buffalo, NY, Mufon case 330227: Multiple witnesses observed strange lights moving in the sky for 20 minutes. Later the power went out, and witnesses saw a "huge disk-shaped object 6 or 7 stories high and as big as a football field with no noise." The police arrived 45 minutes later and everyone witnessed an Air Force jet flying overheard at an extremely low altitude.

There is conflicting information about this NICAP case. It may have occurred on April 19, 1974, or on August 19, in which case it would be the night before the Albany area sightings. In any event, it took place in Altamont, NY, just 20 miles west of Albany.

April or August 19, 1974, 9:30-10:30pm, Altamont, NY: A bright, oval craft sitting on the road, seen by several eyewitnesses. The craft had large, lighted windows and "changes of contrast in this light gave the impression that something was moving around within." The vehicle rose up and accelerated at an "exceptionally high rate of speed." The next day witnesses observed an area of burnt grass approximately 50-75 feet in diameter which may have been related to the craft.

It should also be pointed out that on August 23, 1974, just 3 days after the Albany area sightings, John Lennon had his famous rooftop sighting in New York City of a lighted disk hovering just about 100 yards from him.

And one final case to mention from this time period, as the Albany area sighting involved so many police officers. It is worth noting that in Kingston, NY, about 55 miles south of Albany, on July 9, 1974, a police officer saw an unidentified flying object and shined his light at it. In response, the object beamed a bright light onto his patrol car.

It is clear from all of these cases that the summer of 1974 was an active one in New York.

East Haven, CT
August 1974
NUFORC Report

A police officer of 35 years' experience relates that in August 1974, during the midnight shift, at approx. 3am, Officer A. M. and Officer T.D. saw a brilliantly bright flying object which zigzagged west to east, in the East Haven area. They were on the National Guard rifle range and New Haven Water Company (now known as the Lake Saltonstall, Regional Water Authority) property. The lake is over 100' deep, and there is a ridge which is on the property that runs parallel to I-95 for several miles, with the reservoir (Saltonstall) on the other side. The two officers observed the object for about one minute and lost sight because of its movement over the ridgeline. After it left, the birds began to chirp, and dogs began to howl.

Second night: 5-6+ people, and one officer saw the bright light again, this time flying very low over them, appearing at approximately the same time. Then on the 3rd night, word had gotten out and lots of people were camped out around the rifle range area waiting to see, but it was to no avail.

Harold
Putnam and Westchester Counties, NY
1980s

I received the following letter during the summer of 2014, and have reproduced it below in the witness' own words:

When I saw what I believe to be UFOs, I was working as a Police Officer for the Village of Cold Spring, NY. I observed unidentified flying objects on four different occasions during the 1980s and never said anything to anyone except family and close friends, because I was afraid of being ridiculed by others at the time of the sightings. Three of the sightings were when I was working the 4pm to 12 midnight shift, and the fourth was when I was on my way home from a 4pm to 12 midnight shift. I do not recall the exact times or dates, because I never made a record of them, because I didn't think anyone would believe me. I did read about sightings of UFOs in the area and that they were presumed to be ultralight planes.

I do not recall when the first sighting was, but I believe it was around 1983 and I believe it may have been the same night that there were sightings in Yorktown, NY on March 24, 1983. I believe what I saw at this time were red and yellow lights in a pattern that indicated they were equally spaced apart and they formed a V shape. (See diagram number #1)

The Village of Cold Spring is located along the Hudson River and is on a hillside. I saw the object from a street that gave me a parallel and slightly above view. The object was about 100 feet above the Hudson River and my location was also around the same height. The sky was dark and I could not make out anything other than the red and yellow lights, which were moving in such a manner that they appeared to be moving as one object. There was no sound coming from the object and it was flying slowly and in a southerly direction.

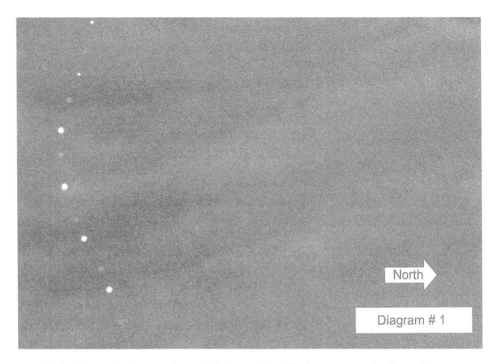

North

Diagram # 1

I had read about the sightings in Yorktown and that they were believed to be ultralight planes out of Stormville Airport. I assumed that was what I might have seen until I had experienced the following sighting.

A few weeks later, while working the 4pm to midnight shift, I saw what I believed be the same object flying over the Hudson River, heading in a southerly direction. I was at a similar location at the time of the sighting, which gave me the same view. This time the object had the same red and yellow lights in a V pattern, however, the second red and yellow lights were not visible giving the appearance of a space, where the ultralight plane could be missing in formation. (See diagram #2). This time there was a slight humming sound coming from the object. I started to believe that what I was seeing were ultralight planes. Then I started to think about what I saw and I rationalized that even though there was a space that gave the appearance of a missing ultralight, they couldn't maintain flying in such a manner to form a perfect V pattern.

I do not know what it was that I saw. It could have been a UFO, it could have been ultralight planes, or maybe it was a classified aircraft project that we may never find out about unless they declassify it after 50 years. However, the next few sightings are even more interesting.

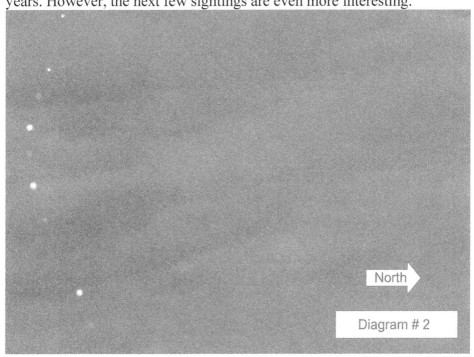

North

Diagram # 2

The next sightings I had of unidentified flying objects were in the mid-1980s, I do not know exactly when I saw them or which of them came first.

The next sighting I had was when I was driving on Route 301 heading home after working the 4pm to 12 midnight shift. I was traveling west on Route 301 in the area of the Fahnestock State Park. I looked out my window and saw the object in the sky traveling in the same direction. As I drove, the object seemed to be going along with me. I stopped my car just before I reached the Taconic State Parkway and got out to observe the object. The object appeared to be moving slowly. I said to myself, "What the heck," and I waved at the object. Then the object turned to the left and flew off rapidly, as if it was a high-speed rocket and then it disappeared. The object was shaped similar to a football or like a blimp without the gondola on the bottom. There were windows visible showing light on the inside, but there were no other lights visible. (See diagram #3)

Diagram # 3

The next sighting I had during a 4pm to 12 midnight shift was while I was patrolling the Metro North Railroad commuter parking lot. I came upon another Officer from another department in the parking lot and stopped to talk to him. As we were talking, he stopped and said, "Look at that." He pointed to the top of a mountain, where we saw a group of lights in a semicircle. I believe they were red and maybe orange or yellow in color and looked square in shape, like windows. I could not see any other shape or form of the object because the object appeared to be within the clouds. I said to the other Officer that we should try to get a closer look, so we tried to relocate to a better spot, but the object disappeared (See diagram #4). I haven't seen any more unidentified flying objects since, but I am still looking and wondering where they are, and what they were.

North

Diagram # 4

Note: My diagrams are not to scale, and they are from what I remember from about 30 years ago.

154

Danbury, CT
July 12, 1984

"This huge, lighted object the size of a football field moved across the sky quite low and made no noise. Some of my officers saw it, too. It was something none of us could explain, and I don't care what anybody says."

Danbury Police Chief Nelson Macedo, regarding his July 12, 1984 sighting.

There's a certain satisfaction when skeptics—usually skeptics who ridicule witnesses—have their own sightings. Such was the case on a large scale when not only did no less than a dozen Danbury police officers have sightings on the night of July 12, 1984, but Police Chief Nelson Macedo saw the enormous craft, as well.

In the active months leading up to the July sighting, people who saw a variety of objects in the sky and called the police to report them, were basically accused of being drunk, were laughed at, and generally made to feel foolish. The common attitude of the Danbury Police was that UFOs were strictly the result of hoaxing pilots, and anyone who believed otherwise was mentally impaired or unbalanced. That is, until they had their own sightings.

Police across Danbury saw an enormous oval with multi-colored lights which was capable of hovering silently in place, and then moving two or three miles in just ten seconds. Chief Macedo was in a boat on Candlewood Lake with three other people, one of whom was a retired cop. Not only did they see a large, grayish, circular craft above them, but it responded to them—when they turned off the boat lights, the craft turned off its lights, and when they flashed the boat lights, the craft also altered the intensity of its lights! There was also the report by a Bethel, CT police officer who shined his car's spotlight at the craft and it responded by hitting him with a bright beam of light.

It was estimated that 5,000 people saw the UFOs on July 12, 1984, making it one of the largest single-night events during those tumultuous years of the 1980s sightings wave. There's no telling how many skeptics were converted to believers that night, but we can probably be fairly certain that after the event, the Danbury Police were not so quick to ridicule witnesses.

9
Abductions, Contact, and Missing Time

Regardless of how you classify these cases and their witnesses—abductees, contactees, or experiencers—they remain quite prevalent in the Hudson Valley and surrounding areas. My very first case involved multi-generational abductions and all of the other stories I have heard over the years continue to amaze me.

However, the most shocking case I have ever dealt with is in this chapter—the case where I discovered I had my own missing time!

Malcom Perry
Somerville, MA?
1938

Note: The following letter does not mention the state in which this sighting occurs. However, the author does mention the town of Somerville, and walking to the "car stop." As Somerville, Massachusetts had streetcars, I believe it makes this the likely location.

This letter in the APRO files was written in 1962 by Malcolm Perry, and while it is a few hours away from the Hudson Valley region, I was compelled to include it in this book because it relates such an astounding close encounter, way back in 1938! This encounter evoked intense feelings of familiarity, and even yearning, which have been expressed by generations of some experiencers. If I had labeled this case with a 1970s date and set it in a New York or Connecticut town, it would fit right in. In short, Mr. Perry's experiences are timeless.

In 1938, after taking my girlfriend to her home in Somerville, I was walking along the street toward the car stop, when, looking over my left shoulder, I saw an object approaching from the east which I thought at first was a Navy blimp.

It was around midnight, the moon was out, and earlier it had been raining. There were low scudding clouds scattered across the sky. I wondered what a blimp would be doing cruising around at that hour, and looking up again, the object was opposite me and I could see several portholes or openings in the side, and I kept looking for a gondola or

156

propeller or something to make it move, but could see nothing, in fact no noise was coming from it at this time.

My attention now became riveted to one of the openings where I could see a person apparently sitting, and he in turn seemed to be watching me.

At this point I had a very strong urge to wave with all my might, so I looked up and down the street to see if anyone else was observing the object, but no one was in sight. Looking back again at the ship, I could also see people moving around as if taking turns looking out of the other openings. I still had an almost irresistible urge to wave with all my strength, as it seemed they were old friends.

At this point, the object moved behind some clouds and was the last I saw of it. I immediately had a peculiar lost or let down feeling.

The next morning I looked in the paper for news of a strange airship or something of that nature, but saw nothing.

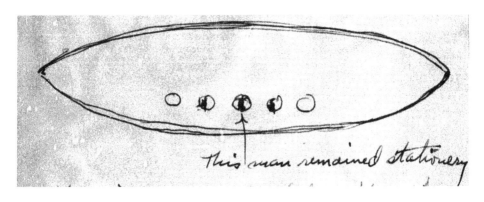

this man remained stationary

I am convinced there are people from other planets that are living with us and visiting us constantly for thousands of years and that their purpose is to preserve peace and improve our way of life without antagonizing, and if they were not afraid of us would make themselves known in ever increasing numbers.

Sincerely, Malcolm B. Perry

An incredible account! In 1938, this man witnessed a silent, saucer-shaped craft with multiple beings inside, and he felt no fear or alarm, only an intense desire to wave at "old friends." And when the craft left, he felt "lost" and "let down."

Other experiencers have expressed the same feelings; that they don't want their contact—in whatever form it may take—to end, and they hope to repeat the experience again. For many of these people, they do have multiple experiences, often beginning in childhood. I would have loved to interview Mr. Perry to find out if anything else had happened to him when he was young, and what may have happened to him after this letter was written.

Note: I did find an obituary of an artist named Malcom B. Perry who passed away in the Boston area in 2014 at the age of 100. He attributed his longevity to the study and use of natural herbs and avoiding pharmaceuticals. He was also a body builder who taught judo to Boston Police cadets.

While I'm sure there have been a lot of 'Malcolm B. Perrys', this man would certainly make an interesting candidate for an experiencer who felt he had some sort of connection with extraterrestrials.

"Bill"
Eastchester, NY
1950s through the 1970s

In April of 2015, I gave a lecture at the Warner Library in Tarrytown, NY, and several people in the audience gave me their contact information, as they had stories to share. One of the most remarkable was from "Bill," with whom I spoke to at length the following week. While I am going to relate the majority of what he told me, I will not reveal all of it, as I strongly suspect he will eventually be telling his own story to the world.

Now in his sixties, in his younger days, Bill had suffered terrible physical ailments for which modern medicine and pharmaceuticals seemed unable to provide any relief. In his forties, he began working with a physical therapist, who saw a connection between emotions and the body and felt that any effective healing needed to take both into consideration. Over the span of about two years, these therapy sessions brought up a lot of childhood issues that were unpleasant, but the overall result was that Bill was finally beginning to feel better. Then the dreams started.

"I kept having dreams about metal spaceships," Bill explained. "And I would say to myself, what's that all about?"

What ensued with his therapist *was not hypnotism*, but a form of relaxation that helped him recall past experiences, and what Bill began to remember was "horrific."

"I remembered being on a table when I was about two years old and people were doing things to me. I was helpless, frozen, and I'd try to pull away from them but I couldn't. This happened again to me when I was about five, ten, thirteen, sixteen and twenty-five. The last one was when I was twenty-five, when they said they were done with me."

Bill said that the experiments from age 16 to 25 involved his reproductive organs, and that he remembers a young woman with brown hair on an adjacent table who was undergoing the same procedures. The beings looked like "six or seven-foot praying mantises" and did not have any sympathy for the pain and suffering they were inflicting. He got the sense they were just the "worker bees" doing their jobs and not caring what was happening to the people on their tables.

As these images began to emerge bit by bit, Bill became physically ill as a result, not to mention being in complete denial. He had no conscious recollection of ever being abducted, only the vague memories of being on the table, the pain and helplessness, and these hideous creatures standing to his right conducting their experiments. It was a very slow and draining process, but once the story emerged, he was able to release the trauma of those experiences, and his long bout with an intestinal illness finally ended, and he was well again.

About ten years later, Bill's revelations had led him toward spiritual practices and he eventually realized that he was 'clairaudient'—now having the ability to "hear" messages. He was able to demonstrate this on numerous occasions when he was able to tell people about their deceased loved ones. For example, a woman handed him a ring, and Bill kept seeing power boats and sailboats and then someone drowning. The woman began sobbing and explained that her boyfriend had given her that ring and that he had both power boats and a sailboat, and had, in fact, drowned.

I asked if Bill thought this ability he now had was the result of something intentional that had been done to him. He said he didn't know, but given the uncaring nature of the beings during his experiences, he would have to guess that it was simply a byproduct of whatever it was they had done to him over the course of 23 years.

I know this all sounds highly bizarre to people who only look for hard evidence of UFO phenomena, but the connection between those who have had intense experiences, whether just once or over the course of a lifetime, and some sort of enhanced sixth sense capabilities, keeps cropping up in my research. Whether these enhanced capabilities are only temporary or permanent, there does appear to be an undeniable connection between UFO experiences and what is commonly referred to as "the paranormal."

Despite his new "gift," however, Bill is not about to forgive and forget what was done to him.

"I would shoot them all if I had the opportunity," he said without hesitation.

For all the healing that has taken place over the last 20 years, he obviously still harbors great anger, hatred, and resentment for the horrors he was forced to endure—and I don't blame him one bit. But for every trial and tribulation that is survived, there are lessons to be learned, and an opportunity to help others. After speaking with Bill, I definitely believe that he is capable of helping many people by sharing all the details of his journey from fear and illness to healing and health, and mercifully finding some degree of peace.

That is why I have resisted the temptation to reveal everything he shared with me, as I feel it would be more powerful and effective coming straight from him. And as I was the first stranger he ever told of these experiences, I feel that this was a first step toward that new journey of transforming the negativity of all that trauma into something positive.

Mr. G., Part 2
New York c. 1950s through to present day in Florida

This is the second part of Mr. G's case which began in Chapter XX with his V-shaped craft sighting. He wrote me that just "Days later we experienced beings in the apartment. This occurred many times after that." He is the rest of his email:

"We later moved to Fort Lauderdale and the 'visits' continued, till one day in our apartment in North Lauderdale, Parrots Landing, a caped being was in our apartment. There is more to describe and how we compared notes with each other, my wife and I. We were interviewed by MUFON and written up, and later I was regressed which brought out

160

many things. I was recently visited here again, and apparently some scar appeared on my inner thigh and what appeared to be a scooped area removed from me.

CAPE

KITCHEN
BEING
NOT EXACT BUT CLOSE

The caped figure he saw in the kitchen of their apartment.

"Lots more details from NY and FL, and we also started seeing orbs, then apparitions down here, too. Been really strange, no room here for me to write it all."

I contacted Mr. G for more information, and the following is a summary of some of his other experiences.

When asked about the sketches he drew, he said he "got a flash of a grey and a chill," as one of the memories came back to him.

Under hypnotic regression, he recalled that when he was about 4 or 5 years old, three small beings conducted tests on him, and caused him considerable pain as they tried to force something up his nose. The next morning his pillowcase was stained with blood. He recalled that as a child, he always had the feeling that there was something in his nose he wanted to get out.

There were other abduction experiences that were brought to light under hypnosis, and for those who don't believe in hypnosis, Mr. G. also had distinct physical evidence years later, as the experiences continued into adulthood, and even when he moved to Florida. In his own words:

"I was in the bathroom sitting, doing my thing, and saw an almost healed scar on my inner right thigh. It was not there before, and it was like it was a cut that was almost healed, but leaving a scar. This was never there before. I showed my wife and she was surprised, too. Since I tend do my thing in the john every day, I know it was not there before. I feel there was another visit, but it is just a feeling and nothing I can feel sure about. Just a strong feeling."

As I have heard from many experiencers, even one episode of intense contact can initiate or enliven a sixth sense, and Mr. G certainly fits the pattern.

"Some things that have been occurring more and more are several different psychic abilities seem to be getting stronger. To others it may be minor, but I seem to predict events or final outcomes of many personal and public things. All are minor, but when I get the 'feelings' I now mention it to the party or others near and close to me."

There are many more details which could be shared here—in fact, a lifetime of them—but the main point is that Mr. G. has had life-altering contact since childhood, and 'they' aren't done with him yet.

162

Kathy

West Taghkanic, NY
1970s to present day

Kathy lived her early years in Yonkers, New York, but her father bought a house "out in the woods" in the small town of West Taghkanic, 90 miles to the north. It sat on five acres and you couldn't see any of the few neighbors that were scattered around the area. Kathy admits she never felt comfortable being so deep into the woods and so isolated, but it was about to get a lot worse.

For some reason, when she was thirteen, she woke up on the floor of her bedroom. She had been screaming in her sleep, and her older brother awakened her.

"What's wrong with you?" he asked, and not too sympathetically, as her screams had awakened him.

She couldn't answer, because she didn't know what had happened. What she did know was that she "felt *so* drugged, dazed, confused, and trapped." It was about this time that she also began to be "terrified of the windows...of something coming through the windows," and "of being taken." She didn't know what it all meant, but spending a lot of time in that house alone didn't help.

In 1983 when she was sixteen, her boyfriend came over one night to keep her company and watch television. They were alone in the house and Kathy started hearing "a very low hum."

"But I can't be sure if I was actually hearing it, or *feeling* a vibration. I had heard it before on other occasions, but only for a few minutes. This time it went on for an hour. My boyfriend couldn't hear it, but it was really getting to me. It was getting me very aggravated."

Kathy finally decided to get up and investigate the source of the provocative sound.

"It was then we saw the lights outside, and I said to my boyfriend, 'Who's in our woods?' The lights were very bright, and they were just piercing through the trees toward the house."

Running into the living room, they saw that the beams of the lights in the woods filled the large window there from end to end, so it wasn't just an individual with a very bright flashlight. They went out onto the deck, and Kathy's boyfriend "wasn't the least bit scared and started flashing a flashlight at whatever it was." When that failed to illicit a response, "he climbed up on the roof and tried to signal with his flashlight."

Meanwhile, Kathy stood on the deck "scared out of my mind," and became even more afraid when her boyfriend came down off the roof and started heading into the woods.

"Get back!" Kathy shouted over and over, her fear level rising off the charts.

However, before her boyfriend could reach the light source, it began to move—straight up!

"This thing went straight up through the trees! And we could definitely see the shape, like a boomerang. It had red and white lights. And it wasn't that big; smaller than the house."

As the craft hovered over the treetops, Kathy's boyfriend continued to wave the flashlight at it to try to get a reaction.

"Then it took off—sideways!—and FAST! We both looked at each other and said, 'Did we just see that!?' It just freaked me out!"

A couple of days later, there was an article in the *Register Star* newspaper about the UFO that night.

"People had followed the UFO along Route 31. Others saw it heading south towards the city down the river. There were many witnesses in Rhinebeck and Poughkeepsie."

From that night, Kathy never went into those woods again. With 30 years of hindsight, she told me she wishes she had examined the area for evidence, but at the time she was simply too afraid. I asked if anything else strange had ever happened to her before or since, and she related more interesting experiences.

"It was that same year, and my friend, Angie, and I had gone to Lake Taghkanic. We stayed until dark, and then were walking back home. Just above the trees we saw lights, like fireflies, but much, much bigger. There were about ten of them, they were white, and they just seemed to be floating and dancing silently over the trees. It scared the crap out of Angie and we ran all the way home."

An interesting point to this story is that Angie and Kathy had drifted apart over the years, and hadn't connected for about a decade. Only recently did they reconnect, and what's one of the first things Angie said?

"I have to talk to you about something. Do you remember those lights we saw that night?"

Apparently, Angie has just recently felt compelled to talk about her experience. It's probably not a coincidence that Kathy also reached out to me because she recently felt compelled to start talking about her experiences, as well. I have heard this time and again over the last several years while conducting interviews—for some reason, *now* is the time that people feel the need to speak out. What it all means I can't even begin to guess, but it is a clear pattern that goes far beyond coincidence.

As for her childhood, Kathy said she has "bits and pieces she just can't remember." Even as a child she had "issues with memory" and had experienced "chunks of time" with no recollection of what had transpired.

As for any physical signs of anything unusual, she said she has "a round, pea-sized object that is as hard as a rock" in the back of her leg, which appeared some time in her teens. Her doctor said it is probably just a cyst, but for some reason "it travels." This small, round object will sometimes be right near the surface where she can actually "get her fingers around it," but then it will go deeper into her skin to the point where she can't feel it for months or years before it reappears.

Kathy now lives in the town of Cairo, and about "three or four times a year" she hears that low humming sound, but never for very long. But when she does hear it, she "jumps out of bed" and wakes up her husband, but he has never heard it. She also "wakes up around 3am *every* night" and often feels compelled to get up and look out the window. She always asks herself, "Why am I doing this?" She has never uncovered the answer.

So, what can we conclude from all of Kathy's experiences? At the very least, she was a witness to a mass sighting of a boomerang-shaped object that landed behind her house. Beyond that, there are certainly common threads of missing time and inexplicable fears of being taken that have been experienced by many other people in the Hudson Valley, and around the world. And as she still hears and feels that low vibrating hum from time to time, and it may very well be that her story will continue.

Lewisboro and Pound Ridge, NY
August 1, 1979

This SBI report could have been included in the chapter on police sightings, as it contains a close encounter by a credible officer who witnessed a craft which exhibited astonishing flight characteristics.

However, I decided to place it in this chapter as it involves some forms of mind-altering contact—including that inexplicable fear that drives so many witnesses to flee.

A Special Report
by Charles Taylor (Chief Investigator in Westchester County, NY)
The SBI Report Issue 1979 Vol. 1 #7

On the afternoon of August 1, 1979, I received a call from Pete Mazzola asking me if I had anyone available to investigate a report of a UFO sighting involving a cop. Being no one else was able to respond, I felt an obligation and responded to document the case myself. Responding the next morning, I learned that a gigantic UFO with a pulsating white light buzzed a car in which Police Officer William O'Shaughnessy was riding in alone. Let me add, the UFO did not pass over the police car once—but *twice*!!

The officer, while being questioned by me, claimed not to believe in men from Mars, however, since the incident he is certainly convinced "we're not alone" in the universe. He states, "There is definitely some kind of advanced civilization trying to make contact with us."

The encounter happened around 1:30am on the morning of August 1, as he patrolled alone in his police cruiser near the Lewsiboro border, just north of New York City in Westchester County. The officer working what is known as the "graveyard shift" (12-midnight to 8am), observed an object larger than a luxury-type car. It was shaped in the form of a doughnut and plainly visible to have a white glow completely encircling the object—like a halo.

As the officer watched the object in awe moving at a fantastic rate of speed from north to south, it suddenly stopped dead in the air. Hovering about 600 feet above the ground for several seconds, it made a right angle turn and went in a westerly direction. The officer attempted to notify his base headquarters by use of his police radio, however, the radio suddenly could not receive or transmit any messages—it was completely dead.

Seeing a nearby telephone booth, the officer decided to call his superiors in this manner. Amazingly enough, this phone was operable. After the notification, he swiftly returned to his police car to watch the object some more.

Without warning once again, the object appeared, only this time it headed with tremendous speed directly at the police car. Shocked, the officer witnessed the object "stop on a dime" 100 feet above his vehicle. Looking out the windshield, O'Shaughnessy saw the strange UFO make another right angle turn and disappear toward the north, heading for the Pound Ridge Reservoir.

O'Shaughnessy states, "I've been on the Westchester Police Department for 9 years and I know that it wasn't a helicopter or small plane." The officer's story was also verified by six other people in the area who observed the same object at approximately the same time of morning. I personally checked with the nearest airport, Westchester Airport, and drew a blank—nothing was seen by radar technicians to indicate a UFO or even a plane or helicopter.

The amazing thing about this case is that not one—I repeat, *not one other UFO Group or organization investigated this case*, or possibly even cared at all about it. That is, all except the SBI. We were on the ball and on the scene once again. Thinking that all I would do was investigate, tape the conversations, have the officer draw diagrams of the object and document the case for SBI headquarters, soon made me believe otherwise.

Calling Pete Mazzola on the telephone explaining the case was being prepared for the files, made me aware that Pete and Jim do their homework. I was asked if I would like to accompany them to interview several other witnesses which they learned about. Pleased with the offer, Pete, Jim, and I proceeded to investigate the other witnesses. The witnesses were located all over town, so after proceeding to several homes together, we split up into teams. I took two more witnesses in the same region of town and Pete and Jim went to another on the other side of town. Pete and Jim investigated a report in which the same object Officer O'Shaughnessy observed may have landed moments before he observed it. They came to the home of Al and Cindy LaMann in the town of Pound Ridge (coincidentally near the reservoir where the officer saw the object disappear). The LaManna family had quite a story to tell them—an incredible story!

The story in itself is complicated, so the basic related points will only be mentioned. Cindy LaManna observed a green glowing glob, perhaps 3 feet in diameter, appearing near her living room window. The object apparently produced a trance-like or hypnotic state in which Cindy recalls similar events as explained by a recent abductee named Betty Andreasson. She recalls being present, possibly out-of-body means, at a city or place of a sort, none like she's ever seen before. Cindy also has no exact idea of how much time elapsed from the time she observed the object until the time she returned.

Telling her husband, Al, about the incident, he quickly assured her that her imagination was running away. At one point, Al had to retrieve a pack of cigarettes from his auto parked outside in his curved driveway. In doing so, he was greeted by a strange sensation to go back into the house. Inside the house he realized or thought he was being dumb, so he attempted to go outside to his car once again. He met the same type of resistance or feeling, this time he looked around to see why he had become so frightened.

He noticed nothing unusual, but heard a large transformer generator, far from the house, humming profusely. Deciding to once again go back into the house, Al turned towards the door to witness an old refrigerator (placed outside to be discarded) glowing bright white. Running into the house, he and his wife were totally baffled for an explanation.

Somewhere between 12:30am and 1am (1/2 to 1 hour prior to O'Shaughnessy's incident), the LaMannas observed a white-glowing object ascend from a wooded area and travel at great speed toward the direction in which the police officer saw the object half an hour later. (The LaManna's residence and the officer's sighting location are about 3-5 miles apart in a straight line.) Amazing that the UFO should travel towards that direction, flying between three mountain peaks (possibly to avoid detection) which formed a pyramid.

By the time the SBI arrived at the LaManna's, many hours of rain had washed away evidence of any such landed craft. But the story does not stop there. The day following the sighting, there were strange events to be considered.

First, their pool was somehow drained of 300 gallons of water (checking for leaks, there were none), their well had gone dry, an area surrounding their enormous property near a pond had suddenly developed a tremendous grassy area, and when either they or relatives entered the pond or pool, they felt a state of tranquil peace. No animal life (birds and deer) went to the pond for several days in the heavily wooded area, and one of the LaManna's children had reoccurring dreams about seeing a spaceship.

What does this all mean? We took soil samples, vegetation samples, water samples from the pond and pool and came up with nothing. The boys even saw the swimming pool for themselves, it was really low filled. Somehow, even through an all-day rainstorm, the water level was very low. They went down to the power generator and while walking there could not hear any sounds being emitted until they were on top of the transformer. They checked for radiation on the grounds, house and in the old refrigerator and could not find anything abnormal. They checked the LaManna's story for flaws, but could not find any after testing with PSE equipment. We don't know much more now than when we began. We can only assume that the incident indeed did happen and that the LaManna family was chosen for some reason to be part of the statistics and trying to unravel the mystery of UFOs.

The case was passed on to me for final documentation, along with the others who witnessed the same object on that early morning. There is not much we can determine except credible people in different locations all saw a UFO. We did not discover any scientific proof for our skeptics to take notice of. But there is proof that UFOs still continue to aggravate us in trying to determine what and who are they. It is only hoped that one day, we shall overcome these obstacles and find out once and for all. However, this cannot be accomplished unless we get up and investigate. Seeking perhaps just one piece of the puzzle to make sense, for a change.

All the names and locations you have read about are true in origin and have not been altered, thanks to the permission of the people involved.

Somers, NY
1979

A man told me about a night he will never forget, although he can't remember all of it. He was sitting in a van with some friends drinking beer. Having to relieve himself, he walked half a block to get to some woods. Just as he was reaching for his zipper, "a huge, round object with lights" appeared over him and hovered silently just a short distance overhead.

Running back to the van, he probably thought his friends wouldn't believe what he had seen—except that a few of them had seen the same craft earlier, in daylight. His friends then asked him why he had been gone so long, and he couldn't understand the question, as he thought he had immediately run back to the van and had only been gone a couple of minutes.

"They told me I had been gone at least 20 minutes," he told me. "I was amazed and flabbergasted!"

Granted, everyone that night was drinking beer, but his friends had been sober earlier in the day when the round craft had first been spotted, so you will have to judge for yourself the validity of this case.

Linda Zimmermann
Nanuet, Lake DeForest, and Harriman State Park, NY
December 9 and 10, 1979

I have interviewed hundreds of eyewitnesses, written three books on UFOs, and given many lectures. I have listened for hours to people's accounts of missing time and blocks of memories that disappeared. I even specifically wrote an entire chapter in my first UFO book, *In the Night Sky*, about the small town of Congers, NY, and its reservoir, Lake DeForest, where so many people have had abduction and missing time experiences since at least the 1950s.

Through all these years of research, writing, and presentations, I was happily going along in the firm belief that at least *I remembered* every detail of my sighting in the 1970s. At least *I never* had one minute of missing time or lost memories. At least *I wouldn't* have to live with that uncomfortable feeling that someone messed with my memories, because *I remembered* everything. Until I found out that I didn't.

One day in 2016, I became determined to go through every page of my diaries from the late 1970s and early 1980s in order to get the exact date of the sighting about which I wrote in the first chapter of *In the Night Sky*. In brief, I, my boyfriend, and his friend, Tony, saw some strange lights pass overhead one night in Nanuet, NY. Recalling that some UFOs had been seen in the 1960s near Lake Tiorati in Harriman State Park, I suggested driving up there. Indeed, the UFOs did approach the north end of the lake and they all came together in bright flashes of light and became

170

a single object that lowered to the top of the mountain. At this point, a cop came by and told us to leave—and he actually passed us in his patrol car because he was so frightened!

It all made for a fascinating personal experience which I have relived in my mind countless times over the decades, and I was confident that I recalled everything about it, except for the actual date. So I sat down with my stacks of diaries and started skimming through them, page by page. It was a very weird and discomforting trip down memory lane reading about my daily life 35-40 years ago, let me tell you! If nothing else, it reminded me what a long, strange road I have traveled!

In any event, I went through all of 1977, then 1978, and was beginning to lose hope when I finally came to Sunday, December 9, 1979, and lo and behold, found that was the date of my sighting. Only something was wrong—something was monumentally, shockingly, impossibly wrong. There were some details that were a bit hazy, which is understandable after all this time, but then there was a full hour about which I have absolutely no recollection! Then the following night there were more experiences about which I also have no memory. It was like reading the words of a complete stranger and I couldn't comprehend what had happened.

While I don't claim to have an eidetic memory, I have been fortunate with my ability to remember all kinds of facts and figures. If you have ever seen one of my lectures, you know I *never* read from a script, and rarely even use notes. But perhaps the best endorsement for my memory comes from my husband, who regularly complains that he "can't get away with *anything*" because I "remember *everything*."

So what happened that was so shocking, something that I can't remember at all? I will let my own words tell the tale from the point of spotting the lights over where I lived in Nanuet:

We all piled into Sue's car and started following them. We followed one to Lake DeForest. I was watching it through the binoculars and it was going fast in one direction, stopped, and went in the opposite direction!

I could live with the fact that I had forgotten that my boyfriend's sister, Sue, had driven. However, what completely stunned me was that we "followed one to Lake DeForest." In my mind that was simply not possible—I was certain that we had gone straight to Lake Tiorati and hadn't been anywhere near Lake DeForest. Perhaps we had just stopped by Lake DeForest for a few minutes, I rationalized, until I read my diary entry for the next day, December 10, which began:

I couldn't believe last night. We watched those things whipping back and forth for an hour.

How could I possibly spend an entire hour standing next to a lake in my bathrobe, on a cold night in December, watching the most incredible thing I had ever seen—UFOs through binoculars, "whipping back and forth"—and not have one second of recollection? I immediately contacted my ex-boyfriend to see what he recalled—and let me state that in many regards, his memory was always even better than mine. His response was alarming.

"Yes, I do recall going to Lake DeForest, but I can't remember anything that happened once we got there."

Yet, he does clearly remember the events by Lake Tiorati in Harriman State Park later that night.

Next, I contacted Sue on Facebook, to see if she had any recollection of Lake DeForest, and her response only deepened the mystery.

"We were all at the lake watching that thing zip back and forth for a really long time. How can you not remember?"

It made no sense. Within hours of the sighting I wrote down all the details in my diary, and then somehow both my boyfriend and I completely forgot about the most intense hour of our lives, yet Sue did remember being there and watching the UFO. And then it got even stranger as I read the next line.

I knew they would go to Harriman.

Reading that made my blood run cold. How exactly did *I know* all the UFOs would go to Harriman? The diary entry continued:

We went up there and sure enough they all converged. There were some bright flashes of white and green light. A cop came and told us to leave.

172

Still reeling from this startling revelation, I read my complete entry for December 10, when I talked about my friend, Harriet, who had first witnessed the UFOs in Hillburn, NY, just minutes before they arrived in Nanuet that Sunday night.

Harriet saw them with some of her friends and she called the police and they said they had a lot of reports.

I contacted a friend and historian who is in the police department in that area, and he kindly did a records search for that date, but unfortunately, apparently none of those eyewitness calls had been officially reported.

In any event, there was even more inexplicable strangeness within the pages of my diary. That Monday evening, December 10, Harriet, Sue, Tony, my boyfriend and I:

went (back) to Harriman. We saw some more of the strange things.

Apparently, we all felt compelled to go back and search for those UFOs again, yet in my mind, that entire night is a complete blank. Unfortunately, Harriet has since passed away, and we lost touch with Tony, but both Sue and my boyfriend can't recall going back to Harriman that Monday night, either.

So there we have it, not quite missing time, as I was able to write about both days in my diary just hours after the sightings occurred, yet very important chunks of those memories are completely gone—so perhaps I should term it "Erased Time." Since discovering this information, I have tried long and hard to remember something of that hour at Lake DeForest, or the second night at Harriman, and the best way I can describe it is like looking at a painting that has had the center cut out of it.

Do I think that we experienced some sort of contact? If someone else had told me this story—especially as it occurred at the infamous Lake DeForest—I wouldn't hesitate to say yes. But honestly, I don't know what to think at this point. At the very least, *something* happened which punched a gaping hole in my memory, and I don't like it one bit!

Perhaps someday it will all come flooding back, or perhaps it is all lost for good. I can only be so very thankful that I compulsively kept a diary every day for all those years, so that some of the truth could later come to light. I think this should be a lesson to everyone who has a sighting or encounter, to write down or record every detail as soon as possible.

This is also a lesson for me—the person who was absolutely certain that I would never end up in this particular chapter of one of my own books. I have said time and again that if someone has had a very intense or unusual experience, there's probably a lot more that they don't remember. It's just that I never thought I was talking about myself.

"Tara"
Massachusetts, Connecticut, and New York
1979-2015

I have repeatedly found that when people have a very intense sighting or encounter, they have more than one, and other family members may also have experiences. The frequency with which this occurs appears to rule out coincidence. Could it mean that entire families are tracked for generations?

The following account by "Tara" could be placed in either the Rectangle or Disc Chapter, but once a witness has a missing time encounter, the case is elevated to another level.

Missing Time: 1979 Massachusetts/Connecticut

"Mom and I went up to Cape Cod and stayed with my godparents for the weekend; they had rented a house up there. I was about 16 years old. I don't remember what time we headed home on Sunday but it was after dinner and I know that we were expecting to be home about 9PM. We lived in Milford, CT. Mom kind of complained about not wanting to leave late because she didn't want to be driving at night in the dark and didn't want to be getting home too late.

"We don't remember much about the trip except for it being a long, dark drive. There was not as much lighting then and there were hardly any other cars on the road after dinner on a Sunday night. It seemed like we were driving forever. When we got home it was around midnight. We both had that kind of road haze or dazed feeling.

"I don't know how to describe it, but we felt like road zombies. We don't remember seeing anything unusual or anything like strange lights in the sky, but the dazed feeling was very odd and we lost 3 hours of time."

[Note: An average, the drive from most locations in Cape Cod to Milford, CT should take about 3 hours. So, the fact that their drive took twice as long, with no traffic, is very unusual.]

Major Sighting: 1980 Milford Connecticut

"My friend and I were walking home from downtown. The road we were on runs basically in a north-south direction and comes along the side of Milford Harbor in Milford, CT (Rogers Avenue). I don't dare ask her if she remembers the day because she was so scared. I was more curious.

"What we saw was very large; it was the shape of 2 squares joined together by, or with, a smaller section in the middle. I would say it was about half the height airline jets fly at, and about 150 to 200 yards to our left. Totally covered with very bright lights; all of which were white.

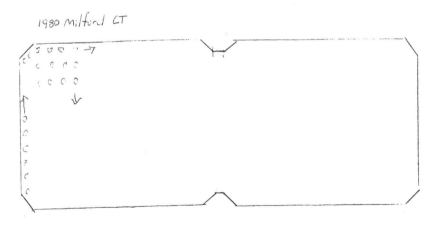

1980 Milford CT

o = Lights
Lights were all over it, and helped define the shape.
Too many to fill in but they may have been larger in size.

175

"It was the middle of the day and the sun was out, but you noticed the lights because they were so bright. It was hard to tell the size, due to the distance and angle that we were from it, but each square was bigger than a football field. Maybe the size of a polo field. Polo fields are the size of 9 football fields. Each section! It was huge.

"It was moving in the same direction we were; south along the harbor, going out to the sound. So it was parallel to us for most of the way home; going about 3 miles an hour. I lived across from the lower end of the harbor and she lived farther down closer to the opening of the channel. It was about a 10-minute walk from where we first spotted it.

"When we got to my house, we met up with another friend who saw the same thing we did, yet still denied the existence of it. We watched it for a minute or two more and then it moved away until the outline of it was only a cigar shape in the distance. It would have been over Long Island at this point. It stayed like this for only a moment and then it zipped off, out of sight. I never heard anything about it after that from anyone."

Illuminated Sky/Barn Invader – May 1987, Bedford Hills, New York

"I had a job taking care of the horses on a property in Bedford Hills. My mother was living in Florida at the time, but came up to visit. While she was staying in my apartment, she slept by the window in this loft space. I was on the opposite side of the room.

"We never saw any unidentified objects, but after some days went by we realized we were both waking up in the early morning or middle of the night hours. I would wake and see light outside, as if the sunrise was very colorful, orange and red, but then I would wake again and it was still dark out and the sunrise would come later.

"My mom would wake up and she said she would see bright red lights lighting up the whole sky. On the third night of these lights, she called to me when she woke up and asked me to look out the window. I did not get up; however, I did see the whole area light up red. She had looked at the clock and it was 3AM.

"This went on for 3 days, and after the third night, that morning the Mt. Kisco newspaper, *The Patent Trader*, had an article on the front page about a ship that was seen just a country block from where I lived.

"Two people saw it up close and said it was the size of the Westchester Hospital, and it was hovering above the hay field at the corner of West Patent Rd. & Broad Brook Rd. I lived on Broad Brook.

"We never put these experiences together until later on, but as it turns out on those same 3 nights, something was happening in the barn…

"The loft apartment was over the stalls so I could hear the horses, and for 3 nights in a row one or more of them had been kicking or thrashing in the stall so violently that it made me run down to the barn to see what was wrong. When I got down there, nothing was out of order. The horses were quiet, but alert, and just stood there looking at me.

"That Tuesday morning, I was getting a horse cleaned up for the owner, and he would not let me near his hind end. Since he was a polo horse and I tied his tail up all the time this was very unusual.

"Then someone noticed there was a little blood on his buttocks. Well, when I finally got him calmed down, I examined him to find a perfectly straight vertical laceration about 4" long and deep enough to cause a lot more blood than there was. Actually, there was only enough blood for us to notice that it was there, though most of the skin layers had been split open as if cut with a razor blade. A very sharp, clean, vertical slice.

"He had a laceration that required stitches, but he wasn't bleeding, so why would he need stitches if he wasn't even bleeding? I think the owner had opted out of calling the vet. We never found anything in the stall that would cut him that way, and he was afraid of people going behind him for a while after that. However, I remember that laceration healed up really fast.

"Boy, did it give me the creeps when I realized I ran down to the barn and someone or something could have been right outside the door; all three nights!"

Mom's version:
"While visiting my daughter in Bedford Hills, I woke up one night thinking it was early dawn, but when I looked at the clock it was 3:00 am and definitely not dawn. The second floor window of the apartment was up high so it looked out to the tree tops, and a bright red light was shining down on the trees and moving slowly from one side of the room to the other. I knew it could not be police or emergency lights because they would be coming from the ground and blinking. Besides, the driveway

was a very long gravel driveway and you could definitely hear any vehicles approaching or even footsteps of people walking. There was no sound at all. It was silent.

"I called out to my daughter and she was awake, too, and saw the trees lit up red also. I recall that the horses downstairs in the barn were very restless. Then the article appeared that week in *The Patent Trader* about a UFO sighting, and it was just down the road from us and on the same night."

[Note: Fortunately, this was not a case of a horse mutilation, but still, something unknown wounded this animal with a deep laceration that mysteriously did not bleed. The fact that both Tara and her mother saw a red light on three successive nights, and the horse was wounded the same night that a UFO was spotted makes this a very compelling case.]

The following is the text and an illustration from *The Patent Trader* article from May 29, 1987:

Summertime is UFO Time is Northern Westchester, by John F. Kelly and Ted Schillinger

UP THERE- The skies over Mt. Kisco are usually like any other; stars, moon, and little that is more controversial than a healthy dose of light pollution.

But last week the unusual happened.

Kicking off what is generally considered the heaviest season for the sightings of UFOs, or unidentified flying objects, area residents with a clear view of the sky above Mount Kisco reported that they had seen a large unidentifiable object flying over the village. According to local police, witnesses called in their sightings from the Sawmill River Parkway, Route I-684 and other locations.

"It was as big as the hospital," said Lysa Schwartz of Pound Ridge. Ms. Schwartz and two companions, Christine Williams of Bedford and David Shea of Mount Kisco, said they were driving toward the village on Broad Brook Road when they noticed a large object above the line of treetops by the road.

178

According to these witnesses, they pulled their car onto West Patent Road and climbed out to get a better look of the object.

They describe it as a large modular craft with white, green and red lights on its surface, hovering and moving soundlessly roughly 1000 feet above the ground. They said that the craft was made up of it least two parts, connected by a narrow attachment between them.

The witnesses stressed that the object's size, unique shape, and soundless motion convinced them that it was not a traditional flying device.

"I think it was a spacecraft," said Ms. Schwartz. "It wasn't anything manmade. That was it. That was the real thing." All three explain that if they had not witnessed the objects themselves, they would doubtless found such reports unlikely.

Compounding the strangeness of their experience, the witnesses described the field from which they observed the object as "completely full of fireflies." "Fireflies don't come out in May," said Ms. Williams. After the three drove to town to report the incident, they returned to the field, but said that the mysterious fireflies were "totally gone."

"Maybe it radiated some kind of energy," conjectured Ms. Williams, accounting for the odd phenomenon.

According to the department of entomology of the University of Florida in Gainesville, it is not uncommon for fireflies to be in evidence at this time of the year, but the excessive fluctuations in weather conditions lately may seriously affect the behavior of the insects.

Police report that many of such sightings result from patterned formation-flying pilots of ultralight planes, small propeller–powered hang-gliders. Responding to these reports, the witnesses said, "This was no glider."

A police officer from the Bedford police department said he witnessed the phenomenon on Thursday, and theorized it was caused by a grouping of ultralight crafts.

According to Department of Federal Aviation Administration (FAA) officials, the ultralights are experimental crafts that use a "lawn mower engine" and a canopy-type body that "is not very sturdy." The FAA said the pilots have been known to use different colored flashlights to create the illusion of a spacecraft, and that ultralights are not allowed to enter controlled airspace.

"These guys are really taking their lives in their hands," said one FAA official who asked not to be identified. "It's just a bunch of guys having fun and games up in the sky, or trying to trick people into believing there's a craft from outer space. It's very hard to stop them... Several times police cars have shown up at landing strips waiting for them and when the pilot sees the cops they just take off into the sky again," he added.

Other sightings have been attributed to highly skilled pilots flying small planes in precise formation out of the Stormville Airport. According to Robert Gribble of the National UFO Reporting Center in Seattle, the reports of the Stormville pilots have been "going on for three or four years."

"I don't know what the purpose of their deception is," Mr. Gribble said, adding "What they're doing is obviously very hazardous and one day their luck is going to run out and they are going to crash into a populated area."

According to Mr. Gribble, the reporting center is a private organization that receives, evaluates and investigates reports of UFOs from all over the world. He said the center is presently receiving approximately "five or six" reports a day.

Mr. Gribble said that that type of craft that was reported last week in Mount Kisco has been identified many times "all over the world."

"This type of craft, while not the most common type, has been identified in the United States, Europe and Africa," he said. "There is not the slightest doubt in my mind that these crafts are real and interplanetary, although I wouldn't have the slightest idea of where they come from...It's a very big universe," he added.

There are also "volumes of evidence of government cover-ups" concerning alien craft evidence, according to Mr. Gribble. He said that reports issued from the heads of Army Intelligence, dating back to as early as 1947, contain eyewitness accounts and radar readings confirming the existence of interplanetary craft.

"There are also military laws specifically devised to cover up UFO information," he said. He claimed there are specific laws relating to military personnel and airplane pilots, laws warning that if any information regarding the sightings of UFOs is leaked out to the public, the informant would receive a minimum of five years in jail and a $70,000 fine.

"If the government told the people what they know today, it would totally devastate all current religious teachings," he said.

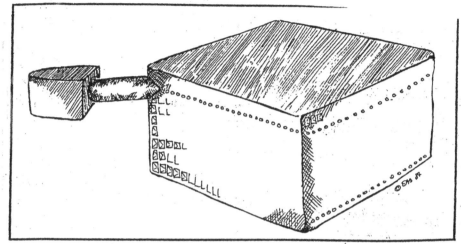

Trader illustration by Ted Schiltinger

Full Moon 3 days after the New Moon: 2015 Brewster, New York

"One evening about a year ago, maybe in October, my boyfriend and I went out to dinner at Las Mananitas Restaurant in Brewster. It was after dark, most likely after 7:30 since we never meet up until after 7 pm. We normally sit outside, but it must have been cold out because we sat inside; so I think it was in the early fall. We had a table right in front of the windows. These windows face east and look out over the East Branch Reservoir.

"I was facing north and my boyfriend was facing south, so I had to look over my right shoulder to see the reservoir. As I was looking out, I couldn't see much in the dark, but I did see the moon. It was full and it was a different color. Kind of orange rather than gray. I kept looking at it to see if I could make out the usual moon details and craters. I didn't see them, however, I didn't want to be rude so I tried not to look; I do like moon gazing. I did mention the moon was there.

"I didn't really think anything of the direction it was coming up because the sun and moon do change locations with the seasons and I am not so well versed with astronomy to know where it should have been, but after our main course I looked over my shoulder again and it was gone.

"At some point during dessert, I realized the darkest night of the New Moon was just a few days ago! My boyfriend still thinks that it was overcast, or that maybe it was a plane, but I know it was not a plane. There is no mistaking a plane for the moon and it did not move.

"I looked at it a few times, it was not moving. And it was round. A round ball of light in the sky that looked like the full moon, but was not the same color, and there could not have been a full moon! I'm not sure he noticed it the same as I did, but he is not always observant of these things like I am. Still, I wonder if he even saw it at all. I know I did."

Continuing the multi-generational concept of sightings, I asked Tara if any other family members ever encountered anything strange, and she replied:

"Thought my dad said he saw ball lighting once when he was a boy and that it stayed in the yard like a gazing ball before it kind of burst/burned out. That was in Bethel, CT."

Coincidence? Like the saying goes, I think not!

***

While the following article does not appear to describe any missing time or abduction experiences, the UFO did have a unique influence on the witness.

Beacon, NY
UFOS Cross Hudson
March 16, 1981
The Evening News

NEWBURGH—Beacon area residents have been seeing UFOs during the past several days, and now the allusive objects have been spotted by a city resident.

Henry Schipp, of 282 First St. here, said he had a close encounter at about 5:00am Saturday when an object which he described as round, about 20 feet wide and with flashing blue lights appeared over his house.

Schipp said the object "flew by and disappeared very fast" and that he felt weakness immediately thereafter although the sensation passed "within a few moments." He said he was taking out garbage cans when he saw the UFO.

Numerous persons in the Beacon and Cold Spring area have called *The Evening News* with similar sightings in the past two weeks.

Shipp said he called Stewart Airport after spotting the UFO and was told by officials that nothing unexpected appeared on their radar screens. But Schipp is unconvinced. "They're not going to tell you anything they don't want you to know about," he observed.

Susan Basilone
Kent Cliffs, NY
c.1982

Susan Basilone didn't care if I used her real name in this story because, as she said, "I know what I saw."

It was in May, around 1982, and Susan was on her way from her home in Kent Cliffs, New York, to a ladies' auxiliary meeting at the fire department. She had just pulled up to a stop sign on Ninham Road when she saw some red lights up ahead. As she drove onto Route 301 by Boyd Corners reservoir, she could see that the lights were so low that it looked like the object "sat in the trees." It was circular, "the size of a high ranch house," and it wasn't moving.

Normally, Susan would have been very much frightened by such an object, but for some reason she "felt compelled to get out of the car and walk across the street," at which point she was no more than 100 feet away from it.

"It was completely out of character for me to get out of the car," Susan explained. "I should have been afraid, but I actually had no feeling. And then the next thing I knew, I was back by my car and one of my neighbors was driving by on his way home from work. He stopped his car and I asked him if he saw what I saw, and he replied, 'I certainly do!' And every time we met after that, like in the supermarket, I would ask him if he remembered what we saw and he would say that he did. So it was good that someone else was there to see it."

The object moved off, and Susan continued on to her meeting. When she arrived, she was very surprised to notice that everyone was relieved to see her. They explained that they had been quite worried that something had happened to her because she was so late, as she was always early for everything.

"I am NEVER late," Susan stated unequivocally. "To give you an idea, the night I met you at your lecture, I had arrived an hour and half early. I didn't think I had been watching the object for very long, but I ended up being 30 to 45 minutes late for my meeting. Somehow, all this time had gone by."

This, of course, sent up some red flags for me once Susan mentioned this missing time. I asked if she had any idea what had transpired during that time, and why she suddenly felt compelled to get out of the car and approach the object. She said she must have just been in such a state that she didn't realize the passage of time.

"Thank heaven they weren't interested in probing me!" Susan joked.

I don't know about the probing part, but in my opinion, the occupants of that craft were obviously *very* interested in Susan.

In any event, she told the other ladies what she had seen, expecting a good natured ribbing, but instead was surprised to hear that they had all seen the round object with the red lights passing over the firehouse about half an hour earlier. If that is the case, then there most definitely were many other witnesses that night. In any event, this is a case with multiple eyewitnesses spanning over half an hour.

I asked if anything else unusual had happened, and she mentioned that many people in her neighborhood had seen lights and strange craft in the area. Susan also said something about water missing from swimming pools, which also caught my attention, as I have dealt with such baffling cases before.

"One morning, we saw that all of the water was out of our pool," she said. "It was an above-ground pool that my husband had built a deck around, so he was able to get underneath it. He was certain there was a leak, but it was completely dry. He couldn't understand it, *there was no leak.*

"Around the same time, our neighbor lost all of the water in his pool," Susan continued. "And it was the same thing—he couldn't find any leaks, and when he filled it back up, it was fine."

I have to admit that I was initially skeptical when I heard for the first time a story about a UFO possibly being responsible for the removal of water from a pool. However, now that I have heard of several cases of sightings and missing water, it seems to be beyond a coincidence.

Many of the UFO sightings in this area over the years have involved bodies of water, and indeed, the round craft Susan saw that night had stopped over a brook that led into the reservoir.

Was there more to Susan's sighting than just an observation of a craft—something to account for the missing time? Was it a coincidence that on another occasion the water from her pool was drained? Without further evidence, or recollections, no one can say, but any time a witness describes feeling compelled to approach a UFO, or doing something out of character, we can't help but wonder.

Nancy
Cold Spring, NY, 1982
Middle Hope, NY 1988

"It was those eyes! Those large, black, piercing eyes that struck me the most," Nancy exclaimed about the entity she encountered.

Aliens were the last thing on her mind that night in 1982 as she and her best friend, Lisa, were driving on Route 9D near Cold Spring along the Hudson River. They were on their way to go shopping in White Plains and the two women were just laughing and talking about nothing in particular when they saw something up ahead.

"There was something in the middle of the road, so I slowed down," Nancy said. "It was over 6 feet tall and very skinny, with really thin limbs. It didn't have any clothes on, and its skin was very gray."

The most startling feature, however, was its "huge head," and the big eyes which were completely black.

"What the hell is that!?" Lisa yelled.

Nancy had no idea what she was looking at, or more importantly, what was *looking at them*.

"I had to slow way down and move over into the other lane to avoid it," Nancy explained. "It just stood there and stared at us with those black eyes. It was looking right at us, and followed us with those piercing eyes. We passed it by no more than one or two feet. I could have hit it, it was so close. Right after we went by it, I looked in the rearview mirror and it was gone."

185

Lisa was "freaking out," claiming that this was definitely "something not of this world." Nancy didn't know what to think, as she had absolutely no interest in UFOs and never heard of Gray Aliens. It wasn't until she moved to California about a decade later and saw a book about them that she realized what she had been eye to eye with one on that dark stretch of road.

"When I saw pictures of the Grays in the book I said, 'Oh my god!' That's what we saw! For years, Lisa and I joked that we must have seen the Elephant Man, because we had no idea at the time."

Six years later, Nancy had another sighting, this time with her mother. It was July 1988, about 8:30pm, and they were driving on Route 9W in Middle Hope, going toward Marlboro to get some pizza. The road was dark, and suddenly they saw something bright. It was a "huge craft hovering over the trees by a pond." The craft was "round with very large, bright, white lights, and it was just hovering silently. My mom pulled over, and I had to get out to look at it. She kept yelling at me to get back in the car. This craft was as big as several houses and it didn't make a sound! And it didn't move!"

Apparently, many other people saw the same round craft hovering silently that night, but the next day a local paper printed the old excuse of it being planes flying in formation, which Nancy says is just completely ridiculous.

Nancy's mother didn't like to talk about this sighting as it was so unusual and so upsetting, but years later, she did tell Nancy's son about it.

"My mother was very old-fashioned; she never lied, and never made up stories," so confirming the details of the sighting was important to Nancy, and her son. This isn't exactly a newsflash, but children don't always believe what their parents tell them! However, when his grandmother told the story of the huge, silent, round craft, he believed her.

During my conversation with Nancy, she told me that she "never, ever did any drugs," and that she had perfect eyesight. I asked if she had ever had any experiences as a child, and there were none that she could recall. I also asked if she had any sort of sixth sense experiences, as I have found that witnesses who have very close encounters often have heightened senses as a result. I wasn't too surprised when she said that she had indeed had numerous experiences, but the nature and extent of those experiences were somewhat remarkable.

"I seem to know when people are going to pass away, even when they appear perfectly healthy, and even people that I don't know very well or who are simply related to friends of mine. It's happened several times over the years."

"Also, when I was living in California, I went to the store one weekend to buy bottled water, canned food, and flashlights. Then I put all of my vases and breakable items that were on cabinets and shelves onto the floor. I just *knew* that a big earthquake was coming, and sure enough, a few days later there was a major earthquake."

Nancy has had numerous other paranormal experiences, and while she can't say the abilities began, or were heightened, that day she locked eyes with the tall Gray, she considers the experience "a big part" of her life.

One final word: as I was interviewing Nancy over the phone about her uncomfortably close encounter, the line went dead. I wish I had kept count over the years of how many times the phone went dead when I was interviewing witnesses about their sightings. The first time it happened was during my very first UFO interview with lifelong abductee, Gary, when I started the *In the Night Sky* project. And in all the years I have lived here, I honestly can't recall having phone trouble and getting cut off during any regular, non-UFO calls—just during the interviews with witnesses.

What does all of this mean? What does any of this mean?

The universe is much stranger than we can ever imagine...

Kent Cliffs, NY
September 1989

To the uninformed and those with just a casual interest in ufology, the following case may seem too incredible to be true. However, if you know your UFO history—particularly in the Hudson Valley—then you realize that families often share years, or even generations, of intense experiences and contact.

Unfortunately, this witness does not elaborate on his family's "missing time and other stranger occurrences," but it is clear this is something they all shared over the course of many years.

187

NUFORC Report
Disc-shaped UFO hovering with red and white alternating lights with planes in chase
Duration: 20 min

I had to have been in 2nd or 3rd grade. As a kid, and somewhat as an adult, I have always been afraid of aliens and the dark. I slept in the same bedroom as my older brother who was 5 years older than me and who always put up with my childish fears. Well, it was a warm night and we had the window to our room open to let some air in. As we were going to bed, (there were two twin beds separated by a couple feet facing the window) I looked out the window and saw a large orange circle with two blinking lights following it. I assumed they were planes. I asked my brother if it was a UFO and, as a typical older brother would say, he told me to shut up and go to bed.

Well, about 10 minutes later, my mom started screaming and told everyone to go to the living room and look out the big window which faced the same direction as my bedroom window. As we all ran to the room to see why my mom was screaming (there were 4 boys and my dad and mom) we heard a humming noise over our house. When we got to the living room, we all saw a disc-shaped object with alternating red and white lights around it in the distance. It seemed like an eternity that it just hovered there. As we watched, we saw some planes getting closer and eventually it seemed as though it wavered a little bit and proceeded to shoot straight up at an enormous speed.

My family has had many sightings living in Putnam, mostly from the same time frame, but many from when I must have been 3 or 4 years old and my memories are a little vague and not as clear about those events, although I do still have memories of them. My family has also experienced missing time and other stranger occurrences.

Janice
Patterson, Kent, and Pawling, NY
November 17, 2016

The night of November 17, 2016 was an active one in the Hudson Valley. In addition to a very close encounter accompanied by intense fear experienced by a man in Montgomery, NY (see next story), Janice also had a close sighting with inexplicable fear. Over the years, many people have expressed to me this same sense of terror and danger, as if they are being warned to not come any closer, or in this case, to *not* obtain any photographic evidence.

The following is in Janice's own words, and includes some follow-up responses to my questions:

"I have to tell you about what I saw last night: First thing, as I was coming home on Rt. 311 in Patterson, up above the tree level in front of me, approaching Rt. 22, I saw a yellow flash that very quickly spread to a thin yellow line, and gone, in all of 1 or 2 seconds. I thought it may have been a reflection off my car window, but I believe it was not. Especially when I told my girlfriend about it this morning and she saw something similar around the same time in Kent, NY. But also as I was going to Pawling around 8:45 or so, on Rt. 22, I saw this low-flying "plane," all lit. As it got closer, I saw it was flying lower and lower, and as it flew over me, I swear it looked like a boomerang. Did I stop to take a picture? No, of course not. *Something told me not to.* I did roll my window down and turned off the radio, no noise; a plane that low, I would have heard. As I watched it fly, it just seemed to go lower and lower."

- "The yellow light happened around 5:15 in the evening."
- "The weird thing was there were no cars on Rt. 22 at that moment; no one behind me or passing me. I was driving very slowly and trying to stay on the road as I was driving. I kept telling myself to stop and my inner voice said, "No, *it's too dangerous.*" Now in hindsight, WHY? I could have easily pulled over."
- "After I picked my daughter up in Pawling, I came straight home and told my husband. I so wish he was with me! The funny thing is, he shared a link of how a boomerang was spotted in NYC last night. I told my coworker about it and that is when she told me about her yellow light experience. Something she would not have remembered if I hadn't mentioned it."
- "The weird thing was, while I was driving up and down Quaker Hill in Pawling to drop her off and pick her up, I am

usually very sharp because of the deer at night, but I felt so disconnected."

NOTE: In the Triangle Chapter, please see the case from New Milford, CT which occurred on the same night, as well as the same time, 8:45pm.

"Dan"
Montgomery, NY
November 17, 2016

It was dusk on the evening of Thursday, November 17, 2016, and "Dan" was out hunting in a field near his home in Montgomery, NY. Suddenly, an "intense and terrifying fear" swept over him and he stopped dead in his tracks. He couldn't understand what was happening to him, because he had spent many nights out in the woods alone, and he is definitely someone who doesn't "spook easily."

The feeling of fear became overwhelming, and it was as if there was someone or something telling him to "LEAVE NOW!" Turning to run for home, Dan spotted a figure about 20 yards ahead. In the fading light, he could only see a silhouette from the waist up, and the figure was about the height of a man. However, there was something strange about this man. The arms appeared to be longer and oddly bent at the elbows, almost "like a monkey." Then it got even stranger.

Racing across the field came three vehicles, which Dan first assumed were SUVs, but then he saw that they weren't behaving at all like conventional vehicles. They were flat-topped, rectangular, and grayish, with no lights, and were making absolutely no sound. Also, the field was rather hilly, yet these vehicles weren't bouncing up and down to follow the contours of the ground—they maintained a flat, smooth course as if they were travelling *above the ground*!

When he got home he had "a wild-eyed look" and "couldn't shake" the feeling of fear, or astonishment at what he witnessed. Dan tried to figure out what he had just seen, and why he had been compelled to leave the field. Then he realized that if the fear hadn't stopped him when it did, he would have walked right into that figure!

The next day he looked for answers. He searched the area where he had seen the three speeding vehicles, but the tall grass was undisturbed—

no tire tracks, no bent or broken plants or bushes. There was simply no indication that anything had driven though that field.

That evening, he refused to go hunting again. In fact, Dan said he will never go out in that field at night again. He can't stop thinking about the mysterious figure and the three rectangular craft, and strongly believes that if he had stayed one minute longer, something "very bad" would have happened.

"I can't shake it," Dan said. "It's something I will take to my grave."

10
Casebook

Sullivan County, NY
1876

The Evening Gazette
Port Jervis, NY
Saturday Evening, March 11, 1876

The Sullivan County papers note from week to week a strange light observed near a lake in that county, and are asking why the mystery is not investigated. It seems to us that the newspapers are forgetting their own calling when they call on others to investigate a proceeding which comes so clearly within their own province. Why don't the editors up there fly around and find out for themselves what they want to know? There may be a first-class newspaper sensation spoiling on their hands. Wake up, gentlemen!

Note: I find it very curious that this article suggests that the editors "fly around" to investigate this strange light. Was some lighted craft flying through the skies of Sullivan County in 1876?

Jersey City Heights, NJ
July 6, 1882

Mr. N.S. Drayton wrote the following letter, which was published in the July 22, 1882 edition of *Scientific American*:

A Supposed Meteor

On the evening of the 6th, while engaged in "sweeping" the vicinity of Ursa Minor for double stars, my attention was drawn to a bright object about the size of a star of second magnitude moving slowly from west to east. It passed within a degree of Polaris and continued steadily in its course eastward, disappearing from view in the neighborhood of Capricornus. In color this object, a meteor doubtless, was deep red, without scintillation or train of any kind, and its slow movement was in marked contrast with the rapid flashing of the common "shooting star."

It was visible to me fully three-fourths of a minute, varying but slightly in brightness during that time. In the closeness of my attention to its movement I neglected to note the time of its appearance, but judge it to have been near half past ten. Perhaps there were others of your readers who observed the phenomenon, and can add more specifically to my testimony.

Perhaps this was just a meteor, but it was certainly an odd one. If you have ever seen a "shooting star," then you know they usually flash across the sky in the blink of an eye, and often flare up and then fizzle out. Some larger meteors or fireballs[1] can leave scintillating tails or break apart, but even those last only a matter of seconds. This object was in view a full 45 seconds, and basically maintained a consistent level of brightness. Drayton doesn't say the object faded or burned out, but just that it disappeared from view, which may mean it simply went out of sight along the horizon.

Using the *Stellarium* program to recreate the sky on the night of July 6, 1882, at 10:30pm, you can trace the path of this object from high in the northern sky by Polaris—the North Star—to Capricornus, which was low on the eastern horizon, just south of due east. To give you a sense of how slow this object was moving over this relatively short expanse of sky, point your finger to the north, and have someone count off 45 seconds while you move your finger to the horizon to the east. This was either one super-slow meteor—or it was something completely different…

***

The following reports of lights on High Mountain, NJ could be dismissed as superstitious nonsense, with fears of the devil and cholera, until one looks at a map and realizes that it is just about seven miles from the Wanaque Reservoir, which was a hotspot for UFO activity in the 1960s. While the reservoir did not come into existence until it was created

---

[1] According to the American Meteor Society, slower moving fireballs tend to be red, but fireballs are meteors with magnitudes brighter than Venus, which has an average magnitude of about -4.0. Drayton stated that the magnitude of this object was about 2.0, which is of similar brightness to Polaris, which he may have used as a magnitude reference.

in 1928, this article may indicate that there was activity in the area way back in 1885, and perhaps even as early as 1836!

High Mountain, NJ
1885

Uncanny Sounds Heard and Mysterious Lights Seen by the Valley Residents
The Evening Gazette
Port Jervis, NY
Friday, March 6, 1885

Superstitious residents of the regions known as Preakness, Haledon, and other suburbs hemmed in by the lofty hills known as High Mountain, writes a Patterson, N.J., correspondent to the New York World, place extra bolts on their doors now o' nights and are careful to be indoors "after hours." Numbers of superstitious ones, and some who are not superstitious by any means, are willing to make affidavits that they have heard uncanny sounds proceeding from the heights, and nearly everybody in the vicinity who has been near the foot of the mountain after dark will vouch for the statement that mysterious lights have been seen flitting to and fro up among the trees.

No soul lives there, and, as it is said that several murders have been perpetrated there, the villages state, with a solemn shake of the head, that "the devil is at work and no mistake," and that there are "spooks on High Mountain."

A party of the braver and brawnier lads of the bailiwick endeavored to solve the mystery a few nights ago, but they soon returned with white faces and quaking limbs, and informed those in waiting by the stove of the place of rendezvous that it was all well enough for them to be sittin' there toastin' their shins and joken', but if they wanted to find out anything about the spooks they had better make the trip themselves. Upon being mollified with "something hot," they became more communicative, and related to their open-mouthed audience the following hair-curdling tale:

They said they had climbed to the top of the mountain, where the lights had been seen, when all at once they were surrounded by lights that jumped around them and climbed the trees and performed other acrobatic feats. Although they appeared to be right in the midst of the flames not a

194

hair on their head was injured and their clothing wasn't even singed. They smelled phosphorous just as plain as it could be smelled, and while they were wondering what to do next the wind whistled through the trees, producing such unearthly sounds that they came right straight away and let the wind have it all to itself.

Doubting Thomases in the audience plucked up courage and firearms enough to make the trip themselves and they, too, soon returned, looking as pale as the historical ghosts and shaking like rattle-boxes. Nobody showed a disposition to go home, and finally, when the host informed them that it was time to close up, they started off in a group and spent the night together by a hospitable neighbor's fire rather than pass the mountain until daylight did appear.

Since then the phenomena have been witnessed by scores of those who were brave enough to approach within sight of the bleak and densely wooded mountain, and the matter has been the chief topic of conversation in the country stores, in the taverns, in the village schools, and has even been referred to by the local dominies. The town hoodlums are now free of going to the stores after dark, for their parents would not think of sending them where they would not go themselves. The jolly hosts of the roadside taverns are jolly no longer, or must be content to be jolly by themselves, for the loungers now lounge at home.

Old residents say that the same thing occurred just before the last cholera epidemic, and that the light presaged another visitation of that dread scourge. Scores of old timers are willing to wager on this, and prominent citizens are willing to encourage them in their belief, for it is on record that the same thing did occur in 1836, just before death stalked through this section of the country.

Reports from Pike County, Pennsylvania, say that the same phenomena have appeared there just as they did in1836, and that the citizens of that place spend most of their night-times in their homes.

Citizens who pretend to be wise assert that the Pike county phenomena are caused by the escape of coal gas from the mountains, and that it is really no phenomenon at all, but are the result of natural causes. They also say that the mysterious lights on High Mountain can be traced to the same cause, and are apparently honest in their belief that a vein of coal would be found by anybody taking the trouble to hunt for it. Should this prove true there is wealth in store for the gentlemen who own High

Mountain, but they will have to seek foreign aid to unearth it, for no native will go within gunshot distance of it since the experiences above related.

Note: According to the Wikipedia article on the Watchung Mountains, which includes High Mountain, they are primarily composed of volcanic basalt, with no mention of coal deposits. This eliminates escaping coal gases as an explanation for the mysterious lights.

Charles Angus
West Haven, CT
Winter 1912

In 1967, Mr. Harvey Courtnay of Stratford, Connecticut, wrote to APRO to report a sighting which had taken place by a Mr. Charles Angus 55 years earlier in 1912, in West Haven, Connecticut.

Night: Clear sky—very cold.

Mr. Angus was ice skating with Beatrice Dedering at the West Haven Reservoir. At least twenty to twenty-six other people also skating.

Saw reflection in ice while skating, then heard swooshing sound. (Reminded him of the sound of pinwheel displays during Fourth of July.)

Everyone looked up and saw five (5) blue colored objects, flying one behind the other in a straight line formation.

Objects passed overhead and disappeared over the horizon.

Direction of travel: North to south.

Duration of sighting: About three to four minutes.

While great aeronautical strides were being made in 1912, this case does not seem to fit any conventional aircraft of the time. For starters, there was the odd "swooshing" sound of the craft, as opposed to that of motors. Also, even if someone had invented a plane with a new form of propulsion, the chances of there being *five* such unknown craft is highly unlikely. Then there is the blue coloration, the lengthy duration of three to four minutes to cross the sky, and the fact that these craft were flying at night toward open water of the Long Island Sound.

Taking all the facts into consideration, these ice skaters clearly witnessed something so extraordinary that they remembered it for the rest of their lives.

Wilton, CT and Philipse Manor, NY
February 23, 1955

PROJECT 10073 RECORD CARD

1. DATE	2. LOCATION	12. CONCLUSIONS
23 February 1955	Wilton, Connecticut	☐ Was Balloon ☐ Probably Balloon ☐ Possibly Balloon
3. DATE-TIME GROUP Local GMT 24/0200Z	4. TYPE OF OBSERVATION X Ground-Visual　☐ Ground-Radar ☐ Air-Visual　☐ Air-Intercept Radar	☐ Was Aircraft ☐ Probably Aircraft ☐ Possibly Aircraft
5. PHOTOS ☐ Yes ☐ No	6. SOURCE Civilian	☐ Was Astronomical Meteor X Probably Astronomical ☐ Possibly Astronomical
7. LENGTH OF OBSERVATION 5-6 seconds	8. NUMBER OF OBJECTS	9. COURSE one	☐ Other ☐ Insufficient Data for Evaluation ☐ Unknown
10. BRIEF SUMMARY OF SIGHTING Round, reddish orange, luminous, described as ball of light. Straight line travel.		11. COMMENTS Two observers at differenct locations. Meteor.

ATIC FORM 329 (REV 26 SEP 52)

According to this Project Blue Book record card, this object seen by multiple witnesses was nothing more than a simple meteor, but perhaps the actual witness testimony indicates something else.

A couple was driving back from a church meeting in Wilton, Connecticut and saw something unusual:

"…returning to my home last Wednesday night, February 23, with my wife, I went on Route 33. About half-way from the center of Wilton to my house (which is about five miles from the center), my wife spotted and pointed out to me a rather peculiar object going across the horizon. It appeared to be a red ball several thousand feet from earth and travelling at a high rate of speed. It was not an airplane. I looked in the papers for some mention of a meteor having come to earth but had seen none.

"Subsequent thereto, however, I spoke to a friend of mine, (name blacked out), who lives on the Hudson River, and he mentioned, in reply to my description, that the same night and about the same time a similar object had apparently passed over his house and crossed the river. This would seem to show that it was not a meteor heading for earth, as the height, speed and distance were such that it would have hit the earth before it reached the location of the river. The time was approximately 10:00 p.m. or slightly thereafter in each case."

The couple went on to describe the object as "decidedly oval" and having the apparent size of a "commercial airline," both of which would seem to further rule out the meteor explanation. It was "reddish orange," with no tail, and no sound.

The New York witness' description is even more compelling:

"At approximately 2200 Eastern Standard Time on 23 February 1955, (name blacked out) was watching television and happened to glance out the window when he saw what he described as a sphere, irregular in shape and orange in color. This object would be about the size of a basketball held in the hand at about arms' length. The only discernible detail (name blacked out) could recall was that the object was a sphere of light shooting across the sky. It had no tail, trail, or exhaust and made no sound whatsoever. The object travelled horizontally across the Hudson River towards Nyack, New York."

This witness was an accountant with a New York City firm, and the Bluebook investigator deemed him to be:

"... a sober minded person who described what he saw to the best of his ability."

A luminous round or oval object the apparent size of a basketball held at arms' length travelling horizontally across the Hudson River at a relatively low altitude does not sound like a meteor! (And one last thing, despite trying to black out all the names, they missed an entry on the last page: The couples name was Hardy, and the accountant was Pabrey.)

Stony Point, NY
1952
MUFON Case
(The following was edited for readability.)

I am 73 years old and suffered a severe head injury so I don't spell too good anymore. I'll do my best. I was with my mother visiting her mom, this was about 30 miles south of Stewart AFB, Newburgh, NY. The Korean War was going on and the F-86 Sabre jets flew out of there and practiced dog fighting over Rockland County. My grandmother went outside to watch the 86s and called us out, all excited. We went outside to see and we saw the Sabres chasing a bright yellow thing in the sky. Every time they got near, it shot away from them. There was a mess of Sabres and only one yellow light thing. After a while, it just shot away and was gone in a split second and the 86s slowed down and milled around for a while and then flew off to the north back to Stewart.

Ossining, NY
c. June 25, 1962, at 2am

This NUFORC report is a classic case in the sense that it not only resulted in what is known as "vehicle disruption," but the street lights also went out. There is a clear cause and effect here with the "balls of light" witnessed and the complete loss of power in the cars and street lights. What that cause is, however, is the question!

NUFORC Report
Refueling in summer 1962, Ossining, NY
Duration: 10-15 minutes

Early morning, car died with several others, 6-7 lights in town on main street (not the name) of Ossining all went out. Everything died, radio, lights, horn, on all vehicles. Full moon aprox. Tried everything, cleaned battery cables, etc., nothing worked...just as sudden as it happened, radio started blasting, lights came on in car, street lights, all other vehicles came alive at same time. At same time balls of light seen at small Con Ed electric plant within several blocks, balls raised to something in the sky.

Newburgh -Vails Gate, NY
c. June 15, 1963, at 10pm

This NUFORC report goes into great detail as to the size, shape, altitude, and movement of the enormous object. If accurate, this was a very early sighting of the type of massive craft that were to become common in the skies of the Hudson Valley and Connecticut twenty years later.

Also, as this sighting occurred just a few miles from Stewart Air Force Base, some kind of connection must be considered. Finally, *The Tonight Show* with Johnny Carson did not start until 11:30pm, so either the sighting began later than this witness recollects, or it lasted a lot longer than he remembers.

NUFORC Report
Duration: 20 minutes

The craft up close was enormous and turned on a semi-circular white light which wrapped around its flattened shape.

I first saw it about 30 degrees from the zenith and to the southwest. At first it was a pinpoint of white light moving towards the horizon. As it moved (maybe in descent), it changed colors in a spectral sequence of white/blue/green/yellow/orange/red. It now appeared as two red lights near the horizon in the southwest. Off to the right, a small plane seemed to be approaching its last position, and then to my astonishment a brilliant white light happened near where they would have met.

Now I was peering intently, thinking an explosion had occurred. But then I saw the two red lights again and now closer and apparently approaching me. It moved slowly and I thought at first I was looking at a large, low flying plane. However, the red lights were steady and not blinking, and as it drew closer I noticed it had only a low buzzing sound.

However, even when it was just above the roadway in front of my house, I still thought it was something from nearby Stewart Air Force Base. But then it turned on a white light, which clearly revealed its shape. The light wrapped around the front of it as a semi-circle, and I could also see it had small wings which were more like fins, and the red lights were at the ends of the fins.

It was 200-250 feet across and 250-300 feet front to back. Its height was 25-50 feet. It was moving very slowly at 150-200 feet above, and maybe 15mph. The white light lit up the roadway. I noticed a slight wobble or hesitancy in its forward motion, as if it were moving within some kind of field. When it turned off its main light, which may have been on for a minute, it began to pivot around one of its fins, and then I was directly beneath it, where I could now see a third red light at its rear, and its full shape from below as a flattened oval, and the fins made it seem triangular. It continued over our house and then to the fields behind. I then

200

ran inside and got my brother, who was watching Johnny Carson. We both watched it disappear, banking behind the trees to the northeast.

**

Any case reported by someone studying "Aircraft Design" deserves extra attention.

Englewood Cliffs, NJ
c. November 1, 1963

NUFORC Case
A row of bright rectangular windows with no visible exterior shape seen on 9W in Englewood Cliffs, NJ
Duration: 3 minutes

We were leaving the 9W bowling alley on Route 9W; it is set below the highway on the west side. So when pulling out onto 9W, the car is inclined up, so you are looking straight out the front windshield over the building on the other side of the road, the Prentice Hall building.

There was a row of bright, large rectangular windows with about a 2:1 height-to-width ratio. At this time, I was finishing my studies in Aircraft Design, so I tried to think of what it was that I saw. The only thing that came to mind was the gondola of a blimp. I don't recall why we couldn't see the shape, but I was most fixed on the windows.

We lowered the (car) windows to see if we could hear the engines, but it was dead silent. We also could not determine as to how far it was from us, so I drove the car across the highway to the left side of the Prentice Hall building, while sticking our heads out and looking up to see if it would pass over us. It had been moving to the north at a crawling speed. We didn't see it pass over us and when we got into the Prentice Hall parking lot, we got out of the car and looked in every direction and there was no sight of it.

When I went to school, I asked a professor if blimps fly at night and he said, "No!" When I got home, I called Lakehurst in NJ where the blimps are and they also told me the same thing.

I've always wondered what we saw that night and when I came across this web site I started checking it out and found several similar reports in this area over the last 30+ years, and one only a few blocks away on the same highway, and one a few miles away near the George Washington Bridge.

(NUFORC Note: Some blimps do fly at night, but they must have standard lighting, in order to do so.)

"Ed"
Highland, NY
1974

I have heard many amazing stories over the years, but this has to rank in the top ten—maybe even the top five. This sighting is the first and only of its kind, as far as I know. It is also the first time a witness made a sketch for me on a paper plate—but hey, researchers take their evidence any way they can get it!

It was 1974 and a few friends in the town of Highland, New York, were cruising in an old Ford Galaxy at around 9:30 or 10pm. They noticed a strange, red, blinking light to the northeast, high above the town of Poughkeepsie, which was just on the other side of the Hudson River.

Pulling the car onto a field, they got out and had a clear view of the light which slowly descended. This small point of light grew in size to something astonishing and unbelievable.

"It was like a mountain in the sky," Ed told me after one of my lectures, as he drew a sketch for me on a paper plate from the refreshment table. "It was like the size of Poughkeepsie and looked like a dark, black volcano."

Ed went on to describe the material in the object as being like "porous volcanic rock that could have just risen up out of the ocean." He also said if it had been in outer space it could be mistaken for an asteroid.

Then it got even stranger: attached to the underside of this mountain was a saucer-shaped, metallic craft, "about the size of a tractor trailer." There were about eight windows, and Ed was very specific that they didn't have sharp edges, that the corners of the windows were rounded.

"Bright, colored lights were flashing clockwise through the windows," Ed continued. "Each window had a different color, and they were never white or black."

202

1974

He said this metallic craft looked as though it could detach from the base of this enormous object, although it remained in place during the entire sighting, which lasted an impressive 15 minutes.

As the mountainous UFO sat over Poughkeepsie, about one mile high, Ed estimates, it was about five miles away. However, it began getting much closer as it moved in their direction until it was no more than about two miles from where they stood. While Ed was entranced and "just in awe," his friends were starting to get very nervous. If it had gotten any closer, he admits they probably would have gotten back in the car and taken off, but the craft suddenly rose up to an altitude of about five miles, then "shot off to the southeast at 'warp speed,' leaving a white tail. And throughout the entire time, there was absolutely *no sound*."

Ed and his friends told a few people about the bizarre sighting, but everyone treated it like a joke and assumed they had all been drunk or stoned. And the fact that nothing appeared in the newspaper or on the radio didn't help their case.

As to all the ridicule, Ed told me, "I just let it go. I know what I saw."

Ed is still in touch with one of the other witnesses from that night, and they still talk about the "Mountain in the Sky." Other than that, however, he doesn't bother to speak about it as he knows the reaction he will receive.

Over 40 years later, Ed can look back on that amazing night and say that the experience did change him in some ways.

"There is a higher intelligence. We are not alone."

A mysterious light hovers in sky near Beacon, NY
August 18, 1976
by Richard Shea
The Evening News

Beacon –It may have been just a star, but it will be hard to convince some residents of the Rombout Ave. area near School Street that they didn't see an unidentified flying object (UFO) last weekend and again Tuesday night.

Diane Pavelock of 124 Rombout Ave. was one of the first to spot the object in the skies to the southwest of Beacon. She called her next-door neighbor, Mrs. Joan Cornett, who in turn called *The Evening News*.

The object they had spotted appeared to the naked eye to be a bright star, but the two women pointed out it was multicolored, a bright greenish blue at the top, white in the middle and bright red in the lower portion.

Viewing the object through high-powered binoculars proved the thing to be vastly different from other stars which were clearly visible because of the fact there was no cloud cover at the time.

Ms. Pavelock and other Rombout Ave. residents said they had seen the UFO, or whatever it was, for the first time last weekend, but in a different part of the sky–more toward the Mt. Beacon area. During its weekend visit, the UFO appeared to be moving from place to place, flashing its bright green, red and white lights.

Tuesday night, the object appeared to be stationary, but did move slowly toward the west, along with other stars. Constant viewing by Ms. Pavelock over a period of half an hour revealed there were two other green-white-red objects, a considerable distance farther away. These two could be clearly seen through the binoculars and both had that greenish blue light at the top, white in the middle and read on the bottom.

Ms. Pavelock and Mrs. Cornett are convinced the object is the same as the one spotted over Mahopac earlier this month. Three Carmel police officers said they were convinced that Robert Jankowski, 14, of Carmel was in earnest when he reported sighting a UFO over nearby Mahopac.

The three officers, Tom Budington, Kenneth Stera and Dennis Freyler went to the area to see the object for themselves and have since submitted a report to the Federal Aviation Administration.

Jankowski described the object as looking exactly like the North Star—but brighter, with a flashing blue, yellow, green and white light. He, too, said the object remained stationary in the sky for about two hours before disappearing.

Jankowski said he also used high-powered binoculars and described the object as looking "like a flying saucer –just like you see in the magazines."

Earlier this summer, two other area residents, one from Glenham and the other from Beacon, reported spotting some kind of unidentified flying object. A woman in Glenham described the light somewhat differently and said the object she saw seemed to disappear into the mountains just east of Glenham rather than go over the mountain.

Neighbors who saw Ms. Pavelock, Mrs. Cornett, and *The Evening News* reporter viewing the object joined and took their turns with the binoculars.

"It's just probably part of our satellites," one (illegible) viewer was convinced. (Illegible) colored object was from (illegible) planet. Most of those who knew they had (illegible) although one young lady said I'll go home and (illegible)—maybe it'll go away.

Danbury, CT
August 30, 1976

Mystery Sky Lights Baffle Earthlings
by Ruth Lockwood
News-Times
August 31, 1976

Danbury—Police were chasing something out of their reach last night.

A "star-sized object" with flickering colored lights zigzagged across the southwestern sky, according to police and residents who live in the area by the airport.

Mrs. Carol Saunders of Wooster Heights, said her son, Randy, 14, was lying in bed about 10:30 PM, looking at the sky through his window.

She said he saw the object and rushed downstairs to wake her up from a nap on the living room couch.

Mrs. Saunders said it looked like the same object she saw August 4, although she had been afraid to admit it at that time.

After Mrs. Saunders, her son, and her husband, Harold, watched the object with blinking red, white, blue and green lights wander across the sky, she called the police.

Four officers, Patrolmen Peter Winter, Robert Paust, Harold Chapman and Elston Dodge watched the object from an area off Mill Plain Road.

Mrs. Saunders said it was quite a distance away and that it was "pretty bright."

Although there were reports that there was more than one object, apparently because of the different colors, Mrs. Saunders said she only saw one. But she added that shortly after midnight an airplane with blinking lights passed the area.

The Federal Aviation Administration tower at the Danbury Airport is manned until 11:00 PM, but officials said they saw no strange objects nor did they have any reports of any. Police said they received reports about the object from dusk to after midnight.

Melvin Goldstein, Western Connecticut State College meteorologist, said visibility last night was "super spectacular" due to the dry Canadian air.

206

Goldstein said there was no haze to prevent a view of objects very, very far away.

Goldstein had no explanation of what the object might have been, but said he had numerous calls about it.

The meteorologist said weather balloons are different colors, but that they do not have flashing lights.

The sighting earlier this month by 14-year-old Robert Jankowski of Carmel, NY was clearer. He, police, and more than 20 neighbors saw a bright object hovering in the southern sky below the moon around 9:30 PM and that it looked exactly like a flying saucer, blinking red, blue and green.

That sighting on August 4 was a week to the day after 14 persons hiking on Blueberry Mountain in Winsted, Connecticut, reported a similar sighting to Connecticut authorities.

UFO Spotted in Danbury
Aug 31, 1976

Danbury, Conn. (AP) –At least four flickering, colored objects dotted the night sky over the city, according to several callers to local and state police.

Danbury police said they received numerous calls from residents who saw the points of light glowing from about 7:00 p.m. Monday night into the morning today.

Several police officers also said they saw the objects, but none would speculate on what the objects were. One policeman photographed the lights and planned to study the film.

State Police in Brewster, N.Y., also said they received calls about the sightings.

Similar sightings were made in the Beacon area recently.

Mid-Hudson Region
1976
Weird Lights and Objects Weave Mystery in Region's Skies
November 21, 1976
by Robert Richards
The Evening News

Earthlings throughout the world have been seen flying saucers since the beginning of recorded history.

While most scientists believe that the vast majority of UFO reports can be easily traced to "natural" causes –from aircraft to optical illusions—the reports continue. And the mid-Hudson area is no exception.

A UFO was reported in the Plattekill area several days ago, spotted by Anthony Martino and his cousin who, coincidentally, is also named Anthony Martino.

Martino said he was traveling in his van when he and his cousin saw "something that looked like a giant Frisbee" fly over and then behind Marlboro Mountain.

Martino said that the object appeared to be "flying faster than the speed a jet would fly at" and was yellow-orange in color. He said the object flew along a straight path and then dipped at a 45-degree angle and disappeared behind the mountain.

There have been several other sightings in the region and few have yet to be explained.

Suffern attorney John Allen, along with policemen, businessmen, schoolteachers and housewives, say they recently saw unidentified flying objects in the skies over Rockland and Putnam Counties.

Allen said he actually saw flying saucers recently as he was leaving the Thruway.

In Tomkins Cove, Dan Cetrone , Publisher of the Rockland County Almanac, and his wife, Barbara, both claim to have seen cylindrical flying objects with red, green and white flashing lights. Cetrone feels these appearing and disappearing UFOs may be drawn to the area by nuclear plants.

During a three-week period in August, 100 possible sightings were recorded in Rockland County with many of them reported to the police. The US Air Force since 1969 has stopped collecting information on UFO sightings

William Patrick, officer in the Stony Point police force, says he has been on the scene of five out of nine UFO sightings.

Patrick said he saw red or green lights rotating as he looked through a telescope. He said seven other Stony Point police officers observed them and described exactly what he saw.

Ken Stern a town of Carmel police officer also described a similar sighting in the skies of Putnam County.

And what about Orange County?

UFOs have been sighted by police in New Windsor –but that was back in 1973. According to Sgt. Dominique d'Egidio, Patrolman William Carrig and Mrs. Pat Gorton, New Windsor police dispatcher, reported sightings on September 30, 1973.

This year Mrs. Betty Hill told a packed audience at Pam's Beauty Shop at Zayre's Shopping Plaza, of meeting a crew of 11 aliens from a flying saucer in New Hampshire.

She showed colored slides of the area where the flying saucer landed. She said that the aliens gave her and her husband medical examinations before they took off for an outer space again.

She described the aliens as having football shaped heads which seemed to be held together with zippers.

Ten years ago in Orange County, hundreds of residents rushed to their telephones and called police and Air Force authorities to describe a brilliant fireball racing across Orange County skies at night.

In the Walden area, an observer said the fireball streaked over that community at a low level and was headed northwest.

A public information officer at Griffiss Air Force Base, Rome, N.Y., affirmed that there was an object flying at tremendous speed which could have been a meteorite or a burned up satellite.

Last summer a mysterious light was reported hovering in the sky near Beacon about the same time many sightings of UFOs were reported in Rockland.

Residents of Rombout Avenue told an *Evening News* reporter that they had seen a UFO on a weekend and again on a Tuesday following the weekend sightings.

Many of the sightings in Orange, Dutchess, Rockland and Putnam have been viewed by persons using high powered binoculars.

According to some scientists, what people are seeing is a bright star, a planet, an airplane or a helicopter.

This has failed to convince most UFO watchers although some are willing to concede they might be looking at a man-made satellite launched from earth.

Bill
Warwick, NY
October 23, 1980

More than a dozen friends had gathered at a house in Warwick, NY near the New Jersey border to have a "Full Moon Party" on October 23, 1980. The sky was "crystal clear" and the moon shone brightly in the southeast. Somewhere between 10-11pm, someone spotted something unusual in the sky to the west.

"It was very large, like a cloud, but reddish in color," Bill told me. "It had defined edges and it was basically oval. There were no other clouds, and no wind."

This cloud-like object had the apparent size of an oval about 8"x12" at arm's length. It was transparent, and everyone could see the stars through it. However, there were two other lights near the top of the cloud, and they were most definitely not stars.

"These two bright lights were emitting beams of light, but they never broke through the edge of the cloud," Bill stated, comparing it to some type of "force field" containing the lights.

Everyone watched this red cloud with the beaming lights in amazement, and offered a variety of explanations from the rational to the absurd—from the aurora borealis to someone "conjuring" up the cloud during the full moon—but nothing seemed to make sense. After watching it for a while and getting a clear look at it, the two lights suddenly went out, and the red cloud began to dissipate until it was completely gone.

What was it all these people witnessed in the sky that night? They don't know, but they all agreed it was very unusual, and defied any conventional explanations. Bill was later to find out that this red cloud and the lights were also seen that same night in the nearby town of Greenwood Lake, NY so it wasn't just the imagination of a bunch of Full Moon partiers!

This is yet another example of some UFOs defying all attempts at categorization, as well as any hope of understanding them.

Josette Diaz
Newtown and Sandy Hook, CT
1983

The following account was written by the witness, and involves a sighting she experienced with her mother and brother:

"We were driving home to Waterbury from Danbury after spending the weekend, so I'm sure it was a Sunday, and being that it was dark and we had school the next day, I would guess it was some time before 9pm.

"We were driving down I-84 and there was a backup of cars and people pulled over on the side of the highway, out of their cars, staring up at the sky. Well, Mom pulled over too! We all got out and looked up and you couldn't see the sky. It was just all black and big white lights. We knew right away that it was a UFO.

"My Mom told us to get back in the car and we drove to the closest exit (Sandy Hook) and pulled into the Blue Colony Diner and immediately saw many, many people out of their cars staring at the UFO. We got out. No one was saying anything. I don't recall us even saying anything to one another. It didn't appear to move. It was just hovering there. As I remember it, it was huge! And very low. I don't recall seeing the sky, only metal and lights.

"We stayed there for a little while and Mom was feeling a bit nervous and said, 'Let's go.' I know that I never felt any fear, just kind of shocked at what I was looking at."

Josette's description of their sighting may just be my favorite, that the entire sky was just "metal and lights." What a marvelous way to convey how massive, how close, and how overwhelming these sightings during the mid-1980s were in the Hudson Valley and western Connecticut! It's no wonder that even after over thirty years, people lined up to share their stories at the Danbury UFO Conference.

Ed Mulholland
Danbury, CT
July 12, 1984

Ed Mulholland's shift at Perkin-Elmer in Danbury was to begin at 11pm on that clear night of July 12, 1984. As he drove to work on Route

84, near Exit 5, he saw "lights to my right, which caught my eye." The apparent size of the object was about that of a tennis ball held at arm's length, and the object was heading towards the west.

Ed described the silent craft as being composed of "seven bluish, soft lights, in a spade configuration."

After I emailed him some questions, he sent the following details of his sighting:

"So when I mention spade shape, it's as in a deck of playing cards spade shape. This single, noiseless, low flying craft, had seven lights, all symmetrically spaced from each other. As I recall, when I exited the I-84 highway, at Exit 3, I parked my car, and actually got out of my vehicle to observe the craft above me. I was alone at this time. No others were with me.

"The lights did change colors from soft blue to white as it made very sharp turns, sort of like a box with 90 degree angles. I returned to my car, went to my place of work, but decided since it was only a two minute or so drive back, I returned [with a coworker from Perkin-Elmer], and it was then that more townsfolks were gathered. I believe the biggest question I overheard at that time was 'What is that?'

"Over the years (32 or so), I made a judgment as to what I thought it might have been. I think that this might have been an experimental aircraft from Stewart Air Force Base, now named Stewart Airport. Again, just my thought. I'm sure I'll never know for sure, but it was an experience that I will never forget. I have not encountered another sighting since, but I do look to the sky each and every morning and night."

When Ed and his coworker returned to Exit 3, there were dozens of people standing there "talking about it." Many hundreds, if not thousands, saw some type of craft that night (see other cases in the Triangle and Cops chapters). In total, Ed's remarkable sighting lasted for twenty minutes, so it's no wonder it has left a lasting impression.

As a final note, I appreciated Ed's closing remarks, when he urged me to, "Continue your quest for the truth."

UFO Events in Fairfield County, Connecticut
March 21, 1985 and August 31, 1989
by Mark Packo, Connecticut MUFON

One of the best parts of being a UFO researcher is to be able to share with other researchers, especially those who have been active in the field for many decades. I had the pleasure of speaking with Mark Packo, who conducted an impressive field study of two separate UFO sighting events in 1985 and 1989, which included many firsthand interviews he conducted personally. In my opinion, there is nothing like the "boots on the ground" approach to studying any case.

He was kind enough to send me a copy of his comprehensive report which contains the detailed descriptions of the sightings and sketches he obtained during these interviews, as well as copies of some newspaper articles from the time, which repeated the standard "planes in formation" excuse. When you sit down and read these accounts, however, which are in chronological order where possible, it becomes clear that something remarkable was occurring.

(To reproduce the full report here would require too many pages, so only a summary is presented. The report is available online at: http://www.ufoevidence.org/documents/doc675.htm)

The first sighting, which occurred between 9-11pm on March 21, 1985, was reported in Brewster, NY, and the Connecticut towns of Danbury, New Fairfield, New Milford, Redding, Newtown, Weston, Easton, Monroe, Shelton, Ansonia, Bridgeport, Stratford, Milford, New Haven, Derby, Seymour, Southbury, Oxford, Wallingford, Hamden, Cheshire, East Haven, North Branford, Middlefield, Naugatuck, and Beacon Falls.

The craft were described as having everything from round, triangular, or rectangular lights and features, to being composed of concentric rings of lights, to being elliptical, U-shaped, H-shaped, cross-shaped, saucer-shaped, or "flattened football shape." They either hovered silently, moved slowly with a slight humming sound, moved forward, stopped, and reversed repeatedly, went straight up and down, or "shot off" at incredible speeds.

The second event of the report involved the night of August 31, 1989, between about 9:30-11:30pm. Witnesses were interviewed in the Connecticut towns of Trumbull, Shelton, Bridgeport, and Stratford. The shapes included spinning circles, boomerangs, chevrons, V-shapes, an amorphous "blob of light," isosceles triangles, "a child's top," and a large, dark structure resembling "the hull of a submarine." Sounds ranged from a low hum, to a "deep rumbling," to "electronic sounds," and a "synthesizer" sound that changed pitch as the object turned, which one witness described as pivoting on its axis ninety degrees "as if it was on a turntable." Another witness said the object hung motionless just 100 feet above the street where she stood—an isosceles triangle covered in white lights, with ruby lights along one edge. Others described the craft they saw as moving over large distances of the sky in an impossibly fast time.

In short, these were remarkable nights of sightings which presented many different sights and sounds to many people over hundreds of square miles of southwestern Connecticut. I urge everyone to read the details of these fascinating sightings and determine for themselves whether they were the result of hoaxing pilots, experimental military craft, or something truly extraordinary—something extraterrestrial.

Westtown, NY
September 12, 1988
MUFON Case

Observed for over 15 minutes, a dark metal, larger than an aircraft carrier, right at tree height, baseball diamond shaped with lights on the entire circumference.

I was working at a TV commercial film shoot. We were last to wrap the location to head back to the Holiday Inn in Middletown, NY, about a 20 minute drive. There was also the truck of electricians, who had left 5 minutes ahead of us. We were in a van of other various film crew departments. There were about 10 of us in the van. It was still light out, but the sun was getting lower.

As we drove on County Rd. 12, we looked out the van window, and at about 11 o'clock in the sky, there was a pinky-orange object that a few of us said at the same time, "What is that?" As we drove, it was getting closer. At first we could not really make out what it was, but we all agreed it was not a plane or anything else we had ever seen. It slowly got bigger and bigger, and it was getting darker and darker as the sun was setting. We kept looking at it, as it was really getting bigger and bigger and we were all freaking out, but at some point the road turns and there was a lot of tree cover so we could not see it.

Then at a small turn in the road, there, stopped in the middle of the road, were the electricians. Their truck just stopped in the middle of the

214

road, and they were out of their truck standing in the middle of the road looking up. We stopped and got out, and there above us was this unbelievably enormous ship hovering quietly right at the tree line.

Around the circumference were different colored lights that changed color, but not in a pattern, they just changed colors, pinky, orangey, bluey, yellowy. We huddled together, gazing up for about 5 minutes. And then in a second it pulled away, without a sound and incredibly fast.

The electricians told us their truck had stopped. When it was gone, the truck started again. We got to the hotel, told everyone else on the crew - they just thought we were nuts. But it was in the paper the next morning, as a crowd in the parking lot of the local supermarket had also seen it.

I still talk occasionally with a few of my fellow witnesses and we are still freaked out, because it was so completely, unmistakably huge; so close and so real. I have told other people in my life, and I am afraid it really has had deleterious effect on my credibility. So I just don't tell people anymore, but it has left a huge mark on my life, and on how I see our place in the universe; I think in a very good way. It really forces you into a bigger perspective!

Peekskill, NY
September 1989

Yet another case where the shape of the craft could not be determined as it was so massive and low.

NUFORC Report
Massive, low flying, slowly moving craft that emitted no sound.
Duration: 1 minute

While travelling a back road through a wooded residential area, I observed a very large object in the sky that appeared to be just above the tree tops. I slowed my car to a near stop. My impression was that it was massive; football field in size. I could almost sense its mass before seeing it.

It moved extremely slowly, there was no sound. There were lights, but I can no longer remember if they were colored or white, nor the configuration. The lights were not extremely bright. Its color was dark, and the shape unknown because of tree cover.

I could not clearly see its details, only a partial outline and impression of tremendous mass. I was perplexed and frightened.

I was following a friend's car. When we reached our destination, her first words to me, unprovoked, were *"Did you see that?"* We were stunned.

I remain stunned to this day.

Ellenville, NY
c. 1989

NUFORC Report
Large, building-type UFO that is tall but rounded, never heard of sighting of a UFO like this one.
Duration: 1-2 minutes

I believe the year was between 1988-90 roughly. I was around 10 or 11 years old, I believe, and was with my 2 younger brothers, roughly 4 and 8 at the time. My mom and dad were taking us through the drive-through of Burger King in Ellenville, NY, to get some food late one night after visiting family members. We saw what I would describe as a huge building in the sky that was rounded but tall, several stories high, with many lights/windows. Besides me and my family seeing this, the girl working the drive-through window also looked out and saw it. It was not like anything I have ever even heard of and have not seen anything else online about UFOs that look like flying buildings, but it was unmistakable. Ellenville is around 12 miles from Pine Bush where there are many UFO sightings, and also where I would have my second sighting of a UFO around 2001 or so, that was more up-close.

Note: See the Rectangle chapter, Waterbury, CT, 1996 for another building-type UFO sighting.

West Point, NY
August 1993
MUFON Case

I would like to state first that I have not told this previously for obvious reasons. In August, 1993, at approximately 2am, I was on duty as a military policeman stationed at West Point Military Academy. I was with two other M.P.s. It was a really slow night as usual, as nothing much ever really happened.

This particular night we were out of our vehicles just talking amongst ourselves. We were parked next to the main parade field. As I was talking I noticed one of the M.P.s was distracted, as he was looking over my shoulder and he asked, "Hey what is that?" I kept talking ignoring him. He repeated, "Hey what is that?"

I turned around and in the background was this mountain. It was a clear night and visibility was excellent, as it was a full moon. When I first saw the object, it was the size that shocked me initially. It was stationary and absolutely silent, it was black in color, the length of it was unbelievable. It had three huge, square lights on the first story. The second story had three square lights on the bottom as well. We observed it for about 3-4 min. We were trying to figure out amongst us what we were looking it, and whether or not we should report it, but not knowing what to report.

I can tell you for certain what it was not. It was not a plane, blimp, helicopter, so on and so forth. As all this is happening, the object all of a sudden flashes a light like a camera flash in rapid sequence three times. However, this light lights up the entire side of mountain. At this time we were very alarmed. We jumped into our vehicles and started toward the object. As we made our way, the object started moving slowly to my left, then it stopped for about 3 seconds and traversed against its flight path, and darted to the right at an incredible speed and it was gone. Within a second it was gone.

We decided not to report the incident, as the military tends to frown upon this type of thing. I was so shaken that at the end of my shift I had to call my father, and reluctantly told him what happened—I had to tell someone. He calmed me down and then told me his story of a sighting while flying on a mission in Vietnam. I felt better at that point. Something is out there and I wish I knew what.

Green Bay Packers Quarterback Aaron Rogers
Cornwall, NY
Winter 2005

It's always interesting when famous people report UFO sightings, especially people who stand to be the brunt of a lot of ridicule. Such is the

217

case of Super Bowl MVP Aaron Rogers of the Green Bay Packers, whose admission probably earned him a healthy dose of ribbing in the locker room. In addition to the high-profile nature of one of the witnesses, this case is also important as it once again implicates military involvement.

The sighting occurred on a snowy night in 2005, in the Cornwall home of Rogers' former teammate, Steve Levy. Also present were Levy's two brothers and parents.

"We started hearing this weird noise and we were like, 'What the hell is that? It's like 12:30-1 at night,' " Levy said. "We popped open the front door and we heard it, but it's coming from the backyard. We go out to the backyard and before you know, within minutes we are in a daze because we are looking at something. It's reddish, yellow, orange-ish and light, and it's moving back and forth and peeking out of the clouds and going back.

"It was absolutely unreal. I don't know what it was—that's why they are called unidentified flying objects.

"We didn't say a damn word to each other; we just looked at it and watched it. It went on for minutes and out of nowhere, it just took off in the direction of my front yard. I googled 'warp speed' and that's the closest that you can come to it when it starts as a dot, takes off in one line and just disappears."

According to a *Times Herald Record* article, "Levy and Rogers ran through the house, screaming toward the front door. They saw nothing. Within 30 seconds, Levy's house started shaking."

Levy reported that, "There were three or four fighter jets that were no higher than 1,500 feet above my house. They were chasing something."

The plot thickened even more, when Rogers explained that the weird sound they had heard was actually warning sirens at the Indian Point nuclear power plant!

"Now, if you know anything about UFO sightings or you've done any research, you know that a lot of times two things are connected to UFO sightings," Rodgers said. "One, is the presence of fighter jets. And two, there's a lot of sightings around nuclear power plants. So to tie it all together, the alarm we heard was from 30 miles out, and a nuclear power plant that had an alarm that went off."

Rogers was naturally hesitant to talk about his sighting at first, but he is absolutely sure that what they witnessed that night was a UFO—and he also seems to know a thing or two about UFO sightings! In the entire history of activity in this area, this case of the famous quarterback, the UFO, the nuclear power plant, and the fighter jets, has to qualify for the Hudson Valley UFO Hall of Fame.

"Nancy"
Montgomery, NY
Summer, c. 2012

"Nancy" and her 11-year-old son were sitting on her parents' deck in Montgomery on a summer's evening when they spotted an unusual whitish-yellow, star-like object. It grew larger and brighter as it appeared to be coming straight toward them, "like in a 3D movie." As Stewart Airport and Orange County Airport are nearby, this easily could have been an aircraft on approach for landing. However, there was something different about this light.

"That is *NOT* an aircraft," Nancy's father stated emphatically.

How could he be so certain? Well, her father knows a thing or two about aircraft, as he is an air traffic controller at Stewart Airport. He has seen commercial, civilian, and military planes and helicopters landing and taking off, in all kinds of weather and conditions.

The light continued to draw closer–much closer than any airplane would have if it was approaching either one of the airports–but they couldn't discern any shape to the craft as they could only see the light. Then it did something quite unusual–it stopped in midair. It continued to silently hang motionless for at least 30 seconds and then it did something the family still can't comprehend.

"It shot *straight up*!" Nancy told me. "It shot straight up and disappeared so quickly!"

Clearly, her father had been correct; this was not any type of conventional aircraft. However, whether this was some sort of secret experimental craft from our government or something alien they could not say. I asked if any of them had been frightened by what they had seen.

"Not in this family!" Nancy said laughing. "We weren't scared, we thought it was awesome!"

Perhaps their attitude needs some explanation: Nancy is the niece of Audrey Harer, whose family members were witnesses to the spectacular March of 1983 sighting of the massive, silent, triangular craft. (See

Triangles chapter.) Once again, this case emphasizes the point that when it comes to UFOs, it is often "all in the family."

Jeff
New Windsor-Newburgh, NY
August 13, 2013

I met Jeff at an event in Albany, NY in June of 2014, and he told me of his impressive background as a former Army Ranger, as well as a civilian flight medic. He mentioned that when he was younger, he had seen a UFO in the Albany area, and had also seen one during a deployment in Iraq in 2004. Then, in 2013, he had yet another remarkable sighting near Stewart Airport, and was willing to share the details with me.

He prefaced his statement by saying that he was "aware of general flight patterns and military responses, and capabilities," and I have no doubt of the validity of that statement, which makes him an excellent witness. The following is his account in his own words:

Well, on August 13, 2013, I had dropped my son off at Newark Airport for his return flight to Switzerland, and was traveling northbound on the New York State Thruway. It was approximately 8:20 pm. It was dusk, the sun was low on the horizon, but it hadn't set yet. As I passed under Route 207 [in New Windsor, NY], I observed about 4 cars pulled over to the side of the road with people out of the cars.

As old habit, I pulled over behind the final car in line to see if there were injuries or if they needed help. I noticed people just looking up, probably 8 people total. As I reached over to put my hazards on, I noticed very bright spot lights illuminating the tree line near where 17K goes over the thruway. I noticed a couple of vehicles on the road with emergency lights going back and forth on 17K.

At that point above the tree line, I noticed a round white light that seemed to envelop whatever the object was. It did not appear to be navigation lights or any other signal lights sitting under or on an aircraft, but it seemed the light itself was moving. I watched as the light hovered about 100 feet above the tree line to the west of I-87, then the light traveled from west to east, crossing I-87. It stopped for about 30 seconds on the east side of I-87, but it seemed to be above 17K.

The overpass as seen on the New York State Thruway (I-87) near exit 17 from Google Maps.

The object then crossed back over to its original position and stayed there about one minute. At that point, I heard what sounded like smaller Huey-type helicopters coming from the south, and turned to see if anything was visible. It looked to be three Lakotas, which appear were based out of Stewart. When I looked back to the object, it blinked three times in rapid succession, like three dots in Morse code, fast, but distinct, and then the object flew up in the sky, quickly hitting the ceiling or turning itself off within 10 seconds. Just zoomed right up.

I got a feeling that something wasn't right (obviously) and noticed that coming south on I-87, was a pair of flashing lights, and saw a couple New York State Police troop cars go flying past, and they looked like they were hitting the U-turn area, so I decided that was a good time to leave (I never left my vehicle during the time of observation) and got myself back onto the road and heading northbound again.

It appeared that the troopers' cars stopped and were approaching the people on the side of the road (I think some more vehicles had stopped behind me but I am not honestly sure). I was able to continue the rest of my drive and returned home to Albany without any incident. I told my wife what I had seen when I got home, but didn't tell anyone else or seek out any information regarding this, as something just struck me as just odd. It appeared that all the activity was happening close to the Air National Guard base and not the civilian airport.

I think this is the majority of what I recall about this. I would say the total observation time was about 6 minutes. I hope that this helps in some way, if I can be of any assistance or provide any more information please don't hesitate to contact me. Also, if you do want to publish anything about this, if you could withhold my last name, as my name is still attached to some classified (or higher) operations from my Army days and I don't want to have any odd visitors thinking I'm spilling secrets or some such nonsense.

By way of my own history if it is of any pertinence: I was in the Army 8 years as a combat medic, seeing deployment in OEF [Operation Enduring Freedom], OIF [Operation Iraqi Freedom] and also in Kosovo. I was medically discharged after being shot a second time in my right leg, and left as a Sergeant First Class with two purple hearts and a bronze star with V device with some other bits and baubles. I also did a whole slew of other stuff so if you need to know any of that just let me know.

My response:
Thank you so much for this. If only all witnesses were this clear and detailed! I will most definitely use the story, and keep your name out of it.

A few questions:

What was the relative size of the object? A plane, a house, a jumbo jet?

At its nearest point, how close were you to the object?

Did it make any sound?

Thanks again, and if you don't mind, I would like to at least mention some of your impressive military credentials, in a way that won't identify you.

Jeff's response:
Hi Linda, Thanks for the quick reply. So I would say the object was about 400 yards from me in general distance. I'm not sure once you figure in the object's height, then my distance from that point would be more, but you know what I mean. I was about 400 yards from the spot the object hovered, however many feet above that point once you figure the height of the trees. It was about the size of a standard raised ranch and made no sound.

And mentioning my military past is fine, just the last name withheld would be fine, and if there was anything you needed to know about me or this just let me know.

So here we have an extraordinary case of a partial-daylight sighting at a major intersection of several highways involving police, emergency vehicles, Lakota helicopters, numerous civilians, and a decorated, former Army Ranger who has seen more than I can imagine in the Middle East and Kosovo. They all observed an object as big as a house, which was able to hover over the road, move silently from side to side, and then accelerate rapidly straight up!

(Also something to note: Jeff described three rapid flashes from the craft, which is exactly what the UFO did over West Point in 1993 in the previous story.)

One would like to think that our own government wouldn't be testing any experimental vehicles over busy New York highways, risking motorists' safety, but then what does that leave? Whatever it was certainly got the attention of the State Police and the Army. And Jeff's account of three Lakota helicopters adds weight to the story, as according to Wikipedia, the "Stewart Army Subpost is also located on Stewart ANGB and supports the U.S. Military Academy, the 1st Battalion/1st Infantry, and the UH-72 Lakota-equipped 2nd Aviation Detachment."

I checked the local newspaper archive and UFO reporting centers, but did not find any reference to this event. I would love to hear from some of the other people who witnessed the object that evening, particularly those who were directly under the UFO on Route 17K. I would also like to hear from any law enforcement officers or first responders who were called to the scene—which makes me wonder what the dispatcher told them! Of course, it would also be wonderful to speak to any of the Lakota pilots, but I hold out little hope of that ever happening.

"Kevin"
Willow, NY
Monday, August 8, 2016

"Kevin" had come up from New York City to spend some time at the family's summer home in Willow, New York. It was about 11pm, and he was sitting on the deck just enjoying the sky, the woods, and pond, when he noticed something odd. With the approach of the Perseid Meteor Shower, there had been a few stray shooting stars, but the bright, stationary object to the south over the pond was something completely different.

As he wondered what this object could be, it suddenly "jerked straight up," moved to the side, and raced back down into its previous position. Startled, Kevin—a former skeptic—admits the object gave him "chills when I realized what I was looking at" and he was completely "fixated" on the object.

Watching something move in such an extreme manner just once is enough to make quite an impression, but this bright, white light repeatedly jerked up, raced over at sharp angles, and then raced back to position over the course of at least *30 to 40 minutes*. Finally, this white light turned red and started to dim until it was a tiny spot and finally disappeared.

He knew he had to tell someone, so the next day Kevin spoke to his mother. She did a Google search and came upon an article which spoke about my UFO research. He contacted me to see if I had any interest in his story, and the next day we spoke on the phone.

Before I had a chance to ask, Kevin assured me that he had been completely sober, with absolutely nothing to drink or smoke for several weeks. He went on to describe his experience to me, and he asked if I had ever heard of such a sighting. In fact, I had interviewed a man from Woodstock, just several miles to the east of the town of Willow, who had a very similar sighting back in November of 1988. (See *In the Night Sky*, page 120) From the picture window of his home, he had watched as a bright, white light zigzagged at sharp angles back and forth across the sky.

As Kevin's sighting took place outside on the deck near the woods and a pond, I had made a mental note to ask if any wildlife acted strangely before, during, or after the sighting. However, before I could ask, Kevin told me that there is a farm next door and that right after the sighting, for about 10 to 15 minutes, "the cows were making a lot of noise, *a lot of noise*, like they were in pain." I said that I hoped the cows were okay, and he said he had also been concerned so he took a walk down by the fence the next day to see the cows and they all seemed to be all right.

As this was a long, intense sighting, I had to ask if any of his family members had ever experienced anything, as is so often the case. His initial reaction was no, but as so many witnesses have done, Kevin thought a second and then said, "Well, actually, my sister saw something once."

He went on to describe that after they had moved into their house in the Bronx somewhere between 2007 and 2009, his sister had told him that she was looking down onto the Hudson River and saw a saucer-shaped craft. "I thought it was complete BS, with her saying it was saucer-shaped and that it hovered in place and then shot off quickly. But then the next day, we saw reports that a lot of other people had seen the same object in New York City."

While the night of August 8th had been crystal clear, with the Milky Way stretching prominently across the sky, unfortunately, the weather for the rest of the week was cloudy and rainy, so Kevin had been unable to look for the object again. I'm sure he didn't need reminding, but I urged him to bring his phone or a couple of cameras or camcorders to try to record this object if it ever returns.

***

Here's something you don't see every day! (And no, I wasn't the one who asked the question.)

Hudson Valley Medical Examiner Claims Jurisdiction Over Crashed UFO
by Todd Bender, January 20, 2017
Hudson Valley Post

Representatives of the Dutchess County Medical Examiner's Office fielded questions from an audience gathered at an educational forum on Thursday night.

When discussing the statutory authority of the ME's office at a mass-casualty incident, one audience member asked if the forensic office would have jurisdiction over a crashed UFO within the county's borders. As it turns out, they would.

The job of the medical examiner's office is to determine the cause and manner of death of any death caused by accident, suicide, or homicide, including any extra-terrestrial beings that succumbed to injuries sustained in a wrecked craft.

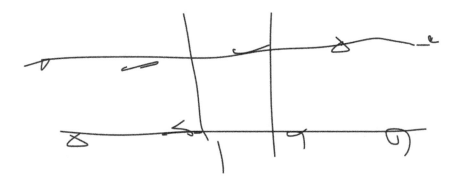

For those who read *In the Night Sky*, you know that Gary was part of one of the most fascinating cases of multi-generational abductions and sightings. What began for him in the 1950s, still continues with sightings to this day, including this bizarre November, 2016 UFO composed of a grid of long, thin sections with lights. His notation "End" with the little circle denotes that there were lights at the tips of these sections. November 2016 was a busy time for UFOs in the Hudson Valley.

Kirk Kristlibas
Congers, NY
Summer, 1988

In April of 2017 as I was putting the finishing touches on the book's manuscript, I received an email from Kirk Kristlibas that really caught my attention, and was worth "holding the presses" if necessary as it hit several hot buttons. (I also felt it was worth its own chapter due to the quality of his writing and ability to express himself.)

Hi Linda, I was wondering if you knew anything about (or were maybe even witness to) a UFO event in the summer of 1988? I can't remember what month it was. Maybe July. Anyway, I lived in Nanuet (well, technically, Pearl River), but the sighting took place in a cornfield in Congers. I was 18 yrs old, hanging out with three close friends. We first sighted it just at twilight in the eastern skies (I suppose this 'object' would have been over Croton at that point, or the Hudson River), so it had to be around 7:30 pm, I'm guessing?

My response: Kirk, This Is fascinating, especially because I lived in Pearl River and Nanuet and had a very intense sighting at Lake DeForest in Congers (which I recently discovered from an old diary involved missing time). Congers has been the location of so many sightings over the decades that I wrote an entire chapter for it.

I asked Kirk if he could sketch the craft, and was thrilled to find out that he was a professional graphic artist, and he was able to create an accurate representation of what they saw that night. He also volunteered to rewrite the account he had initially emailed me with more details. As Kirk's writing skills and ability to express himself is way above the average eyewitness, and his friends also agreed to share their recollections of the event, I decided to include this story in a separate chapter.

The following is in Kirk's own words:

It was the summer of 1988. The event took place in the town of Congers in Rockland County, New York. I was 18 years old. I am almost a 47 year-old man now, but I remember that night like it was yesterday, and it is among the most important, terrifying, bizarre, and beautiful experiences of my life.

It was mid to late July, I believe (I've never been good with days and months) and I was spending the day with my three closest friends, Corey, Brett, and Ida. Ida lived in Congers, and beyond her backyard was a large, rather derelict cornfield, some attractive woods, and a reservoir [the reservoir was lake DeForest]: a perfect environment in which four teenagers might frolic on a carefree summer day.

I might add that we were not exactly typical teenagers. All of us were very artistic, spiritually inclined, 'outsider' types. It would not have been unusual for us to spend a Saturday afternoon in one of the 'New Age' bookstores in nearby Nyack, make a day trip up to the Gurumayi ashram in South Fallsburg, or just sit around discussing topics like astral projection, witchcraft, UFO's, etc. We were the weird kids–and we looked the part, too. In fact, for any average citizen of Congers that might have spotted us traipsing around in the woods, we would have constituted an altogether different sort of 'sighting.'

I digress. To my mind, the weirdness really began in the earlier that afternoon. It was a hot, clear summer day, and the cornfield was dry. The few cornstalks that still stood were dead. I can still feel the gritty dust coating my teeth from kicking up so much dirt. But it was a beautiful day. Once we entered the woods, the dappled shade made everything cooler. Ida decided she wanted to go for a dip in the nearby reservoir. None of us boys went in the water; we were afraid of getting caught swimming in a public reservoir (okay, maybe we dipped our toes).

I remember looking up at the trees, breathing in the fresh air, and just enjoying the setting. I was never much of a nature person, and didn't feel especially comfortable in the outdoors, but with my friends I felt safe. Besides, this was still suburbia. What could happen? While Ida slipped into the water, Brett entertained us with one of his improvised nonsense songs. We all laughed. Brett could have been a successful stand-up comedian. So could Ida for that matter, and Corey, too. I was in a very good mood.

Later that afternoon, we hiked back to the farthest edge of the cornfield. In the distance was an apple orchard (Concklin Orchards?), and straight ahead, the looming High-Tor and Low-Tor mountains. To our right would have been Haverstraw and the Hudson River, so I suppose we were facing north. We could see the orchard and the apple trees from where we stood, and not having eaten for a few hours, Corey and Brett

228

thought it was a good idea to go and pick some apples. But in Ida's experience, the owner did not take kindly to trespassers. I don't comfortable stealing anything (not even apples), so I didn't want to go. The orchards seemed too far away, anyway, and the day was now getting too hot to walk such a distance.

As we gazed out at the orchard, still debating an apple picking crime-spree, we noticed three figures standing by one of the trees. Even though they were very far away, I took the tall one to be 'the farmer' (whoever that might have been?), and the two shorter ones to be, perhaps, his 'children.' I noted they looked a bit overdressed considering the weather, like they were wearing heavy, leather overalls. For some reason, Ida suddenly became very anxious (Ida was not the paranoid type), and absolutely refused to trespass on the orchard. Ultimately, she forbade us to venture any further; something about the presence of those three people upset her. We dropped the subject.

It is at this point that the general mood of the day "shifts."

Later that afternoon we're still in the woods, not doing much of anything. We're pretty drained, having not eaten (certainly not any apples) all day. Naturally, we begin to consider calling it a day and going back to Ida's house. Ida, a very good cook, promises to make fresh hummus and fried kibbeh (my favorite). I vote for going back. I don't know why, but Brett and Corey really push for us to stay outdoors *just a little longer*. I think this is strange. These guys love to eat, and we're all starving. Ida and I agree to linger a little bit longer, and the long summer afternoon begins its slow, almost imperceptible, descent into twilight.

Finally, we agree it's time go back to Ida's house. But first (again, why?) we have to stay in the cornfield and look at the sky for "just a few more minutes," Corey and Brett insist. I really can't understand why Corey and Brett are so adamant. At this point I'm just standing there, bored, staring at High-Tor Mountain. My body is feeling heavy and tired, but my mind is clear. I can really sense my boots in the rocky dirt beneath me (I wore heavy motorcycle boots all year long), and I have a sense of having achieved something staying outside all day like that, like I'd passed some test. The sky at this point is becoming a sort of deep, milky blue, with only the faintest orange streaks on the horizon. One or two stars (Venus, I suppose) are just beginning to peep out, but only just barely.

My three friends stand to my right, facing east in the direction of the

229

Hudson, and I am still looking north, gazing at the mountain. I'd always been fascinated by these particular mountains ever since I was a kid. Before my family moved to a different town in Rockland, I had grown up on the opposite side of them. As a kid back in the mid-seventies, I was convinced that Bigfoot lived in the woods around South Mountain Road, and when I would see UFO documentaries on TV I would run to a window and imagine flying saucers hovering over the ridges. I suppose I had always been rather preoccupied with UFO's in general. Purely out of habit, I begin to think to myself how wonderful it would be to see a UFO. I look up at the sky above the mountains, seeing nothing but blue, and sigh, "Oh well..."

It is at this moment that my friends' alarmed chatter finally rouses me from my reverie. I don't know why, but I didn't seem to care what they've been so talking so excited about the past few minutes. Finally, Brett grabs me and he points east, out to the distance. I don't see anything at first. But Brett carefully guides my gaze. "See? Look at that!" he exclaims. It is low, just over the horizon line of the trees. But it is very far away, probably all the way on the other side of the Hudson River. It's much too far away to really get a sense of it, but it certainly seems unusual. What I see appears to be a small cluster of red and green lights, sort of 'curled' into a tight spiral, like a snail.

"What could that be?" I wonder to myself. As we continue watching the lights, the spiral begins to very slowly unravel into a dancing or undulating chain of lights, now moving north. The sky is deepening into a darker blue now, and the strange lights soon appear brighter. I begin to feel slightly concerned. They, or it, is clearly heading in our direction, undulating across the sky toward the mountains where I had previously been looking. It moves very, very slowly. It's like watching a giant electric water moccasin swimming through the air. The lights are alternately red and green, fading in-and-out, very, very slowly, in no particular order. Now it's turning in our direction, and we see that it has one, bright, white head light. Its length is maybe that of a football field, perhaps even longer. It moves in complete silence. Yet, what is most alarming is that it somehow seems to be alive. It feels like a living creature.

We unanimously agree this is not anything we can identify whatsoever, which is when I begin to seriously panic. I have the sense of this massive 'string of Christmas lights' as being a predator, like it is hunting for something (or someone?), and taking its sweet time about it at that. I suddenly feel very, very threatened.

After a few more minutes, it is now 'dancing' over the mountain. "It's going to land!" Corey and Brett shout, "It's going to land right here in the cornfield!" We all agree on that. We just 'know' that's what it intends. It seems to have heard us, because at that exact moment, its 'head' turns, its white light looking right in our direction. At this point it can't be more than two miles away, and maybe only two hundred feet up. I am now completely and totally terrified in a way that I have never experienced before.

The sky is now completely dark. It's time for me to take serious inventory of this situation. We have been watching this thing for at least fifteen or twenty minutes already. It is not a plane or series of planes. I know that. It isn't a bunch of helicopters. It isn't a bunch of lanterns, or a massive Chinese kite. I'm racking my brains. I want very badly for it to be *something*. I don't care what. Anything. I just do not want it to be what it is –and it's coming for us, and we know it. I think what a fool I was for ever wanting to see a UFO. I do not want to be seeing this thing.

The only sound is that of dogs howling crazily far away in the distance. This is when the fear really hits me hard. It isn't like any kind of fear I had ever felt before. I am going to be devoured body and soul. However, instead of falling apart, I find I am extremely alert and lucid.

Corey and Brett take off running into the darkness. They're going to try and 'flag it down.' They'll be the first to get beamed up, obviously. I turn to Ida. She's now collapsed on the ground, hyperventilating, tears streaming down her face. I say something to her, but she can't hear me. She seems to be catatonic. I quickly weigh running back to her house and just hiding under her bed. But something inside says, "No." I can't abandon my friends. This is my fate. There's no escape.

Thoughts are rushing through my head, all at once. This thing is going to either land or 'beam us up' any second now. They probably have Corey and Brett already, because I can't hear their insane hooting and hollering anymore. I am never going to see Earth, or my parents, ever again. I am going to be taken to some other planet where I am going to be made into a slave. Like watching shadow puppets on a screen, I see my new overlords with their long whips. And I'm just standing here, like a stupid deer caught in headlights. What else can I do?

Suddenly, a memory flies into my head. Oddly, it is an episode of the Oprah Winfrey show which I had seen some time recently. Back in the eighties, before Dr. Phil, car giveaways, or the hysterical audiences we've come to associate with that program, Oprah often interviewed all sorts of interesting people, and occasionally even broached 'occult' subjects. But there was one particular show in which Oprah interviewed a woman who claimed to have seen a flying saucer right outside her apartment window, and from very close range.

What the woman said on the program really struck me: She said it occurred to her that this could very well be a unique incident, that she'd probably never see a flying saucer again, so why be frightened? Instead, she decided to use all of her powers of concentration and perception, and just 'imprint' what she was experiencing on her mind. Every little detail. That way, even though she didn't have a photograph, she would always have the memory stored in her mind's eye forever, like a perfectly preserved mental keepsake.

I decide this is a better option than just quaking in my boots (so, thank you, Oprah?). I begin to jog forward. I want to try to get more-or-less beneath it as it floats overhead. But the rocky terrain is difficult to run on while looking upwards, and I'm stumbling. I would rather have a clear view of it than chance falling down or twisting an ankle. I stop and just look straight up at it. I don't know how to explain this, but I sort of direct my whole awareness at it: not just my eyes or my mind, but my whole being. I want to turn my body into a sort of 'recording device.' I stare at it, hard. I take in the lights, their round shape and perfect colors, the dark girders that seem to connect its segments, the brilliance of the one, bright headlight, and its smooth, silent, slithering movement as it traverses the sky above me. Craning my neck, I take it all in as it passes over and push it as far inside as it will go (if that makes any sense?).

There is no laser blast or tractor beam. Soundlessly, it snakes its way back in direction it came from. Before long, Corey and Brett come running back. The looks on their faces...they are positively glowing. It's funny, but the way I remember it, it's like I could see light glistening off of them. Ida recovers her senses (I still don't know exactly what she went through –she would never really talk about it), and we all sort of huddle together under the night sky, amazed at what we'd just been through. I feel like I've cheated death.

The dogs of Rockland are still going out of their skulls, however. And as we make note of that fact, we notice a shooting star. It crosses the sky above us in a long, smooth arc. And then another. The sky is now filled with shooting stars. Dozens of them. None of us know a lot –or anything, really– about astronomy, but it strikes us as very strange. Next, we're looking straight up overhead. Very high up in the atmosphere, there is a swarm of tiny lights, like mosquitos buzzing around a street lamp. One of us suggests these are fighter jets sent from a local military airport...

A ludicrous idea. Jets can't fly like that, and these lights are at least as high as a satellite. But our minds can't handle another UFO. It's just too much. We decide it simply has to be the military. I have no memory whatsoever of the rest of the night.

In the days that followed, Corey, Brett and I talked a lot about our experience. Apparently, when they had run out into the woods they saw other people there. When I asked who they were, neither of them seemed to have a clear idea of who these people might have been. "We were all just running," Corey said. Alarmed locals, we decided.

Ida didn't seem quite as keen to discuss the event.

I told my parents about it. I have a memory of showing them an article in the local newspaper. They didn't really know what to think.

It might have been the day after the incident that I was in the car with my mother. We were listening to WRKL, the local radio station, when the announcer reported on the sighting. "Mom, did you hear that?" I exclaimed. "Yeah," she replied, and changed the station. A day or so later, she claimed she never heard anything about a UFO on the radio nor did she see any newspaper article. I really don't think she was pretending not to remember.

A week later we went back to the cornfield with some drums and maybe some tambourines… I think we were going to try and 'call it back'. We brought a few more friends with us and we started drumming around ten o'clock at night. After a few minutes, we saw some flashlights or something in the woods, and we ran back to Ida's house and locked the doors. Personally, I was glad it didn't return.

It was during the months following our sighting that some odd things started happening to me. I felt then (and still feel) that they are directly connected in some way. Now, I was aware of the *Communion* book, but I had not yet read it. I was, however, familiar with Whitley Strieber because my general circle was very much into a film based on his vampire novel, 'The Hunger.' Between David Bowie, vampires, and Peter Murphy of the band Bauhaus, this was a movie we rented and viewed together, often. I did not read a whole lot of fiction, horror, or fantasy novels at that age. My nightstand would more likely have had something by Carlos Castaneda, Robert Monroe, Yogananda, or Margot Adler on it.

Now, around this time, very often, usually early in the morning, I would awaken to the sound of something like a metal gong rolling through my head, from ear to ear, accompanied by a blue light. Following this, my body would become filled with violent vibrations, and then I would hear a soft, woman's voice telling me it was "time to go." I would then 'roll out' of my body and fly out of my bedroom window. I have no memories of where we went, except up into the sky.

I began to have recurring dreams of being in some kind of classroom. It felt like a community college setting. The teacher (a woman) would have us perform this strange dance. We would be seated on the floor, or be hovering low to the ground, and we would start spinning and moving in a circle. I had the impression we were imitating the planets of a solar system.

I also had many dreams of strange beings (only sort of like the one on the Communion cover). They had large eyes (but not black) filled with wild, prism-like patterns of color. One time they took me to the top of the World Trade Center (where my father worked in reality, incidentally. Thankfully, he survived 9/11). The leader, the tallest of them, was dressed in a long robe with a peaked, stand-up collar. He had me look down. The city below was filled with smoke and flowing lava, pouring out from the building below. I thought it was the end of the world. Then he took his claw and traced a bunch of scratches across my face.

My little sister frequently reported seeing balls of blue or purple lights floating in her bedroom upstairs, which she seemed to attribute to me, somehow. Pretty soon, my house gained the reputation among my friends for being a place where strange things happened.

After reading this fascinating account, I asked Kirk if this incident had any influence on the last 30 years of his life, and he gave me this thoughtful reply:

As to your question, I would really have to say this experience changed my life completely. I think there is something that happens when we confront the truly unknown, maybe especially at a young age before our brains are fully developed. For me, the reaction was abject terror. And yet, somehow, I managed to force myself to open to it. And that openness, I think, seemed to catalyze my spiritual trajectory for the remainder of my young adulthood. Even now, thirty years later, I often find myself reflecting on the event, and notice the experience still feeds me in subtle ways.

I know that sounds vague and 'new age' so I'll give you another example: I like to play a game with myself when I am outdoors and alone. I look up and imagine sighting another craft or unknown intelligence in the air. I just notice my immediate gut reaction. Sometimes my reaction is to find the nearest shelter and hide. Other times I try to make mental contact with it. This serves as a sort of barometer for where I'm at in terms of my inner health, and simply how I'm handling stress at that time. I mean, life itself is an unknown.

There have been times when I've visited India when I was very afraid for my safety. Again, I managed to maintain balance and push through, and trust. Obviously, I'm still here. Also, over the past few years, I've been having problems with 'poltergeist' activity in my apartment. The experience in '88 very much informs how I've been handling it. Those who I trust enough to tell always say the same thing: "You should move!" That really cracks me up.

And maybe more than anything, the experience redefined reality for me. I live in a much larger universe than most people I know. I work in a university, so I talk to a lot of young people. It has surprised me to learn that most of them would not *want* to live in a larger universe. But I think, at some point, they'll no longer have a choice.

I hope that answers your question?

I was very interested in reading the accounts from Kirk's friends, Corey and Brett, who agreed to share their memories. One story I did not expect, however, was the one from Ida, as Kirk told me she never wanted to talk about it. Wouldn't you know, hers was the only one I received! However, whereas Kirk vividly recalls Ida passing out, she does not even mention that happening, so she may have no recollection of it. I also want to point out that Kirk and Ida did not compare stories, yet they use many of the same descriptions:

We were taking our usual walk down by the reservoir behind my house. The town had to lay pipe, so they cut a path, and replanted the grass and some small trees. My friends and I had taken walks down there whenever they would come to hang out. The path led back up to the cornfields behind my house. There were acres and acres of open space, which is no longer there, having been replaced with McMansions.

From the cornfields you could see out to the apple orchards, and out to Route 304. There was a mountain, just past 304 that they had been blasting for as long as I could remember. There is a quarry down by the Hudson River, about 4 miles from my mother's house. It was dark enough that you could really see a great deal of sky. I was so grateful for that nature outside our back door, it was a great escape from our teenaged lives.

On this particular night, something beyond explanation happened, and we've been trying to make sense of it ever since. It's got to be thirty years since the sighting, but I can recall all the feelings, as if it just happened.

We were returning to the cornfield from the reservoir promenade, (We, being my friends, Kirk, Corey, Brett and myself). As we reached the edge of the cornfield, what caught my eye was a cluster of lights that seemed to be illuminating the top of the trees. The usual chorus of, "What IS that? Are you seeing what I am seeing?!" happened as we started walking faster towards it to get a better look. It was as if Christmas lights had been dropped on the tree tops. Dogs were barking and howling and making a total racket.

Something was not normal.

We would pause and watch, the configuration would sort of hover, coming closer to the center of the cornfield. I have no sense of how long it took for them to appear above us. I remember the lights being bright enough to illuminate us. There was no sound. I vaguely remember maybe some red lights amongst the trail of white lights. They just kind of undulated, hovered and slowly started toward the mountain on the other side of 304.

I don't remember us even talking while it was happening. It was so subtle, not scary, totally captivating, and I think if they dropped a tractor beam, all 4 of us would have just flown away.

It was really like watching a string of super bright Christmas lights gently fly in the night sky. I had a sense that they were separate, as opposed to being part of a larger craft. The silence was kind of surprising as well, being that the lights were close enough to cast light down on the cornfield.

After it was gone, I remember feeling a huge surge of adrenaline. We had just witnessed something inexplicable, and astonishing. We ran home to my mother's house, and with breathless excitement, recounted what we had seen.

The memories are still magical, and in the decades of gazing up at the night sky, I have never seen anything like it, since.

12
Gravitational Anomaly?
Hartford and Woodbridge, CT
September 4, 1960

I have dealt with so many remarkable UFO cases with such surprising and startling eyewitness testimony, that you would think that nothing would faze me anymore. But then something comes along that just knocks you for a loop and you wonder if this is something truly earthshattering, or just a lot of nonsense.

Such was the case with something I found in the Project Blue Book files. When I expanded my research into western Connecticut, I decided to do a thorough study of all the Blue Book cases to see what the type and level of activity was for those decades of the project records. There were quite a few of varying importance, and then I came across a case from Hartford, CT from September 4, 1960 that immediately sent up some red flags, although I had no idea how far down the rabbit hole it would take me.

The information on the official Project Record Card stated:

Observer heard loud swish in air. Looked and saw object falling like green flame. Object landed and appeared to be cone about 1 foot high. This started a fire in a shed in the backyard. Janitor put out the fire and had police called. The material was subsequently turned over to the police and obtained for analysis.

Obviously, things don't fall out of the air and start fires every day, so when this did occur—and in the middle of the Cold War, no less—there should be a high degree of curiosity. Was this a piece of a Soviet satellite? Or some U.S. technology that fell out of orbit? Or was it a natural meteorite, or something very unnaturally extraterrestrial? Surely, it must be one of the four.

Well, according to Project Blue Book, it was actually none of the above:

Material analysis showed substance to be furnace slag.

238

This would have been the first piece of furnace slag in history to somehow launch itself into orbit so that it could re-enter the atmosphere with such an impressive and fiery display—so right off the bat I knew the official conclusion was absurd. Then there was the fact that the PBB file contained 73 pages—a rather massive accumulation of data and photos for a lowly piece of slag. Clearly, there was something here that was never supposed to see the light of day.

I read the various descriptions of eyewitnesses who saw the "fall." One woman, who was working at the White Cedar Restaurant at 817 Albany Ave. in Hartford, looked out the window of the dishwashing room to see a "comma-shaped, brilliant green flame about sixteen inches long" plummeting through the sky from south to west. The leading edge was "round, and the size of a grapefruit" with "an orange tail."

Other witnesses reported seeing the green flame and hearing a "swishing sound" as it fell, and then hearing a loud "thud" when it impacted the ground near a shed. The building's janitor threw water on the object to put out the small flames, and when the metallic object, or objects, cooled enough to handle them, he placed them in containers and called the police. (Interestingly, one report stated that two female witnesses kept fragments for themselves. Could they still be out there in private hands?)

With some speculation that this could have been a piece of Sputnik IV, which had launched on May 15, 1960, word spread quickly. Professor Robert L. Brown of Southern Connecticut State College was soon involved, as was the famous astronomer Dr. Fred Whipple of the Harvard Observatory, and Major R.J. Friend, the head of Project Blue Book. Most interesting of all, however, was that the samples were soon in the hands of the brilliant and controversial Townsend Brown, Chairman of the Science Advisory Committee of Whitehall Rand. Townsend Brown's claim to fame is that he believed he had discovered an antigravity field.

As I don't pretend to fully grasp the subject, here is the Wikipedia entry on Brown:

An American inventor whose research into odd electrical effects led him to believe he had discovered a connection between strong electric fields and gravity, a type of antigravity effect. For most of his life he attempted to develop devices based on his ideas, trying to promote them for use by industry and the military. He came up with the name "Biefeld–

Brown effect" for the phenomenon he had discovered and called the field of study electrogravitics.

Instead of being an antigravity force, what Brown observed has generally been attributed to electrohydrodynamics, the movement of charged particles that transfers their momentum to surrounding neutral particles in air, also called "ionic drift" or "ionic wind."

Townsend Brown with one his metallic discs he believed he could propel with an antigravity force.

As baffling and complicated as this all sounds, the key is that Townsend Brown believed there were anti-gravitational forces, and that he could harness them to propel aircraft—particularly disc-shaped, metallic aircraft. This may have influenced his work on this Connecticut case—or, even more compelling, this case may have influenced his future work on anti-gravity.

The PBB file contained several pages of the chemical analysis of the mysterious substance, which turned out to be aluminum with high amounts of barium and strontium, with a variety of other elements, although the scientist who wrote the report cautioned that only the crust of the samples was tested, so this may not be the exact composition of the entire sample.

Such analysis was interesting, but hardly worthy of getting all excited about something extraterrestrial. However, a letter in the file from Townsend Brown to Major Friend alluded to something else that was unusual about this material.

October 12, 1960
Major R. J. Friend
Aerospace Technical Intelligence Center
AFCIN 4E2X
Wright-Patterson Air Force Base, Ohio

Dear Major Friend.

It was a pleasure to be with you last Wednesday. I was glad to have the opportunity to give you some information on the Hartford fall. It has been an engaging subject to me for the reasons I explained to you.

Professor Robert Brown telephoned me upon my return to Washington and mentioned that your office had requested additional samples. I told him of our visit and that no samples are available because of work in progress. I assured him, however, that you would be furnished complete reports of our investigation, and that our efforts would be closely coordinated with the Air Force.

Sincerely yours, T. Townsend Brown, President

Unfortunately, Brown does not elaborate on the "reasons I explained" during their meeting, but clearly the Air Force, and project Blue Book, was very interested. A letter dated the following day to Dr. Whipple shows that analysis of the samples had begun within days of the fall, with the Air Force being involved from the beginning.

October 13, 1960
Dr. Fred L. Whipple
Smithsonian Astrophysical Laboratory
Harvard Observatory
60 Garden Street
Cambridge 38, Massachusetts

Dear Dr. Whipple,

It was a pleasure to be with you on September 8 and to have the opportunity to examine the material which fell at Hartford, Connecticut, on September 4. After careful consideration, you expressed the opinion, I believe, that this material was not meteoritic, and therefore no further interest to your group,

You will recall that, during my visit, I was in touch with the Air Force and personally delivered samples of the material to the Air Force research center at Bedford. I promised to send Dr. McCrosky of your laboratory, copies of the Hartford police reports and other papers for your permanent file, and these are enclosed.

Thank you very much for your participation and cooperation in this matter.

Very truly yours, T. Townsend Brown, President

Once again, however, there is no mention of any unusual properties of the Hartford sample. The real bombshell would come in a letter from Townsend Brown to Professor Brown, where it is revealed there was a second, related fall in Woodbridge, CT, by New Haven. Before exploring that letter, however, here is the description of that Woodbridge fall by Professor Brown in a letter to Townsend Brown:

Dear Dr. Brown,

I should like to clarify some aspects of the particle sent you from New Haven.

It is not part of the Hartford fall, but a distinct fall both spatially and with reference to time. It is my opinion, however, that both falls are related to the same orbiting object. The relatively larger particles sent to you through the mails fell in Woodbridge, a suburb of New Haven. The airline distance between the two falls (Hartford and Woodbridge) is

242

roughly 47 miles along the line whose heading is approximately 30° (E-N 30° E). Certain aspects of the fall are the same as those of the Hartford fall. However, the Woodbridge particle fell essentially intact with only a slight general scattering of the metallic dust noted in the earlier fall. Since it landed in an area (asphalt driveway) that had been carefully swept the night before, the impact area was clearly defined. It created a "burned" circle 6½ inches in diameter with a slight elongation to the north. Contained within the circle were several "splotches of the metallic material" with a larger particle slightly off center. The time of the fall could easily be established as between 8:30 AM and 12:30 PM local time, since the discoverer Mrs. (Name blacked out) had walked there and noted nothing unusual, whereas upon returning from a drive into New Haven was astounded at noting when she returned at 12:30 the object within the burned circle. She had first kicked it aside, then picked it up. Surmising that this anomalous material might be of interest to others, she phoned a friend, Professor (name blacked out), Curator of the Peabody Museum at Yale University, who in turn suggested she notify me. I recovered the particle after noting the conditions, returned to the college and notified you by phone. I might add that the time of the fall can be relegated to the earlier portion of the interval in as much as it was not warm when picked up.

Professor Brown then goes into a detailed description of how the sample was packed for shipment—through the regular post office mail!—and how there was a crust on the material that could have flaked off in transit, thereby slightly altering the weight. This was important to note, as this Woodbridge sample appeared to not only be inexplicably losing mass, but also affecting the mass of objects with which it came into contact! Had Townsend Brown finally found proof of anti-gravity?

October 26, 1960
Mr. Robert L. Brown
Associate Professor, Earth Sciences
Southern Connecticut State College
New Haven 15, Connecticut

Subject: "Woodbridge" Fall of Suspected Gravitationally Anomalous Material

Dear Professor Brown:

Thank you for your letter of October 22 and the additional information concerning the Woodbridge fall. I am inclined to agree with you, and this seems to be borne out by tests currently underway, that this fall is indeed of great scientific importance.

This object has not been officially classified (to the best of my knowledge), but I suspect that it may soon be, and I will ask you to retain (except to authorized personnel) any information I may give you in strictest confidence until this matter can be finally decided.

We are continuing the chemical and physical tests of the chunk of material which you sent to us. Even though capsulated by glass, so as to eliminate the possible effects of moisture or occluded gases, the weight of the sample is still changing. Observers also agree that the amount of white surface incrustation is increasing, and, as I mentioned over the telephone (for your information only), the incrustation appears to contain certain nuclides of barium and strontium in amazingly high percentages. What all this means, of course, remains to be determined.

The continuing change in weight is startling and indisputable. Since Dr. Kuslan weighed the sample at Hartford, it has lost over 3% and is still decreasing. A most surprising recent finding is that the material appears to have the power (perhaps by virtue of its B radiation) to induce a weight change in certain receptor materials with which it is associated. We now have an example of ten-fold leverage in the gross weight-change of a large volume of material, induced merely by contact or close proximity with the sample. Many other intriguing facts are coming out of this investigation. Perhaps soon you may have the opportunity to come to Washington to see these things for yourself. We are deeply grateful to you for sending this sample.

In the rereading your letter, there are certain questions or concerns which occur:

1. What was the date of the Woodbridge fall? Perhaps you covered this in a telephone conversation, but I have no record of it. I note

that you believe the material probably fell between 8:30 and 10:00 a.m., and that it did not seem to be directly related to the Hartford fall of September 4, 1960.

2. You mention "splotches of the metallic material" at the area of impact—what has become of that metal and are the samples available to us?

3. Would Dr. Kuslan give me an affidavit covering the weighing operation, so as to have a formal record of its accuracy and authenticity?

4. When I received the material from you (between the two watch glasses), I looked closely for any flaking or evidence of detached particles. Nothing was found.

5. I am greatly interested in your thoughts of an oscillating trend in the weight-change following impact. While the observed curves show some irregularity, the steady trend is definitely downward, and there is no evidence so far of any regular oscillation.

While we are deeply grateful to Mrs. (name blacked out) for her alertness, and for turning the material over to you, and for her interest, I expect, in the interests of science, that it will be some time before this piece of material can be released from its busy schedule. Time is all the more important, because, from theoretical considerations, the material would appear to have a definite (half-life) rate of decay, and every effort is being made to utilize it while it is "hot".

Major Friend tells me that he makes frequent trips to Washington, so by copy of this letter, I wish to invite him to stop in upon his next visit to learn more in detail what is happening. I would be very glad to see him. Again, thank you for your kind collaboration, and I shall look forward to your visit in the near future.

Sincerely yours, Townsend Brown, Whitehall-Rand, Inc.

I was hardly able to believe what I was reading in this letter. While there could be a number of scientific reasons why a sample of material is losing mass, I was dumbfounded by its ability to "induce a weight change in certain receptor materials with which it is associated. We now have an example of ten-fold leverage in the gross weight-change of a large volume of material, induced merely by contact or close proximity with the sample."

These lines are worth rereading, as several very capable scientists are asserting that some metallic substance that fell out of the sky had the power to change the weight of things around it! Was Townsend Brown blinded by his belief in anti-gravity, or did the data truly prove a "continuing change in weight" that was "startling and indisputable"? Had some extraterrestrial craft expelled some material over Hartford and Woodbridge, Connecticut, material which could have revolutionized the aerospace industry and allowed us to build our own anti-gravity vehicles?

We may never know, as frustratingly, this is where the information in the Project Blue Book file ends. There is no final report as promised, no conclusions, and no mention of what ultimately happened to the samples. I have been unable to find any other information on this case, and no other references to gravitationally anomalous material found in Connecticut in 1960.

I wish I could state that this is one of the most important cases in UFO history, but there is simply not enough evidence. However, there is certainly enough evidence say that—unless every scientist working on the samples was inept and completely wrong—something strange fell into a backyard in Hartford and a driveway in Woodbridge. Unfortunately, the only thing I can say without any doubt is that it wasn't furnace slag.

About the Author

Linda Zimmermann is a former research scientist and an award-winning author of over 30 books on science, history, and the paranormal, as well as several works of fiction. She enjoys lecturing on a wide variety of topics, and has spoken at the Smithsonian Institution, Gettysburg, West Point, the Northeast Astronomy Forum, and national Mensa conventions. Linda has also made numerous appearances on radio and television.

When she isn't glued to her computer writing books, Linda goes cycling, kayaking, cross country skiing, and snowshoeing. She is a lifelong NY Mets and NY Giants fan, so don't even think of trying to call her when a game is on.

http://www.facebook.com/pages/Linda-Zimmermann/116636310250

www.gotozim.com

Linda Zimmermann's books are available from her website, Amazon, Barnes & Noble, and most major retailers. They are also available for Kindle, Apple, NookBook, Kobo, and other E-book formats.

Bad Science:
A Brief History of Bizarre Misconceptions, Totally Wrong Conclusions, and Incredibly Stupid Theories

Winner of the 2011 Silver Medal for Humor
in the international Independent Publisher Awards

Amazon.com Review:

"*Bad Science* is simultaneously informative and ever-so-entertaining. Riveting! Enthralling! Hilarious! I highly recommend this book if you like a jaw dropping read that is a LAUGH OUT LOUD."

CPSIA information can be obtained
at www.ICGtesting.com
Printed in the USA
BVHW031926180819
556170BV00001B/24/P